Redirections in organizational analysis

Redirections in organizational analysis

Michael Reed

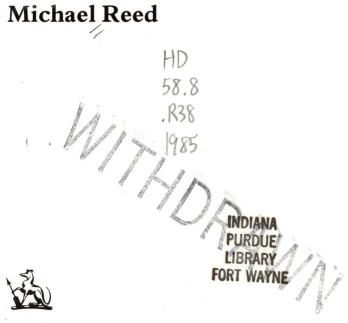

Tavistock Publications
London and New York

To Ceris and Cara

First published in 1985 by
Tavistock Publications Ltd
11 New Fetter Lane,
London EC4P 4EE

Published in the USA by
Tavistock Publications
in association with
Methuen, Inc.
29 West 35th Street,
New York, NY 10001

Photoset by Rowland
Phototypesetting Ltd
Bury St Edmunds, Suffolk
Printed in Great Britain
by Richard Clay (The Chaucer
Press) Ltd
Bungay, Suffolk

*British Library Cataloguing in
Publication Data*

Reed, M. I.
Redirections in organizational
    analysis. –
(Social science paperback; 293)
1. Organization – Research
I. Title   II. Series
302.3'5   HM131

ISBN 0-422-78940-2

*Library of Congress Cataloging in
Publication Data*

Reed, M. I. (Michael I.)
Redirections in organizational
    analysis.
(Social science paperbacks; 293)
Bibliography: p.
Includes index.
1. Organizational change.
    I. Title.   II. Series
HD58.8.R38   1985
    658.4'06   85-14736

ISBN 0-422-78940-2

10-28-86

Contents

Preface

A number of people have contributed to the writing of this book, although they may not wish to be reminded of it in public. First, I must thank Peter Anthony and Tom Keenoy – two close colleagues in the Department of Industrial Relations and Management Studies, University College, Cardiff – for the help and encouragement which they have given over a number of years. I also owe a great deal to past colleagues in the Department of Administration, University of Strathclyde, who encouraged me to develop a much broader conception of organizational analysis than is often the case in other institutions which have a declared interest in this area. Mrs Mair Price has shown great patience and skill in typing and re-typing an often disorderly and almost illegible manuscript. Finally, I must thank my wife, Ceris, for putting up with the inevitable absences and dislocations entailed in the writing of a book.

Michael Reed 1985

Introduction

I have three objectives in writing this book. First, to provide an evaluation of the most significant developments in the field of organizational analysis that have occurred over the last forty years or so. Second, to develop an approach to the study of organizations which avoids the more debilitating weaknesses of existing perspectives and offers a more coherent and subtle understanding of the process whereby collective social action becomes organized. Third, to provide an assessment of the current situation within the field of organizational studies and, more speculatively, the direction that it is likely to take in the future.

Before providing some indication as to the way in which these aims are to be realized, it is necessary to state, somewhat baldly, the underlying conception of 'organizational analysis' which informs the arguments that follow.

The analysis conducted in this book rests on the fundamental proposition that the most significant developments within the field of organizational studies are those involving theoretical change – that is, changes (of varying degrees of magnitude) in the conceptual structures whereby 'organizations' are characterized as common members of specifiable ontological categories or domains and subsequently subjected to various forms of rational analysis and appraisal.

The justification for this assumption is derived from Gouldner's analysis of the contingent relationship between the 'infrastructure' of

2   Redirections in organizational analysis

social theory on the one hand and its 'technical structure' on the other (Gouldner 1971). The former consists of clusters of 'domain assumptions' or tacitly accepted beliefs held by identifiable groups of social theorists at specific points in time concerning the nature of and relationship between man and society in its most general sense. They are shared with and shaped by the encompassing culture and society within which social analysis is practised. In turn, they shape the explicit technical structure of social theory – the formally articulated propositions (and accompanying methodological apparatus) specifying the links between objects within the domain and the conditions under which they hold. In this way, 'articulated theories in part derive from, rest on, and are sustained by the usually tacit assumptions that theorists make about the domains with which they concern themselves' (Gouldner 1971: 34).

Thus the most far-reaching and consequential transformations in social theory are those involving basic changes in the conceptual schemes which are embedded in and internally embody new background assumptions concerning the object domain to which they are directed. The process of theorizing has to be seen as 'a doing and making by persons caught up in some specific historical era' (Gouldner 1980: 9); as a precarious combination of individual imagination and technical production located within a dynamic social context which is always liable to subvert shared assumptions which have petrified into unreflectively accepted intellectual orthodoxies. While the technical structure of social theory may attain some degree of epistemological independence from its social location, it is always vulnerable to successive waves of penetration by the culture and society of which it is a part in that the sub-theoretical matrix of assumptions in which it is grounded is pervious to general shifts of opinion taking place within the larger community.[1] In this sense, theoretical development in the field of organizational analysis has to be understood as the outcome of a complex interaction between what Toulmin (1972) has called 'socio-historical' processes and intellectual or disciplinary procedures – between the conditions which enable (and constrain) certain forms of intellectual develop-

---

1 This position contrasts with the 'reductionist' account of the relationship between ideas and context offered by a number of theorists reviewed in chapter 2 who tend to see the former as a direct reflection of the latter.

ment to occur and the rational procedures whereby some intellectual 'variants' rather than others are selectively perpetrated.

Undoubtedly, the most intellectually powerful domain assumption on which the study of organizations has traded is that which maintians that, 'once firmly organized, an organization tends to assume an identity of its own which makes it independent of the people who have founded it or of those who constitute its membership' (Blau 1968: 54). As Gouldner notes, while this proposition is offered as an empirical generalization, its true significance lies in its status as a domain assumption – as a universal characterization of all formal organizations in which supporting empirical evidence 'is trivial in comparison to the scope of the generalization' (Gouldner 1971: 51). Gouldner also maintains that the assumed ontological autonomy of organizations is itself embedded in a larger domain assumption which has proved to be intellectually dominant within the historical development of social theory *per se* – that is, the assumed ontological autonomy of social structures and the dependent status of the 'raw material' on which they work, individual human beings. In turn, this has facilitated a broad acceptance of a research methodology and an associated technology of social control which treats human beings as objects or things to be manipulated in the furtherance of higher-order goals such as national military, economic, and political power. While this 'technocratic' view of social theory has been under attack in recent years, its survival capabilities should not be underestimated given its congenial resonance with dominant cultural values extolling the virtues of scientific and technological achievement and, more importantly, with 'the sentiments of any modern elite in bureaucratized societies who view social problems in terms of technological paradigms, as a kind of engineering task' (Gouldner 1971: 52).

As a number of previous commentators have noted (Waldo 1948, Wolin 1961, Mayntz 1964, Albrow 1968), the historical development of organizational analysis provides a particularly instructive case-study illustration of the process whereby the 'technocratic paradigm' came to dominate Western social theory during the course of the earlier decades of the twentieth century. As we shall see, from a present–day vantage point, organizational analysis looks like a very miscellaneous, not to say fragmented, affair. However, the comparative disarray characteristic of the contemporary situation has to be viewed against a backdrop in which the status of organizational studies as 'an interdisciplinary science of man in organizations' (Pugh

1966) seemed assured, even at a time (the second half of the 1960s) when social science's credentials as a fully paid-up member of the scientific fraternity were looking increasingly shaky. Pugh's panegyric to 'modern organization theory' implied that the 'Comtean vision' which had informed the work of successive generations of organization theorists – beginning with Saint-Simon and culminating in the work of modern systems theorists such as Blau, Etzioni, and Thompson – was on the verge of being fulfilled. Wolin represented the motivating force of this vision in the following terms:

> 'Organization as power over things – this was the lesson taught by Saint-Simon. The new order would be governed not by men but by scientific "principles" based on the "nature of things" and therefore absolutely independent of human will. In this way, organizational society promised the rule of scientific laws rather than men and the eventual disappearance of the political element entirely. . . . According to contemporary writers, organization does more than increase man's power or compensate for his shortcomings; it is the "grand device" for transforming human irrationalities into rational behaviour. . . . Pervading much of the recent theorizing on method is the promise that right method will enhance and extend man's power over nature and society: method provides us with the power to predict the course of phenomena and hence to put them under our control.'
>
> (Wolin 1961: 378–83)

Wolin contends that the unintended consequence of the intellectual dominance assumed by the technocratic vision of organizational studies during the course of the twentieth century was the sublimation, if not explicit assimilation, of specifically 'political' practices and associations into non-political forms which reached its zenith in the 'technocratic managerialism' of the 1940s and 1950s. The ethical and political dilemmas raised by the complex relationship between the individual and society in the social conditions characteristic of mass industrialization and politicization in the twentieth century were transformed into engineering problems and tasks to be dealt with by an enlightened bureaucratic elite which controlled the levers of economic and political power in the 'new administrative state' (Waldo 1948). The links between the individual's organizational membership on the one hand and his membership of an identifiable political community on the other were gradually severed by an intellectual system which denied the relevance of a whole range of ideas and practices associated with 'the political' – citizenship, obligation, authority, justice, and power – and treated the new 'organizational Leviathans' as closed social systems. Organizations were islands of rationality in a sea of human irrationality; their triumph over the surrounding environment assured by their vastly superior technical capacity for co-ordinating and controlling the individual actions of millions of human beings in the furtherance of the 'general good'. Thus the 'technocratic' vision of organizational studies embodies an image of an objective, value-free social science of organizational behaviour directed at the solution of technical problems which simply require the vastly superior cognitive capacity of a method of analysis facilitating the location and treatment of 'pathological' or 'deviant' behavioural patterns. In this sense, the development of organizational analysis as a legitimate intellectual endeavour requiring material and social support from its host society had traded on a promise which has never been realized – the rationalization of politics and the elimination of social conflict. The failure to provide the technical means and normative foundations for achieving a radically different form of social and moral integration in a modern industrial society to that achieved in traditional society has to be related to a changing mosaic of socio-historical conditions which constantly threatened the reconstruction of social order around the values associated with bureaucratic or formal organization and the promise of systematic rational control which it seemed to offer. However, this failure also has to be seen in the light of the 'intellectual schizophrenia' which has bedevilled organizational studies' historical development. The *Zeitgeist* of the modern age may have seemed to possess an elective affinity with the technocratic conception of organizational analysis's historical role and substantive practice. Yet this conception was itself fatally flawed by its claim to provide a new collective morality as well as a set of more refined and sophisticated techniques of social control.

The view of organizational analysis as an applied science of organizational structure and functioning, directed to the manipulative needs of an enlightened managerial elite, became the dominant ethos of the 1950s and underwent subsequent refinement and extension during the 'heyday' of modern systems theory in the 1960s. Yet its grip – ideological, theoretical, methodological, or technical – was never entirely complete. This was true to the extent that it originated in an intellectual aspiration which was never consciously put to one side but was played in an increasingly *pianissimo* tone as the stubborn resistance of human beings to further extensions of technocratic control became evident. This aspiration rested on the belief that organizations could provide, at one and the same time, mechanisms of rational control and sources of collective moral identity (Wolin 1961: 368). To put the same point another way, organizations were rationally conceived means for the achievement of collective ends which, potentially at least, facilitated the institutionalization of group values and norms to which individual ends and action could be initially subordinated and eventually assimilated. The ideal situation in which the immolation of 'the self' within the organizational community is realized at the minimum individual or social cost could be achieved if the elite controllers were sufficiently sensitive to the need to strike an acceptable *modus vivendi* between general imperatives and particular wants and desires. In this ideal situation individual moral choice and collective decision-making would be fused; organizational analysis would provide the theoretical foundations for an amoral administrative practice through which individual behaviour could be scientifically manipulated in the furtherance of collective social goals (Storing 1962).

However, successive generations of organization theorists were forced to recognize the practical obstacles which stood in the way of constructing and administering an organizational form in which the need for control and the need for commitment – for association and community – could be neatly combined in a novel institutional synthesis in which the endemic conflict between individual freedom and collective constraint would become redundant. Both Barnard (1938) and Simon (1945) – the true 'founding fathers' of modern organization theory – substantially modify their original theoretical conceptions of organizations as naturally co-operative social systems operating according to a universal logic by incorporating elements of ideological indoctrination and structural control to deal with an irredeemable human recalcitrance on the part of 'lower participants'. A highly manipulative strategy of organizational control is relocated within the conceptual husk of an organicist social theory presupposing natural harmony and consensus as universal features of all formal organizations. As a result, organization theory is bequeathed a general theoretical framework which is forced to reconcile the contradictions generated by a metaphysic that assumes collective moral consensus as a social given and at the same time advocates the adoption of techniques whereby this may be engineered.

An uncritical acceptance of formal organization as equally functional for all participants (and the moralizing which flows from this problematic assumption) quickly became ingrained within the intellectual foundations on which organization theory was developed between the 1940s and early 1960s (Perrow 1972). The unquestioned assumption of the social value of imperatively co-ordinated institutions encouraged the formulation and promulgation of a systems model of organization in which many of the most distinctive features of organizational life – structured inequality, social conflict, individual resentment, collective deceit, and outright coercion – are selectively filtered out in favour of a concentrated focus on the cognitive and motivational aspects of organizational behaviour (Krupp 1961). The political and moral dilemmas ingrained in the structure of bureaucratic organizations are sublimated within a conceptual vocabulary and an analytical framework which preclude any open and rational assessment of the priorities that usually inform organized social action and the intellectual tools whereby their complexity can be more fully appreciated. In Barnard's terms, organizational elites are naturally assumed to possess the superior co-ordinating rationality through which the 'organizational personality' can be protected against internal and external threats to its integrity. This assumption is carried over into the elaboration of a more sophisticated systems approach during the 1950s and 1960s so that its status as a theoretical presupposition of dubious empirical validity is never admitted, much less questioned.

However, the attempt to sublimate the traditional concerns of political philosophy within a technocratic rhetoric was not entirely successful; the deafening 'silence' which systems theorists maintained in relation to many of the most significant features of organizational existence provided an opening through which those offering a very different conception of organizational analysis could pour during the course of the late 1960s and 1970s. Yet an awareness of its failure to establish a general theoretical framework free from contamination by value-judgements is important to the extent that it highlights one of the most critical recurring themes discovered in organizational analysis's historical development – the successive attempts which have been made to resolve the internal tensions and contradictions contained within a conception of 'organization' as entailing necessary institutional restraint and as, potentially at least, moral community. The emphasis on restraint conveys the nature of organization as providing that social machinery required to control antisocial and potentially destructive human desires in an unstable social environment which positively encourages unregulated egotistical behaviour – a machinery of constraint and control as necessary to those who would transform society as to those who wish to preserve the status quo. The alternative image of organization – as constituting a somewhat fragile moral order reproduced through the unconstrained practices of its members – implies a social condition characterized by natural co-operation between free and equal ethical agents (Dawe 1979).

Consequently, 'organizational man' – at least as an ideal-typical theoretical construct – remains an unstable and unpredictable composite of unrestrained egotistical desire and spontaneous ethical and social concern. While the institutional arrangements associated with formal or 'complex' organizations are assumed to reflect the tensions arising out of the contradictions between these opposed 'models of man',[2] the history of organizational analysis (up until the present time at least) seems condemned to stress the importance of externally imposed regulation and discipline.[3] The 'pragmatics' of organizational power win out over seemingly idealistic, and hence unrealistic, Utopian sentiment.

A major contention maintained throughout this work is that the comparative disarray presently found within the field of organizational studies – an outcome in part due to a very thin diet of positivistic[4] epistemology and technocratic ideology unrelieved by the rediscovery and renewal of alternatives until the last fifteen years

---

2 Hollis suggests that a 'model of man' provides a reasonably coherent package of assumptions concerning the defining characteristics of human nature. These link up with assumptions concerning the nature of scientific explanations to form what Hollis labels a 'metaphysic' (Hollis 1977).

3 This deterministic epistemological tradition continues to flourish in organizational analysis, though it appears in different theoretical guises. Indeed, it has been the dominant philosophical theme in the historical development of organizational analysis and has helped set the theoretical agenda to which succeeding generations of organization theorists have been forced to respond.

4 The term 'positivist' has become an instrument of philosophical and ideological abuse rather than a useful concept with a clear analytical meaning and purpose. For two recent commentaries which achieve a more balanced exposition and treatment see Giddens (1979) and Keat (1981).

or so – is a symptom of the sustained capacity of its practitioners, young and old alike, to engage in a highly selective process of historical reinterpretation and reconstruction in which the underlying tensions and contradictions previously identified are filtered out in support of a particular version of its historical development and role. As a result, the field of organizational studies has been dominated by intellectual perspectives characterized by a distinct lack of historical depth and a marked inclination grossly to oversimplify the subtle interaction between intellectual and social change.[5]

The following six chapters plot the intellectual, institutional, and contextual factors which have interlaced to produce this existing state of affairs. The book is also rash enough to offer some provisional advice as to possible strategies for future theoretical innovation which may help us to avoid repeating the more glaring mistakes of previous generations.

The first three chapters of this book provide an exposition and evaluation of the most significant theoretical developments which have taken place in the field of organizational studies since the late 1950s. Chapter 1 charts the selective incorporation of the legacy of classical social theory within a systems framework and the gradual erosion (and subsequent breakdown) of the intellectual hold which the latter had exerted over the field for much of the preceding thirty years. Chapter 2 outlines the development of a critical theory of organizations during the course of the 1970s as offering the most explicit challenge to the weakening intellectual domination of the systems perspective. Chapter 3 provides an overall evaluation of the major developments which have been identified in chapters 1 and 2, while indicating the need for theoretical reconstruction of the concept of organization as a particular form of social practice.

Chapter 4 suggests such an alternative conception of organizational analysis as an intellectual practice focused on the secondary social practices through which collective social action becomes organized. Chapter 5 grounds this theoretical approach within a detailed and systematic reworking of a number of well-known case studies where its advantage can be more clearly displayed. Chapter 6

---

5 This lack of historical imagination and vision owes as much, if not more, to the pervasive intellectual influence of philosophical doctrines which legitimize static and deterministic theoretical approaches as it does to any other factor.

assesses the most prominent strategies for future development which are currently on offer and indicates its preference for the form of understanding which the practice framework promises.

A brief concluding section argues that a more open recognition of the internal contradictions and limitations of organizational analysis can provide a source of intellectual strength which can be drawn on in future work that attempts to improve our understanding of the dilemmas of organizational life and their implications for intervention on the part of human agents.

1
Redirections in organizational analysis

Introduction

Between the late 1940s and the early 1960s a relatively small number of works were published which have attained the status of classics in their own right within the field of organizational studies, such as Selznick's *TVA and the Grass Roots* (1949), Gouldner's *Patterns of Industrial Bureaucracy* (1954a), and Crozier's *The Bureaucratic Phenomenon* (1964). These books were classics in the sense that they were clearly directed to problems which had provided a focus for the Western European tradition in social and political thought stretching over two millennia (Wolin 1961) and they promised the construction and development of 'a theory of organizations which had identifiable links with the study of social class on the one hand and the study of elites on the other' (Perry 1977: 1). In other words, the authors of these studies were attempting to monitor and assess the complex interaction between institutional and organizational change from the point of view of a social philosophy which focused on the increasingly tenuous relationship between the individual citizen and the political community in the destabilizing social conditions created by twentieth-century industrial capitalism.

However, this continuity in intellectual preoccupations and conceptual frameworks has remained submerged within the 'official history' of organizational analysis's development until the last fifteen years or so. This is true to the extent that the latter has obscured the link between social and organizational theory by selectively incorporating only those elements or 'residues' of the European tradition which would serve in the formulation and codification of a systems framework as providing the conceptual base from which a general theory of organizations could be constructed (see Pugh 1966).

The initial purpose of this chapter is to chart the process whereby the original link between social and organization theory was partially severed in pursuit of the Holy Grail of an 'interdisciplinary science of man in organizations' (Pugh 1966). This is followed by an assessment of the debilitating effect which this act of 'intellectual parenticide' had on the capacity of systems theorists to cope with the severe internal contradictions generated within their self-constructed orthodoxy in the course of resisting the challenge presented by those who rejected a positivistic interpretation of organizational analysis's form and content. While this attack has been almost totally successful, the chapter indicates that the cost has been substantial in the sense that it has shattered any illusions which may have remained concerning the viability of reconstructing a general theory of organizations which is universal in its empirical scope and unified in terms of its logical structure. It has also helped to produce a fragmentation of theoretical perspectives and substantive concerns in which any pretence to intellectual coherence seems absurd.

Perhaps somewhat paradoxically, the chapter indicates that the search for an all-embracing theoretical structure in which organizational studies can be faithfully pursued as an integrated intellectual practice is not entirely dead and buried. It suggests that 'post-interregnum' organizational studies may be witnessing the resurrection of an attempt to provide a general theory of organizations which finds inspiration in the work of one who has been largely ignored by mainstream organization theorists – Karl Marx.

Before this latter response to the perceived fragmentation, not to say dissolution, of organizational studies as an identifiable field of study in its own right can be evaluated, it is necessary to examine the way in which the intellectual legacy provided by classical social theory was selectively assimilated within the substantive concerns and conceptual structures of conventional organization theorists during the course of the 1950s and 1960s.

The classical legacy

Insofar as organizational analysis can claim to have any 'founding fathers', then the seminal works of Marx, Durkheim, and Weber have better claim than most to this exalted, if somewhat uncertain, status.[6] They have provided the intellectual resources which succeeding generations of organizational theorists have drawn upon to characterize and account for what they consider to be the leitmotifs which give the field some degree of intellectual coherence and continuity.

The way in which these resources are utilized varies in relation to the specific purposes to which they are put and the location of the latter within particular socio-historical contexts. As such, the writings of the 'founding fathers' fulfil both a technical and legitimatory function; they identify certain problems as being of sufficient significance to merit the investment of considerable material and human resources, and they justify this investment in relation to substantive concerns which stretch beyond the relatively narrow confines of academia.[7] In this way, the practice of organizational analysis and the resources which it requires are legitimated both in terms of the contribution which it makes to improving the 'effectiveness' of the technical means by which collective social action is carried through and the 'reflectiveness' of the intellectual processes through which the valued social ends directing the use of these means are chosen. While the former may have proved to be the predominant justification during certain historical periods, a concentrated focus on technical means to the exclusion of socially valued ends has proved to be insufficient intellectual sustenance for a viable and coherent field of study. The intimate intellectual and historical connections between social and organizational theory have proved

---

6 The problem as to who is to be included in the category of organizational analysis's 'founding fathers' is a vexed question. I have drawn a distinction between a relatively recent systems-based orthodoxy in which Barnard and Simon are the key figures and a more broadly based tradition of socio-political theorizing which finds its intellectual source and sustenance in the 'holy trinity' of Marx, Durkheim, and Weber.

7 Child has used the terms 'technical' and 'legitimatory' functions in a slightly different way to refer to the dual role of British management theory in improving organizational performance and maintaining the status of organizational managers (Child 1969).

too strong for those who have attempted a 'technocratic' reading of the latter's role.

Two interrelated themes dominate the contributions of the 'founding fathers': first, the social and psychological consequences of a more complex division of labour under industrial capitalism; second, the related development of rational bureaucracy as providing that organizational mechanism through which administrative co-ordination and control of specialized functional roles can be realized on a continuous and calculated basis (Giddens 1971, Lukes 1977a).

For Marx, the division of labour produced by modern capitalism is the source of human alienation. It results in an extreme fragmentation of work tasks so that they are broken down into routine and meaningless units of productive activity. In addition, it requires the structuring of productive relations within an organizational form through which a dominant capitalist class systematically exploits a class of wage-earners. Both of these alienating features of a capitalist mode of production can only be overcome through a fundamental transformation in the structural organization of society brought about by revolutionary change.

In Durkheim's case, the work alienation and class conflict resulting from the extreme occupational specialization and bureaucratized forms of organizational control practised under modern capitalism are interpreted as 'abnormal' or 'pathological' deviations from the 'natural' state of affairs postulated by the model of 'organic solidarity' – increased functional interdependence and social integration through a more technologically advanced division of labour. The dehumanization of work and the social disintegration which it generates are rooted in the anomic position of the individual worker under modern factory conditions. The solution to the problem is not to be found in the dismantling of the structure of social relations prevailing under a capitalist mode of production. Rather, it is to be discovered in the development of a network of intermediate occupational groups and associations linking the individual more firmly into the wider social structure. This configuration of interlocking intermediate groupings needs to be overlaid by a more sophisticated 'conscience collective' of 'moral individualism', balancing out the competing ethical claims of self-interest and the 'general good' (Giddens 1976). This will establish a normative framework within which the social and occupational inequality required by a highly differentiated social structure can be legitimized on the basis of an ethic of individual achievement and merit rather than through the rigid collective discipline imposed under 'mechanical solidarity'. In this way, Durkheim argues, social stability under a technologically advanced division of labour can be, somewhat precariously, preserved.

The central structural principle of Weber's sociology of modern capitalism is the systematic specialization of work tasks and their recombination in the form of an administrative control system which drastically minimizes the scope for discretionary behaviour on the part of the individual 'operative'.

Thus, as Giddens remarks, 'Weber gives to the organization of relationships of domination and subordination the prominence which Marx attributes to relations of production' (Giddens 1971: 234). In Weber's view, the development of a greatly expanded division of labour under the pressure exerted by technological and commercial change, as well as the realization of a bureaucratized means of administration, are interlocking aspects of the same long-term historical process – the rationalization of Western civilization and its contemporary institutional manifestation in the shape of industrial capitalism:

> 'What is distinctive about modern, large-scale "rational" capital-
> ism – in contrast to earlier, partial forms – is that it is methodical
> and predictable, reducing all areas of production and distribution
> as much as possible to a routine. This is also Weber's criterion for
> calling bureaucracy the most "rational" form of organisation.'
> (Collins 1980: 927)

Each of the 'founding fathers' has received very unequal treatment at the hands of their interpreters within the field of organizational studies. Marx, until of late, has been largely ignored or his conception and account of work alienation under industrial capitalism have been theoretically and ideologically assimilated within a social-psychological model of organizational behaviour (Eldridge 1971). As a consequence, the structural and ethical aspects of his analysis of the alienating features of industrial capitalism have been largely programmed out of the theoretical preoccupations which have dominated mainstream organizational analysis. In addition, he has been roundly criticized for failing to appreciate the full significance of the 'organizational revolution' and its implications for the long-term management of industrial capitalism through large-scale bureaucracies (Gerth and Mills 1952). In this way, Marx is either consigned to the pre-history of managerial social science or a highly selective interpretation of his analysis of work alienation is combined with a technological determinist account of his focus on changing forms of work organization (Zwerman 1970) so that he becomes a precursor of modern 'contingent theory' (see Donaldson 1976). On the whole, Durkheim has been treated more favourably. His interest in a type of 'descriptive functionalism' has been eagerly seized upon and transformed into the 'explanatory functionalism' which provides the conceptual core of modern systems theory (Parsons 1951, 1956). His support for a form of provisional descriptive analysis which maps the functional interdependencies between social institutions has been transformed into an explanatory theory in which the functional interrelations between units within a social system assume the logical position once occupied by causal linkages between structural components (Durkheim 1938). Within this explanatory framework, anomie is reconceptualized as a psychological syndrome produced by the imbalance between technical and social needs within the organization of modern industry. This imbalance, it was argued, could only be repaired by an enlightened managerial elite well versed in the complex interaction between 'formal' and 'informal' organization (Barnard 1938, Roethlisberger and Dickson 1939).

However, it is Weber's concept of 'rationality' and its expression in modern bureaucracy which provided the main 'intellectual capital' from which organizational theory developed during the course of the 1940s and 1950s. Yet each of these aspects of Weber's analysis of rational bureaucracy – his conceptual distinction between 'formal' and 'substantive' rationality, and his belief in bureaucracy as a technically superior form of administration which was absolutely indispensable to the functioning of a modern industrial society, whatever its cost in human terms – has been the subject of a great deal of controversial debate.

The analytical differentiation which Weber offers between 'formal' and 'substantive' rationality has been criticized on the grounds of being conceptually confused, and of providing an elaborate theoretical disguise for his ideological commitment to bourgeois values in particular and the capitalist system in general (Marcuse 1971, Binns 1977, Eisen 1978, Clegg and Dunkerley 1980). To this extent, the distinction between 'formal rationality' as instrumental technique and 'substantive rationality' as valued social ends is interpreted as an intellectual rationalization of Weber's preference for

bureaucratized capitalism over state socialism. In turn, this theoretical rationalization of underlying value commitments, Weber's
critics contend, leads to an illegitimate narrowing of the institutional
options open to modern industrial man – either a stultifying system
of centralized state control or the endemic power conflicts generated
under large-scale capitalism. Consequently, Marcuse maintains that:

> 'Weber's analysis of bureaucracy was not value-free enough, in
> that it imported values and norms specific to capitalism into the
> "pure" definitions of formal rationality. Thus, the contradictions
> developed between formal and substantive rationality, and its
> obverse: the "neutrality" of technical reason against all external
> material values. This neutrality made it possible for Weber to
> accept the (reified) interests of the nation and its political power as
> the values determining technical reason.'
>
> (Marcuse 1971: 149)

Weber's undoubted admiration for the technical superiority and
functional indispensability of rational bureaucracy – as theoretically
mediated through the ideal-type – has been the intellectual source for
a great deal of debate within the field of organizational studies
(Merton 1952, Gouldner 1954a, Blau 1955, Crozier 1964). The value
commitments supposedly smuggled into his analytical identification
of formal rationality are seen to compromise Weber's arguments for
the separation of the 'cognitive' and 'evaluative' spheres in social
science. In addition, it results in an unimaginative 'Hobson's choice'
between equaly unattractive institutional packages for future social
development. The causal link which he is thought to have identified
between rational bureaucracy and technical efficiency provided a
substantive focus and a theoretical bone of contention from which a
general theory of organizations, based on a systems frame of reference, could be constructed in the course of the 1950s.

However, the assimilation of Weber's analysis of bureaucracy
within modern organization theory could only be achieved through
a very special form of theoretical mediation on the part of its
practitioners. This process of assimilation consisted of a series of
'operations' whereby Weber's contribution could be incorporated
within the conceptual structures and methodological conventions of
an applied science of organizations in the 1930s and 1940s, and
subsequently elaborated within a systems framework during the
1950s and 1960s.

First, the broader theoretical context in which Weber's analysis of bureaucracy was situated – his sociology of domination – had to be selectively ignored in justifying a purely 'technical' interpretation of the complex link that he forged between formal rationality, organizational structure, and managerial control. Second, the relationship between this analysis and his methodological predilections, particularly in relation to the aims and procedural rules of ideal-type construction and the logic of sociological explanation (in terms of meaningful social action and its institutional outcomes), is either discreetly misinterpreted or simply dismissed as a manifestation of early 'intellectual immaturity' which is eventually superseded by a firm commitment to sociological positivism. Third, the neglect of his sociology of domination and a positivistic reading of his methodological position encouraged the lazy acceptance of the stereotypical image of Weber as the supreme prophet of bureaucratic rationalization. This results in a complete disregard for the deep ambivalence that his work reveals over the long-term social consequences of such a development. Finally, each of these previous 'operations' facilitated the insertion of an emasculated reading of Weber's contribution within a functionalist model of organization – derived, in part, from a rather tendentious interpretation of 'descriptive functionalism'. In time, this would provide the basis for further elaboration of a systems frame of reference which presumed to possess the conceptual resources and methodological rigour necessary to construct a general theory of organizations.

It is to these subsequent developments and their implications for an assessment of the current situation in the field of organizational studies that we must now turn in the following sections of this chapter.

Towards a science of organizations

Between the late 1930s and the mid-1960s a number of key publications were issued which attempted to provide the intellectual foundations of a 'science of organizations' and to justify the institutional support which such an enterprise would require.

Three developmental phases can be identified in this body of writing. First, a period of 'foundation' between 1938 and 1945. Second, a period of 'expansion' between 1945 and 1958. Third, a period of 'consolidation' between 1958 and 1967.

Three publications dominate the foundational period: Barnard's

The Functions of the Executive (1938), Roethlisberger and Dickson's *Management and the Worker* (1939), and Simon's *Administrative Behaviour* (1945). The expansionary phase is marked by Selznick's *TVA and the Grass Roots* (1949), Blau's *The Dynamics of Bureaucracy* (1955), and March and Simon's *Organizations* (1958). The period of consolidation is organized around Etzioni's *Comparative Analysis of Complex Organizations* (1961), and Thompson's *Organizations in Action* (1967).

The foundation period saw the emergence of a coherent theoretical framework for organizational analysis which was focused on a domain of substantive social problems and suggested a potential control strategy whereby they could be contained if not totally eradicated. The theoretical framework indicated that 'organizations' should be conceptualized as adaptive social systems which had to cope with the threat to 'equilibrium' resulting from the imbalance between formal or instrumental rationality and non-rational human needs. The social and psychological disruption caused by this imbalance, it was further argued, could only be effectively managed through the ministrations of an enlightened controlling elite trained in the theories and techniques of the new 'administrative' or 'organizational science'. An alternative *Weltanschauung* for an emerging class of professional managers and administrators was in the making. It was a process in which a growing band of 'organizational scientists' were going to play an important intellectual and political role.

The expansionary phase consisted of the 'grafting on' of the remaining theoretical residue of a Weberian approach to the study of bureaucracy to an embryonic science of organizational behaviour which had been developed by the mid-1940s. This intellectual operation was carried out relying upon a structural–functionalist sociology and a behavioural–social psychology. It gradually evolved into a generalizable conceptual framework applicable across a wide range of organizational types and settings.

This provided the basis for a consolidatory period in which a 'comparative' perspective, focused on the interaction between structural and processual variables, could be further developed and applied to recurring problems of organizational design and control. However, the theoretical advances made during this period also served to intensify internal tensions prevailing within the system's orthodoxy which had come to dominate the field by the end of the 1950s. Bringing these, largely submerged, tensions to the surface of explicit debate and analysis was the catalyst for a fundamental reworking of the epistemological and methodological foundations of organizational analysis as they had been codified and practised over the course of the previous forty years. This reworking would culminate in a radical theoretical reformulation and intellectual reorientation around the problems of 'meaning' and 'action' in organizational life during the course of the 1970s.

FOUNDATION

The immediate intellectual backdrop to the development of a science of organizational behaviour within a systems frame of reference is provided by that body of writing conventionally labelled the 'classical or traditional theory of organizations' (Massie 1965). The contributions to the literature had focused on formal organization structure as a mechanism for controlling the performance of work tasks on a rational and continuous basis (Mouzelis 1967). As such, their work constitutes a somewhat uneasy synthesis of the 'positivist spirit' informing a great deal of social and political writing at the beginning of the twentieth century (Waldo 1948, Wolin 1961) and 'operational practicability' in conditions of fundamental socio-economic change (Massie 1965). Considered in these terms, it can be seen as an aspect of a 'general movement to extend the methods and spirit of science to an ever-widening range of man's concepts' (Waldo 1948: 47). Yet it also eschewed theoretical complexity and empirical verification in favour of an overriding desire to provide useful practical guides for managers faced with the operational problems generated by a radically different form of industrial technology and organization under modern factory conditions (Tillet 1970).

This intellectual pot-pourri of formalism, positivism, and pragmatism was retained by Barnard, but transposed into a conceptual framework which would come to dominate the field of organizational studies for the next three decades (see Perrow 1972). His book, *The Functions of the Executive* (1938), is a key text in the intellectual development of organization theory for a number of reasons.

First, his conceptualization of organizations as constituting 'co-operative social systems' would provide an analytical base from which succeeding generations could construct more complex theoretical structures. Second, his recognition of the political importance of maintaining the subtle balance between the constraints imposed by formal organization and the demands arising out of informal group behaviour for the long-term preservation of 'natural co-operation' established a common theoretical reference point around which a wide range of managerial problems would crystallize. Third, the strategic role which he assigns to 'the executive stratum' within the organization in maintaining this delicate balance established a theoretical justification for the existence and power of management as that elite group charged with protecting the moral integrity of the institution – that is, preserving the coherence of the 'organizational personality' in the face of internal or external threat. Their technical and social skills were regarded by Barnard as a necessary condition for protecting the moral foundations of organized social action in an industrial society. This was enough to legitimate the economic and political power which they wielded. Finally, and perhaps more critically for the future development of organization theory, it introduced a seemingly incurably 'intellectual schizophrenia' within the systems tradition which was to dominate the field for much of the next three decades or so. This can be traced to the 'dual vision' informing Barnard's approach which was to reappear in the work of other prominent contributors operating within the systems tradition such as Simon (1945), Selznick (1949), and Parsons (1956).

The pivotal assumption underlying Barnard's conception of 'organization' is that the concept of organization logically entails the concept of social co-operation between its members – the two are mutually implicated as a matter of logical necessity rather than contingent variation. This assumption establishes the analytical justification for the construction of a model of organization as a naturally co-operative social system in which the general purpose or 'personality' of the social collectivity dominates individual thought and action. In this way, any conflicts of interest and value within the organization are settled by 'organization codes and personal codes are not directly involved' (Barnard 1938: 77).

However, this logical construction is heavily qualified by a recognition of the fact that organizational members, particularly those excluded from the executive stratum, are unevenly socialized into an acceptance of the overriding purpose or mission which is embodied in the 'organizational personality'. Indoctrination of the rank and file member into the 'collective conscience' of the organization is required to counter the recalcitrant leanings of the 'lower participants'. It is the most difficult problem in the overall operation of co-operative social systems and calls for high levels of technical and social skills from the managerial elite. In this context, the communication function performed by informal organization and the spontaneous legitimation of executive power 'from below' are combined with the 'objective' characteristics of formal organization structure to form an integrated social unit in which actual or potential rejections of the organization codes laid down by managerial elites can be resisted.

Herein lies the source of Barnard's 'dual vision'. On the one hand, his conception of organization logically presupposes natural and spontaneous human co-operation as the defining analytical property of organized social action. On the other hand, this 'domain assumption' (and the moral loading which it carries for how organizational members *ought* to behave to one another) has to be drastically modified to accommodate to the fact that people subscribe to the dictates of the 'organizational personality' – the institutional repository of the organization's moral integrity – with widely varying degrees of rational foresight. Fortunately for the executive, however, this inclination for deviant behaviour is largely concentrated in the lower levels of the organizational hierarchy. Yet human recalcitrance is a practical problem which Barnard, as well as those who followed in a similar theoretical tradition, could not afford to ignore.

This leaves an opening for an extended discourse on the techniques of ideological indoctrination and social control which the managerial elite must rely on to secure routine compliance through a complex process of psychological and social conditioning which the original model of organization would seem to disallow. The material inducements and ideological control systems required to achieve an acceptable degree of compliance from lower participants, divorced from any concern with the link between conflicting social values or structural constraints and internal decision-making processes, becomes the central issue, and a systems conception of formal or complex organization the theoretical means to its resolution.

Barnard's attempt to contain both 'co-operative' and 'conflict' models of organization within an organicist framework (based on the axiomatic status of natural and spontaneous consensus between members which is subsequently modified to accommodate the need for managerial control over potential or actual recalcitrance) is repeated by succeeding generations of systems theorists. In turn, the theoretical and ideological contradictions implicit in this 'dual vision' become embedded within the conceptual infrastructure within which the dominant school of thought in organizational studies is developed during the course of the next thirty years. The struggle to accommodate a model of organizations emphasizing natural consensus and co-operation and a model stressing diametrically opposed features of rational manipulation and control within a functionalist framework could be contained as long as systems theorists retained control over the 'agenda' for organizational studies. When their grip loosened, the inherent problems in this accommodative strategy would become too difficult to manage.

This 'dual vision' reappears in Roethlisberger and Dickson's (1939) subtle interweaving of theoretical reflection and empirical research which stands in sharp contrast to the abstract and 'bloodless' analytical constructions characteristic of the contributions forthcoming from so many working within the systems tradition. Industrial organizations are viewed as adaptive social systems in which the main function of management is to maintain internal equilibrium through the securing of a common social purpose for the enterprise and ensuring willing co-operation on the part of the members so that individual needs and organizational demands neatly coincide.

The most substantial threat to this delicate balance between the individual and the organization is a recurring intellectual failure on the part of management to appreciate the sophisticated control mechanisms necessary to create and sustain a viable *modus vivendi* between formal management systems and workshop behaviour. This can be traced to the psychological and ideological hold which reductionist modes of thinking exercised over contemporary management practice in the forms of explanatory models of work behaviour that were limited to physiological and economic variables. The alternative intellectual construction which Roethlisberger and Dickson offered in place of this conventional wisdom was a model of organization as a socio-technical system in which the psychological needs of human beings and the structural constraints implicit in technical and social conditions are subjected to a process of continual readjustment through intelligent managerial intervention.

It is in this context that the explanatory and engineering implications of 'social factors' – particularly the importance of internal group networks on the shop floor for organizational socialization and control – takes on such significance for Roethlisberger and Dickson. The 'logic of efficiency' underlying the technical operations of the industrial organization and the 'logic of sentiments' informing the social behaviour of industrial man had to be integrated with a stable factory environment. Here, the active intervention of an enlightened managerial elite whose practical skills were based upon the most advanced forms of theoretical knowledge was absolutely crucial. This knowledge was codified in a model of industrial organization which stressed the functional interdependence between members and the acceptance of common goals within a social system operating on the basis of a 'dynamic equilibrium' between its constituent elements.

The *Management and the Worker* monograph was to provide an extremely profitable theoretical resource for succeeding generations of writers holding very different normative and analytical commitments to those of its authors (see Eldridge 1971). It would also have a catalytic effect upon the future development of industrial sociology and organizational analysis, in terms of both the heated theoretical and methodological controversies which it generated and the ideological rationale that it provided for institutional expansion in the area of managerial social science (see Rose 1975). Yet the social philosophy which underpinned the study, and its intimate connection with the theoretical strategy that it recommended as providing a coherent intellectual foundation for managerial action, has not been subjected to the same close scrutiny.

It has been argued that the concept of anomie, though central to an appreciation of Mayo's work (Smith 1975), was of only tangential relevance to Roethlisberger and Dickson in that their monograph contains little direct comment on the imminent social disintegration of the industrial order or on the role of the factory community in stemming, if not reversing, the disruptive impact of industrialization upon established structures (Landsberger 1958). Instead, the authors are seen to concentrate on 'technical' issues of managerial design and control, while studiously avoiding the more grandiose claims of Mayo's social philosophy (Carey 1967).

Nevertheless, their overriding interest in preserving the precarious balance between managerial direction and workshop organization forces them to consider the intensification of social conflict resulting from the social upheavals occasioned by the onward march of industrial capitalism during the late nineteenth and early twentieth centuries. Their analysis of social conflict in contemporary social conditions focuses on the lack of structural and ideological integration between formal and informal organization within a unitary conception of social order which resonates with Barnard's organicist philosophy. The conception of industrial organization as an adaptive social system, dominated by an overarching normative consensus fashioned and maintained by management, is consistent with an analysis of social conflict concentrated on the factory's technical division of labour, but excluding any concern with the conflicts of interest and value which may be grounded within a particular mode of production and the authority relations it requires. Thus they maintain that:

> 'no simple dichotomous classification of the company's personnel could be made. The personnel could not be divided into an employer and employee class because there was no employer class. Every person in the company from top to bottom was an employee.'
>
> (Roethlisberger and Dickson 1939: 542)

As in the case of Barnard, a particular theoretical tradition provides the intellectual means whereby the potentially divergent implications of recognized social problems and a preferred ideological rationale can be contained within a reasonably coherent analytical framework. Roethlisberger and Dickson do not ignore the economic and political context in which the relationship between work organization and work behaviour must be located, as some commentators have argued (Kerr and Fisher 1957). Rather, they manage to maintain the coherence of their position by separating out 'social problems' from 'social causes' and then reworking the former within an analytical framework that permits a redescription of structural constraints in terms of a neutral technical vocabulary in which they are 'laundered' of any unpalatable ethical and political connotations. The structured antagonism between employers and employees situated within a capitalist mode of production is redescribed in terms of the functional dislocations arising out of the organizational disequilibrium generated by rapid socio-economic change and a managerial elite whose traditional modes of thinking still lag behind environmental developments.

In both cases, systems theory provided an extremely useful intellectual device whereby explanation of the severe strain and pressure placed upon existing social structures by the destructive predilections of industrial capitalism could be accommodated within a social philosophy that no longer corresponded to the realities of industrial life which the theory *implicitly* recognized. The use of abstract

technical jargon could not completely disguise the perception of a
social order in danger of 'coming apart at the seams' and the inability
of prevailing intellectual frameworks to come to terms with these
developments.

However, the underlying contradictions contained within this
pragmatic reconciliation between social awareness and theoretical
commitments would become increasingly evident as the direction
and pace of socio-economic change in the second half of the twentieth century forced a fundamental reconsideration of accepted
intellectual conventions and their philosophical foundations.

There is certainly no hint of impending intellectual discontinuity
and revolution in Simon's *Administrative Behaviour*, published in
1945. Indeed, Barnard's foreword to the first edition of the text
indicates that Simon's:

> 'apprehension of the structure of organized action [is] consonant
> with my own experience. . . . Its ultimate practical view is great,
> sharpening observation, preventing the neglect of important
> factors, giving the advantages of a more general language and
> reducing the inconsistencies between behaviour and its verbal
> description.'
>
> (Simon 1945: I.iii)

Barnard's eulogy conveys a consistency of intellectual purpose
between his own work and that of Simon, as well as support for the
combination of theoretical advance and practical intent embodied in
the burgeoning 'science of administrative behaviour'.

Simon's treatise attempts to construct a general vocabulary for the
analysis of administrative behaviour which is derived from the logic
and psychology of rational choice within an organizational setting. It
rests on a model of organization as a social unit in which a complex
network of interlocking decisional processes are coherently structured through the provision of distributive, allocative, and authori-
tative control mechanisms. Such a unit is deemed necessary not only
because of the relatively 'ordered' pattern of decision-making sequences it facilitates or the reasonably 'rational' outcome which they
produce, but more importantly because of the key role which it plays
in ensuring that the 'subjective rationality' of the individual and the
'objective rationality' of the social collectively coincide (Simon
1945).

The coincidence of these two rationalities is seen to be a problem in
the sense that the decision-making calculus which the individual

relies upon may not correspond, in terms of either formal principles or substantive content, to that informing collective decision-making. The possibility that individual values, alternative options and informational inputs may diverge from those of the collectivity is a recurring one. The organization provides a structured social environment in which 'that behaviour which is rational from the standpoint of this environment is also rational from the standpoint of group values and group situation' (Simon 1945: 243).

To this extent, Simon's decision-making approach offers a solution to a problem which had haunted Durkheim, Barnard, and Roethlisberger and Dickson – that modern industrial society provided the social and economic conditions in which the innate and irrational motivational drives of 'industrial man' were now free from the conventional normative and material restraints of traditional society. This comparative lack of social and normative regulation encouraged the rise of a militant individualism (Giddens 1976) which threatened to destroy the psychological foundations and structural supports of civilized life.

The importance of formal or bureaucratic organization lay not so much in its functional or technical significance, but rather in the alternative institutional source of order and discipline that it provided in a social environment encouraging the spread of rabid individualism at an alarming pace. This neo-conservative reaction (see Wolin 1961) to the destabilizing consequences of industrialization provided the ideological foundations for the construction of an analytical framework which combined the methodological virtues of 'positive science' with a conceptual vocabulary treating organizations as organic entities operating on the basis of an independent social logic which could be internalized by its members. In turn, the essentially partial and limited 'organizational learning' which the average member could hope to achieve established both the intellectual and political justification for a highly manipulative strategy of social control and indoctrination within this organicist perspective. The 'model of man' justified a control strategy which the 'model of organization' refused to admit.

In Simon's terms, organizations set the psychological premises and structural mechanisms necessary to achieve the correspondence between subjective and objective rationality. Between the dangerously idiosyncratic predilections of the individual organizational member and the collective goals of the institution in which he is socially located:

'The organization takes from the individual some of his decisional autonomy and substitutes for it an organizational decision-making process. . . . Organization limits the natural autonomy of the individual by placing him in an environment and by providing him with the information needed to make decisions correctly. By limiting the range within which an individual's decisions and activities are to lie, the organization reduces his decisional problems to manageable proportions.'

(Simon 1945: 199)

The potentially unlimited wants and desires of the individual are constrained by a tightly structured organizational environment that channels human thought and action in the direction of institutionalized goals. There is some recognition of the fact that the latter will be influenced by considerations of political power in the shape of the values and material interests of the 'dominant coalition' within the organization (Simon 1964). But Simon translates these interests into organizationally specific criteria in terms of which individual actions are to be evaluated in relation to the degree of 'objective rationality' they exhibit. These criteria are contained in his notion of the 'principle of efficiency', which provides an overall measure of positive ratios between inputs and outputs over a series of 'decision-making sequences'. The ratios are measured in relation to the effectiveness with which the organization uses a wide range of resources, including money, materials, and manpower, in the achievement of collective goals. The latter are taken as 'theoretical givens'. This is based on the assumption that members, given the constraining influence of a structured decision-taking environment, will strive to realize a 'satisfactory' level of cost-minimization rather than a consistent maximization of output over inputs. Hence, the contrast between the social fact of 'bounded rationality' and the theoretical hypothesis of 'global or perfect rationality' (Simon 1945).

Each of the authors we have examined in this section contributes towards the construction of a theory of organizational behaviour and administrative control through which the ethical disagreement and ideological conflict characteristic of modern industrial life can be rendered socially obsolete. This theory emphasizes its close relationship with the procedural conventions of natural science as exhibited in the intellectual rigour of its mode of reasoning and the methodological precision of its scientific practice. These qualities are combined with a conceptual vocabulary which substitutes the abstract terminology of systems theory for the ambiguous and tendentious normative ingredients of traditional moral and political theory. The knowledge which this emerging administrative science provides is regarded as being morally neutral in the sense that it treats the valued ends informing social action as outside the purview of its theoretical focus – that is, as statistically random and socially given. It concentrates instead on the rational manipulation of psychological needs and institutional structures necessary to achieve that organizational equilibrium which is a precondition for the realization of 'objective rationality' in the conduct of social affairs.

EXPANSION

The works of Barnard, Roethlisberger and Dickson, and Simon provided the intellectual foundations on which a more sophisticated theoretical structure would be erected between the mid-1940s and mid-1960s. Selznick provides the link between the 'administrative science' approach of Barnard and Simon, leavened with the organicist rhetoric of Roethlisberger and Dickson, and the 'Weberian' interest in bureaucratic domination. The theoretical means whereby this link is first forged and then transformed into an integrated conceptual framework is structural–functionalist sociology. The latter provided the intellectual resource necessary to couple the neo-rationalists' concern with the technical problems of organizational control to the moral and political issues embodied in the leitmotif of the Weberian corpus – the rationalization of the social world under the driving force of Western capitalism and its paradigmatic institutional expression in bureaucratic organization. While Selznick would strive to contain an analysis of these issues within a neutral scientific vocabulary of 'systems adaptability', 'organizational disequilibrium', and 'functional dilemmas', they would continually reappear in their original guise and disrupt the objectivist technical veneer with which they were overlaid.

This can be seen in his attempt to translate the conflict between bureaucratic rationality and democratic values (the central theme of *TVA and the Grass Roots*) into a theoretical problem which can be accommodated within the analytical structure of a structural–functionalist sociology as providing a general theoretical framework for comparative organizational analysis. The theoretical problem is the 'recalcitrance of the tools of action':

'Social action is always mediated by human structures which generate new centres of need and power and interpose themselves between the actor and his goal. Commitments to others are indispensable in action: at the same time, the process of commitment results in tensions which have always had to be overcome.'

(Selznick 1949: 253)

Weber's interest in the potential conflict between 'formal' and 'substantive' rationality – between technical means and valued social ends – is clearly echoed in this statement, but in a very different theoretical idiom. Social structures, originally developed as institutional means to the realization of substantively valued ends, are transformed into ends in themselves and subsequently subvert the projects for which they were intended. However, the theoretical resolution of this dilemma by Selznick, or at least its tentative accommodation within a systems frame of reference, could not disguise the deep (and characteristically Weberian-like) pessimism which he displays with regard to its practical resolution. The call for 'institutional leadership' and flexible organizational socialization, conveyed in the mode of Barnard, could not hide Selznick's conviction that the triumph of bureaucratic power politics over direct participatory democracy seemed inevitable. The necessary institutional restraint on the worst excesses of human irrationality provided by bureaucratic organization, something which had been so loudly proclaimed by the 'administrative scientists', was now revealed for what it really was – an artificial human contrivance always liable to escape the control of its creators and to wreak havoc upon their most cherished hopes and ideals. What had once been thought of as an impartial technical instrument for extending institutional control over potentially destructive human desires had been recast in the form of a power resource ensuring the domination of formal rationality and the social interests it protects.

Blau's work also expresses a deepening sociological concern in bureaucratic organization and its implications for social action framed within a systems perspective. However, it lacks the intellectual subtlety of Selznick's contribution and helps prepare the ground for the formulation of a behaviourist view of organizational analysis in the hands of March and Simon.

Blau's contribution to the study of organizations – as originally formulated in *The Dynamics of Bureaucracy*, first published in 1955 (second edition 1963), and extended over a series of publications during the next twenty years (Blau 1974) – is based on a critical response to Weber's work on bureaucracy and a reworking of the 'middle range' functionalist paradigm constructed by Merton (Merton 1949).

The critique of Weber focuses on the putative methodological inadequacies of ideal-type construction and its use in the study of bureaucratic organizations. The ideal-type, Blau contends, mixes formal definitions and empirical hypotheses. This encouraged Weber to assume the factual existence of bureaucratic efficiency on the basis of logical necessity rather than empirical investigation. In turn, this led him to neglect bureaucratic innovation and change as a recurrent social phenomenon continually modifying prevailing organizational structures over time.

This criticism of the Weberian approach and its corresponding ignorance of 'emergent' organizational forms is coupled to a reworking of Mertonian functionalism. In this reworking, the operational linkages between theoretical categories such as 'function' and 'dysfunction' and participants' categorizations of the same social events and phenomena to which these terms refer are more clearly established. Merton's middle-range functionalist approach – which is focused on the problem of whether the social consequences of social action enhance or prejudice the structural adaptation of a social unit to the external social conditions that it faces – is deemed insufficient by Blau to furnish precise empirical criteria for supporting clear conceptual distinctions and the theoretical explanations they imply.

In Blau's view, functional analysis of organizational behaviour must consider the evaluations of the consequences of social action which are offered by organizational members for prevailing structural arrangements. These evaluations will necessarily be regulated by the specific location of members within a complex web of power relations, affording systematically constrained access to scarce resources and the range of opportunities it provides for social intervention:

> 'It is not possible to account for the persistence of needs, for practices that have serious dysfunctions, or for the fact that one pattern rather than another serves a given function, without enquiring into their differential effect on groups variously located within the power structure.'
>
> (Blau 1963: 13)

However, Blau is extremely reluctant to jettison the conceptual core of the Mertonian paradigm. He admits that a reformulated functionalist approach to organizational behaviour and bureaucratic change must concern itself with the explanatory significance of social action for structural innovation. Yet the analysis of social action must be conducted within the theoretical parameters set by a functionalism which predefines a set of explicit organizational goals (and an implicit range of functional needs) that structures the investigator's empirical research into intra-organizational power processes and relations. In this way, Blau offers a number of minor modifications to the core theoretical categories of Mertonian functionalism – 'function'/'dysfunction', 'manifest'/'latent' function, 'functional alternatives' – while retaining the underlying logic of functional analysis. The latter requires that social structures are to be accounted for in terms of the predefined functional needs which they fulfil. The social actions through which these structures are reproduced must be reinterpreted as emergent behavioural patterns which make an unequal contribution to system survival.

Nevertheless, Blau's determination to preserve the theoretical integrity of functionalism, while at the same time incorporating an explanation for a range of empirical phenomena that had often slipped the grasp of more orthodox functionalists, has certain unintended consequences for his reworking of the functionalist approach. This comes in the form of a resulting inability to perceive the ambiguous relationship which Selznick had identified between bureaucratic means and valued social ends. A recognition of the way in which existing structural arrangements (and the social inequalities they contain) severely limit the scope for social action is overlaid with a complacent reassertion of the recuperative capacities of social institutions and their ability to respond to changing social needs. New supervisory practices may lead to even greater discrimination against disadvantaged ethnic groups in their quest to secure employment in the local labour market. The collusion between agency officials and business managers may result in a less effective enforcement of legislation directed at improving working conditions (Blau 1963: 188). Yet the in-built capacity of bureaucratic organizations to meet emerging social needs through structural adaptation is repeatedly displayed as a reassuring manifestation of the social responsiveness of such institutions. Selznick's reflected vision of bureaucracy as constituting a pervasive and potentially destructive political force is transposed by Blau into a model of a somewhat wayward but none the less manageable social unit in which small groups construct a maze of transactions and supporting 'understandings' through which collective social action is made possible.

By the time we reach the work of March and Simon (1958) the projected 'depoliticization' of organizational analysis is all but complete and the triumph of a technocratic vision over remaining philosophical doubts seemingly assured. Their achievement lay in the skilled assimilation of a series of sociological works on the functioning of bureaucratic organizations within a behaviourist social psychology based on universalistic assumptions concerning the nature of individual rational choice (March and Simon 1958: 36–7). The reductionist methodology inherent in this theoretical programme would be substantially qualified, if not totally rejected, by a number of organizational theorists working within a related frame of reference (see Perrow 1972, Crozier and Friedberg 1980). However, the aspiration for a general conceptual framework for the analysis of organizational behaviour, encompassing both structural and motivational 'variables', provided a rationale for successive waves of theoretical consolidation in the late 1950s and early 1960s. In addition, it was also envisaged that such a framework would permit a more precise analytical identification of those psychological and sociological constraints which restricted the degree of formal rationality exhibited in goal–directed behaviour. This would create further intellectual legitimation for practical interventions in the course of collective social life aimed at extending the reach of institutional control over social action.

March and Simon's exposition of the general analytical structure underlying the work of Merton (1940), Selznick (1949), and Gouldner (1954a) is framed within a model of 'organizational learning' focused on individual behavioural response patterns to the disruptive influence exerted on established organizational routines by a changing set of environmental stimuli. The independent variable within this model is conceptualized as 'some form of organization or organizational procedure designed to control the activities of organizational members' (March and Simon 1958: 37). The implementation of these procedures, based upon a 'machine model' of human behaviour (interpreting the human organism as a simple machine responding in a predictable manner to a well-defined system of external stimuli), is shown to have both anticipated and unanticipated consequences for the operation of the dependent variable – that is, the range of behaviour-response patterns exhibited by the individual organizational member. The unanticipated consequences – increased rigidity and defensiveness on the part of the individual member to organizational instructions and constraints – reinforces the tendency for management to rely on control devices which reproduce, in a heightened form, the deviant behaviour they were originally meant to counteract.

The impact of March and Simon's 'synthesis' of sociological theories of organizational functioning and social–psychological theories of 'satisficing' behaviour on succeeding developments within the field of organizational studies during the 1960s should not be underestimated (see Whitely 1977b). First, it provided an interpretation of a number of empirical case studies on the dynamics of bureaucracy which selectively ignored their interest in 'power politics' and its impact upon the practical realization of democratic accountability and control over modern administrative institutions. Second, it reinforced the search for a general theory of organizational behaviour based on a behaviourist social psychology appropriately modified to accommodate the influence of structural stimuli on the cognitive operations of the individual decision-maker. Third, it encouraged the unreflective acceptance of an 'empiricist' epistemology and an 'instrumentalist' methodology as providing the necessary philosophical infrastructure for a science of organizational behaviour fashioned on behaviourist lines. 'Organizations' were to be treated as independently existing empirical phenomena which could be analysed from the perspectives provided by a range of theoretical approaches. In this way, a categorical separation was maintained between 'theory' and the empirical phenomena to which it was directed. 'Organization theory' constituted a systematic body of propositions concerning the structure and functioning of such independent entities which was produced through the application of accepted scientific practices such as experimentation and replication. These propositions would, in time, establish the 'knowledge base' from which more effective strategies of managerial intervention and planning could be implemented. Finally, the commitment to an empiricist epistemology and an instrumentalist view of scientific practice neatly dovetailed with a pragmatic incorporation of the dominant social priorities embodied in prevailing organizational structures within the normative substructure of organizational analysis. This helped to deflect any systematic reflection on the relationship between the aims that informed the practice of organizational analysis and the institutional and ideological constraints to which it was subjected.

It is against the intellectual background provided by the extension of an integrated systems approach to organizational analysis between 1945 and 1958 that the theoretical and practical prominence afforded to the systems concept during the following decade needs to be understood. It provided a conceptual vocabulary that facilitated a much more sophisticated appreciation of the sources of 'leverage' open to managerial intervention and the constraints limiting the scope of managerial action when dealing with problems of organizational design and control. These concerns converged to some extent with those of theorists relying upon the concept of system as a way of more clearly establishing the interrelationships between bureaucratic action and broader institutional parameters within a middle-range functionalist paradigm. What had once been a problem of engineering the appropriate man/machine relationship had become an issue for the social psychology of small-group behaviour, then a question of intergroup relations and organizational structure, and eventually progressed into the theme of 'environmental determinism'.

However, the community of systems theorists which had dominated organizational analysis since the 1930s began to show signs during the 1960s of a destabilizing coalition which identified some common interests, but not necessarily a common history or intellectual heritage. The consolidation of hard-won gains could not erase the creeping realization that organization theory had singularly failed to deliver the ambitious programme that its pioneers had so rashly promised. There was a need to take stock and to reconsider the short-term achievements which had been made as a prelude to realizing more long-term objectives which had yet to be fulfilled. Pugh's conviction that the *Zeitgeist* was with the practioners of organizational analysis may have been correct in its identification of the symbolic link between their aims and those of the society at large – or at least its managerial and administrative elites – but in need of readjustment when it came to predicting the time span in which the goal of 'unified science of man in organization' would actually come to fruition.

CONSOLIDATION

Etzioni's *Comparative Analysis of Complex Organizations* was published in 1961 and gave little indication of the disputes over methodological foundations, theoretical predilections, and normative commitments which were to emerge by the end of the decade.

In the preface to the first edition, Etzioni clearly spelled out the need to consolidate the past achievements of those attempting to rework and integrate a middle-range functionalist approach and a behaviourist social psychology with a systems framework. This process of consolidation would establish a firmer empirical and theoretical base for the achievement of the much more ambitious project that had been a recurring theme in the historical evolution of organization theory – a general theoretical framework specifying universal propositions holding for all categories of organization. The strategy of consolidation would have both a negative and a positive aspect. The former would be found in the reduction of over-generalized propositions to lower-level, middle-range statements. The positive aspect would be realized in the elaboration of an analytical framework permitting the formulation of propositional statements identifying general relationships between 'structural' and 'behavioural' dimensions of organization.

The conceptual germ for this middle-range analytical framework was the notion of 'compliance' consisting of two theoretically distinct but interrelated elements – the mode of power applied by 'higher participants' in securing the required behaviour of 'lower participants' (a structural variable) and the form of involvement forthcoming from the latter in response to the type of power resource to which they are subjected (a socio-psychological variable). On the basis of the possible logical relationships between these two key analytical elements, Etzioni constructed a typology of compliance structures consisting of three 'congruent' forms – 'Coercive' (coercive power–alienative involvement), 'Utilitarian' (remunerative power–calculative involvement), and 'Normative' (normative power–moral involvement).

This typology provides Etzioni with a classificatory device through which different empirical examples of complex organizations can be categorized on the basis of the predominant form of compliance pattern which they exhibit. The application of this typology also rests on the assumption that there will be a 'strain towards congruency' between the form of compliance pattern which an organization adopts and the goals it attempts to achieve. The ineffectiveness in resource allocation and utilization which would result from the imbalances created by incongruent patterns – such as

the application of a set of primarily coercive sanctions in an organization requiring moral involvement for the realization of its objectives – produces a self-regulating tendency towards congruency
between compliance structures and organizational goals.

Etzioni's framework is based on a firm rejection of commonsense
categories as providing an adequate conceptual base for theorizing
about organizations, given their lack of analytical precision and
logical coherence. Instead, he advocates the construction of a form of
abstract theoretical discourse which identifies its particular object of
concern and establishes the analytical categories through which it is
to be studied. This discourse is firmly located within a functionalist
tradition of sociological analysis focused on the problem of 'social
order' at the level of the individual organizational unit rather than the
social system as a whole. This tradition, according to Etzioni,
provided the conceptual resources necessary for integrating the three
main perspectives which have dominated the study of social order:
Elite theory and its primary concern with physical force as an
instrument of power; Marxist theory and its interest in economic
coercion as establishing the grounds for political and military power
structures; and finally Weberian theory and its focus on access to and
control over ideological and symbolic resources as a foundation for
the exercise of social power on an organized basis.

He accepted that the Weberian approach, particularly in its functionalist form in the USA, had tended to dominate work on this issue
to the virtual exclusion of the alternative perspectives. However, he
insisted that his own brand of functionalism could provide a means
for integrating this range of approaches in one coherent analytical
framework. This is so to the extent that it treats the three major
'power resources' on which compliance structures are dependent
(physical coercion, economic assets, and institutionalized values) as
'theoretical equals'. They provide the basic conceptual material for
the construction of a middle-range comparative framework in that
they constitute 'universal' features of social organization. They
regulate social behaviour with regard to three possible 'dysfunctional' behaviour patterns found in all social systems – social interaction based on asymmetrical values, conflict over relatively scarce
economic resources, and the deviant behaviour resulting from imperfect socialization processes within societies and their constituent
organizational units.

In this way, Etzioni concluded, his own version of a middle-range
functionalist approach avoided the theoretical difficulties associated

with Weber's three-fold distinction between 'class', 'status', and 'power', and his focus on 'the individual's moral judgements about the source and nature of the directives he receives' (Etzioni 1961: XVII). It provided a comparative analytical framework for the study of organizational compliance structures without having to consider the relationship between the categories relied on by the analyst and the interpretations of empirical forms of compliance patterns offered by organizational members. The methodological problems associated with this relationship are thus disposed of through a strategy of definitional fiat as opposed to systematic argument.

Yet the first edition of the *Comparative Analysis* (1961) did indicate an awareness of a number of methodological problems associated with the analysis which its author presented. Indeed, Etzioni's premature dismissal of these difficulties anticipated the kind of methodological critique to be offered of functionalism from the late 1960s onwards that provided the opening for a number of alternative approaches to be developed in the course of the 1970s.

The most pressing of these problems, for Etzioni at least, was the methodological question concerning the relationship between the analytical dimensions that provided the conceptual core of his comparative framework and the manner in which they were to be operationalized in empirical research:

> 'The major hindrance lies in transferring instruments from the study of one organization type to another while research is oriented to comparative propositions from the start. . . . There are not very many questions which would be meaningful in all three contexts (when weighting relative compliance patterns). . . . The crux of the problem is not that the units to be compared differ markedly and in many ways because we can compare them with respect to a limited number of variables at a time. The problem is that the *concrete indicators* for the same variable often differ greatly from one type of organization to another.'
>
> (Etzioni 1961: 301)

However, this methodological problem over the operational link between analytical dimensions and empirical indicators could not be resolved within the terms of the theoretical discourse which Etzioni had set himself – a revised middle-range functionalism – because it logically precluded any systematic reflection upon the link between sociological categorizations and those used by organizational participants in the course of their everyday lives. Weber's theoretical commitment to 'an action frame of reference' was firmly rejected as a basis for thinking about the relationship which exists between 'theoretical' and 'practical' forms of discourse. Weber's typology of domination and related organizational forms is based on the various strategies of social legitimation which 'rulers' implement through the promulgation of certain belief systems and their (partial and provisional) acceptance by 'followers'. Etzioni's typology of organizational compliance structures is the outcome of a theoretical exercise in conceptual classification based on the notion of 'organizational goals' as derived from a functionalist conception of the 'needs' of a social system. Once more, the metaphysical presuppositions locked into the vocabulary of systems theory prevent an honest recognition of the realities of organizational life which its exponents are struggling to come to terms with in their research.

This elision between the 'conservative' implications of metaphysical commitments and the 'radical' path of theoretical rejuvenation generates a range of internal contradictions which manifest themselves in various forms – methodological, theoretical, and substantive. Thus the unresolved problem of the link between theoretical and practical discourses also raised a number of additional issues to which Etzioni would have cause to return in the second edition of the *Comparative Analysis*, published fourteen years later. In particular, the static bias inherent in his approach and its effect on a number of key conceptualizations such as 'power' (Harris 1969) prompted a deeper re-evaluation of the functionalist perspective than he was prepared to undertake. In turn, this led to the provision of a more sophisticated formulation of the systems approach which incorporated phenomena that were explicitly recognized as characteristic features of organizational life. That form of functional analysis which was theoretically and normatively wedded to the domain assumptions of institutional integration and value consensus (at least at the level of the 'central value system' if not at the level of the individual organizational unit) became even more irrelevant at a time when social conflict and structural transformation were reclassified from the analytical status of 'deviant' and relatively minor disturbances into integral empirical features of organized social action (see Giddens 1979).

The significance of Thompson's *Organizations in Action* (1967) lay in its attempted synthesis of 'classical' and 'modern' traditions within an open-systems framework:

'The open-systems strategy shifts attention from goal attainment to survival and incorporates uncertainty by recognizing organizational interdependence with the environment. This newer tradition enables us to conceive of the organization as an open system, indeterminate and faced with uncertainty but subject to criteria of rationality and hence needing certainty.'

(Thompson 1967: 13)

Thompson's belief that the applied and theoretical strands in the field of organizational studies needed to be brought more closely together in a coherent and wide-ranging theoretical synthesis had been prompted by a number of developments taking place during the course of the 1960s. The contribution of the 'socio-technical school' (Trist *et al.* 1963) and that of 'contingency theorists' (Lawrence and Lorsch 1967) indicated that the unreformed neo-rationalism of Barnard and Simon or the closed-systems logic of 'bureaucratic theory' had to be considerably broadened to incorporate an interest in the 'environment' as the primary analytical element in a newly emerging open-systems approach. The latter also suggested that existing interpretations of the systems approach needed to be substantially reformulated to accommodate external variables which had been largely excluded from its purview. This process of theoretical elaboration, it had been argued, would also require the assimilation of many concepts which had either been reduced to the status of minor explanatory status or completely ignored, such as 'power', 'conflict', 'political bargaining', and 'organizational change'.

Thompson responded with great enthusiasm to this challenge. Closely associated with the 'administrative science' movement in America from the second half of the 1950s onwards (Thompson 1956), he developed his approach with sufficient skill to have largely avoided the label of 'technological determinist'. As a result, he was in a position to offer himself as a prominent contributor to an increasingly popular theoretical perspective which promised to synthesize key elements of those approaches that had dominated the field up until the mid-1960s, but were now in need of a conceptual overhaul.

Consequently, the open-systems strategy which Thompson recommended seemed equipped to analyse the central problem which faced all modern organizations – that is, the need to cope with the 'uncertainty' arising out of a dynamic socio-technical environment in which management have to ameliorate the disruptive impact of external 'turbulence' on internal operations through implementing the appropriate form of organizational design.

The problem of uncertainty stemmed from three main sources – the culture at large, the particular socio-technical domain in which the organization was located, and the internal interdependencies prevailing between operational sub-units. Thompson suggests a range of managerial strategies whereby the informational and organizational uncertainties resulting from these sources can be effectively managed. Taken together, they constitute a form of 'bounded rationality' through which organizational management can 'gear' its social structure to the demands of its technological base, as well as to those originating in its wider socio-technical context. Uncertainties which are presented to the management of complex organizations originate in a number of sources: a lack of cause/effect understanding in the culture at large, contingencies located in the socio-technical context, and the interdependency between organizational components. Each of these requires a control strategy – systematic organizational intelligence, a structured environmental domain, and administrative co-ordination – facilitating the realization of organizational rationality.

Up to this point, Thompson's 'conceptual inventory' merely reads like a more sophisticated version of Simonian neo-rationalism. However, he attempts to provide a more sophisticated theoretical gloss on this conceptual framework by introducing a systematic analysis of both the internal and external political contexts in which the formulation and implementation of managerial control strategies are located. This leads him into a consideration of a theme which had dominated, in rather different ways, the works of both Blau and Etzioni – that is, the concept of power and its implications for our understanding of organizational behaviour within an open-systems framework.

This analysis entails a rejection of the 'unitary' model of organization informing the work of the classical theorists with its monolithic control structure and associated processes of rational decision-making on the part of a seemingly omnipotent managerial elite. In its place, Thompson offers a pluralistic conception of intra-organizational coalition behaviour and a reworking of the concept of power within a 'power-dependence' framework (Emerson 1962). Organizational decision-making becomes much less a matter of unquestioned command or rational appraisal and much more a process of political bargaining and negotiation in which the exercise of power plays a key role.

The theoretical devices that Thompson uses are focused on the way in which the discretionary power of the 'dominant coalition' within an organization is severely circumscribed by a range of factors (incomplete knowledge, limited control over technological operations, prevailing political interests and commitments, and a dynamic socio-technical environment) which result in imperfect coping strategies being implemented. This implies a clear recognition of the political constraints in which organizational management are forced to operate. Indeed, the latter constitutes a complex coalition of interests which have to bargain with other coalitions before a policy can be formulated or implemented.

The power of the 'dominant coalition' rests on its ability to cope with internally and externally induced uncertainty with a minimum degree of reliance on the informational resources, technical knowledge, and skill of other organizational coalitions. It remains in a dominant political position as long as it is able to maintain a network of dependency relationships with other coalitions in which its scope for autonomous action is maximized by reducing its reliance on the contributions of others when managing uncertainty. Thus the dominant coalition and other intra-organizational sub-units are able to exercise a degree of power relative to their capacity in coping with sources of uncertainty affecting the task performance of other sub-units. This capacity is determined by such factors as their structural location (are they in a position to gain and retain access to information enabling them to monitor the environment?), the political skill they display in using this knowledge, and the importance of their technical skills to the undisturbed operation of the organization (Thompson 1967: 31). The resulting structure of power-dependence relations within the organization will determine the sort of response which it makes to the environmental pressures that it has to face. It forms the political interface between environmental change and the implementation of a particular strategic response on the part of organizational elites who are forced to negotiate with other interests.

Thompson's open-system approach is an attempt to rework and integrate aspects of both neo-rationalist decision-making theory and structural–functionalist sociology within a conceptual framework equipped to analyse 'organizations in action'. The conceptual shell of neo-rationalism is preserved, while elements of functionalism and exchange theory are inserted with the aim of providing a more sophisticated and realistic appraisal of the structural and processual constraints which limit the realization of 'bounded rationality'.

The contributions of Etzioni and Thompson can be interpreted as representations of a collective attempt to consolidate the theoretical gains which had been made during the course of the 1950s. In particular, the formal commitment to a general theory of organizations which the systems approach entailed was maintained, although the time span in which this objective was to be achieved became considerably extended. However, the perceived need to extend the theoretical scope of the systems approach to incorporate factors that had been relatively neglected was substantially reinforced. It culminated in a number of major modifications and extensions to the conceptual apparatus which the advocates of the former had managed to construct. At the same time, the integrity of its underlying assumptions concerning the defining characteristics of 'organization' and the structure of the scientific method through which they were to be researched were preserved through an attitude, if not a policy, of benign neglect. The compromise between a somewhat frenetic process of conceptual retooling and the easy acceptance of methodological and ideological orthodoxy could only be sustained as long as the internal tensions which this generated were regarded as being containable within the organicist metaphysic in which the systems approach had been developed.

The nagging doubts as to the capacity of a considerably reconstructed systems approach to cope with the constantly widening agenda of organizational analysis is evident to varying degrees in the contributions of both Etzioni and Thompson. In each case, the explanatory limitations of Parsonian functionalism and Simonian rationalism, both grounded in a model of organization emphasizing structural integration and value consensus, are clearly recognized. Various modifications are introduced in an attempt to overcome the perceived inadequacies of established perspectives. Yet the implications of this process of theoretical reformulation for the viability of the methodological and normative foundations on which the 'systems enterprise' rested are either ignored or have to wait upon later developments in an intellectual milieu much more conducive to reflection upon philosophical fundamentals – a time when implicit 'domain assumptions' are explicitly articulated and defended against external attack.

A renewed faith in the quintessential flexibility and adaptability of the systems approach in the face of increasing pressure for further theoretical innovation is cautiously expressed. Those who worked within the systems tradition had to perform a somewhat hazardous balancing act between contained theoretical reform and judicious philosophical neglect. This ability to maintain a strict division of labour between theoretical redevelopment and implicit philosophical stagnation would become increasingly precarious when the strength and range of external criticism became more intensive and extensive. The philosophical incubus which had remained dormant as long as the underlying contradictions between 'rationalism' and 'naturalism' could be contained within the conceptual shell of modern systems theory (see Gouldner 1959) was about to be awakened as a result, initially at least, of a methodological critique which seemed to pose little, if any, direct threat to the dominant intellectual position which the latter had achieved by the middle of the 1960s.

The revolt against science

By the end of the 1960s the intellectual hold which the systems perspective had enjoyed within the field of organizational studies was beginning to weaken. While work had been carried out in the 1950s and 1960s which resisted its embrace and criticized its limiting influence (Krupp 1961, Strauss 1963, Bittner 1965), the late 1960s and early 1970s witnessed a spate of publications in which this somewhat muted criticism was transformed into open challenge and subsequent elaboration.

As has already been indicated, the major factor contributing to this increasingly destabilized situation was a growing recognition that systems theorists were unable to resolve certain fundamental problems within the terms of reference set by the form of discourse which they had constructed over a period of thirty years or so. A point seemed to have been reached where any further extension of the intellectual parameters in which this discourse was located would inevitably call into question its core 'domain assumptions' concerning the nature of organization, the structure of scientific reasoning, and the technocratic value system on which it relied to provide ideological justification for its promulgation.

It would be at this point that the 'separatist strategy' of conceptual renovation and philosophical neglect would be jeopardized in that it would be explictly revealed for what it was and would have to be defended as a viable and honourable practice for organizational theorists to follow in the future.

However, it is important not to over-dramatize and simplify these changes in terms of some 'paradigm shift' or 'gestalt conversion' from one reigning intellectual orthodoxy into another framework in which the whole basis of intellectual work is fundamentally transformed (as suggested in Benson 1977b). Instead, what we have is:

> 'an untidy but characteristic unevenness of development. What is important is the significant breaks. . . . Changes in problematic do significantly transform the nature of the questions asked, the forms in which they are proposed, and the manner in which they can be adequately answered.'
>
> (Hall 1980: 57)

Thus the gradual change in problematic occurring within the field of organizational studies during the course of the second half of the 1960s and early 1970s has to be understood and interpreted in terms of the escalating internal difficulties which the dominant perspective had been experiencing and the intellectual space which this afforded for alternative frameworks to be developed.

It is also significant that similar changes were concurrently taking place in a number of fields of social scientific endeavour (Eldridge 1980). Indeed, some have even suggested that the 1960s were a watershed in the intellectual development of a wide range of fields:

> 'Intellectual, artistic and social movements which dominated their respective fields throughout the first half of the twentieth century finally petered out or ran into the sand to be replaced by other streams, many in quite different and quite often opposite directions.'
>
> (Toulmin 1971: 53)

In relation to the development of English-speaking sociology, Giddens has argued that the period can be characterized in terms of the 'dissolution of the orthodox consensus' which had dominated the discipline up to the late 1960s (Giddens 1979). This orthodoxy, Giddens suggests, had three main components – one substantive, one theoretical, and one methodological. The substantive component was contained in the 'theory of industrial society', the theoretical component in 'functionalism', and the philosophical component in 'naturalism'.[8] The first of these suggested that class conflict had become institutionalized and had subsequently transformed the terms of 'ideological' debate from class conflict into small-scale technical issues. 'Functionalism' characterized the subject matter of sociological analysis in terms of self-regulating social systems which operated on the basis of their own internal logic, while 'naturalism' adhered to the proposition that the logical frameworks of natural and social science were essentially the same (Giddens 1979: 235–38). The previous section of this chapter has illustrated the substantial contribution which organizational analysis made to each of these components of the orthodox consensus between the late 1930s and the mid-1960s. Yet this had to be paid for at a price; and the price to be paid was an undeniable credibility gap which had opened up between the 'promise' of a science of organizations which would prove to be the intellectual midwife of a rational technocracy and the actual 'delivery' of an intellectual practice which displayed all the signs of latent immaturity and retarded development. In short, it was a field of study characterized by deep-seated doubts and uncertainties over fundamental assumptions concerning the questions which are asked, the forms in which they are posed, and the manner in which they can be adequately answered. As long as these doubts, and the tensions which they generated, could be contained within a mainstream orthodoxy which actively discouraged detailed self-reflection over philosophical fundamentals, or managed selectively to diffuse the large implications of those that actually got through, then the project of a general science of organizations along systems lines could just about be held together. However, it became more and more evident as the 1960s gave way to the 1970s that this delicate balancing act would be very difficult, if not impossible, to sustain in the future without detailed re-examination of the domain assumptions in which the systems approach had been embedded.

A number of commentaries published during this period (Mayntz 1964, Mouzelis 1967, Albrow 1974, Burns 1969, Child 1973b, Crozier 1974) revealed the intensifying strain under which the propagators of

---

8 Giddens's use of the term 'naturalism' needs to be distinguished from the usage followed in this chapter in relation to Barnard. Giddens is using the term to refer to a particular methodological doctrine, while I have used it to characterize the broad tradition of socio-political thought in which Barnard's work is located.

orthodoxy laboured. These overviews of the 'state of the art' also helped to pinpoint the most vulnerable positions occupied by the latter. This was so in relation to two strategic areas: first, the sustained methodological commitment of systems theorists to a naturalistic (or positivistic) conception of social scientific reasoning as welcome relief from nagging doubts over the epistemological status of the knowledge which these efforts produced; second, their ideological commitment to a pluralistic model of industrial society as a necessary intellectual solvent for a nascent Marxist critique which was growing in strength and influence.

Mayntz's survey (Mayntz 1964) of the condition of organizational studies in the mid-1960s identified these weaknesses with great clarity and precision. Modern organization theory, she argued, depended on a highly abstract and ahistorical model of organization as a social system which was justified (in methodological terms) by the search for a general theoretical scheme similar to that discovered in the natural sciences. In turn, this model encouraged a disinterest in the 'power aspect of organizational control' and reinforced the official image of organization as a 'small-scale replica of the societal model of pluralism' (Mayntz 1964: 105). Both of these extremely contentious domain assumptions, Mayntz concluded, acted as a restraining influence upon the strong centrifugal tendencies within the field which threatened the fragile unity and integration that systems theory had provided: 'contrary to the promise of the theoretical approach, the unity and coherence of the field of organizational research is highly precarious' (Mayntz 1964: 111).

Mayntz suggested that two developmental trends were beginning to emerge at that time which offered alternative intellectual roads for organizational theorists to tread from that laid down by orthodox systems theorists: 'towards a prescriptive theory focusing on efficiency on the one hand, and towards the systematic linkage with problems on the societal level on the other hand' (Mayntz 1964: 118). The former, she believed, would be dominated by management science and business administration, while the latter would be strongly influenced by sociology and politics. Both would continue to rely on a view of the organization as a social system, but with the aim of developing analytical models and empirical propositions applicable to a particular class or type of organization rather than a universally valid general theoretical framework.

While Mayntz had displayed a considerable degree of prescience in locating the critical sources of weakness within the orthodox approach during a period when it seemed to be at the zenith of its powers, she substantially underestimated the extent to which they would be exploited to produce, in the fullness of time, a far deeper and wider fracture (or series of fissures) within the field than she had ever envisaged. The first wave of criticism and subsequent reformulation would coalesce around the methodological strategy through which systems theorists had attempted to shore up the philosophical foundations of their analytical edifice. The second wave would focus on the ideological character of their theorizing and would produce a much more searching, if radically flawed, examination of the relationship between 'analysis' and 'values' in the study of organizations.

The second of these critiques and reformulations must wait until the next chapter. It is time to turn to the first wave of criticism and its eventual crystallization in the form of an action approach to the study of organizations.

THE ACTION CRITIQUE

The initial critique of mainstream orthodoxy focused on the positivistic conception of social science on which systems theorists had traded, and the theoretical and substantive distortions which this reproduced. This provided the justification for a thorough-going reorientation of research effort aimed at greater clarification of the 'first order' interpretations of organizational life provided by members and their expression in 'second order' structural components such as technology and managerial control systems. Eventually, the original interest in the link between actors' interpretations and structural constraints would be buried in an obsessive concern with the minutiae of 'everyday life' as exemplified in the intricacies of organizational routine. This methodological critique and its subsequent elaboration into an alternative theoretical frame of reference had intellectual roots in a much earlier and far-reaching critique of positivism which it tended to plunder, somewhat indiscriminately, in search of philosophical support for its sociological arguments. Thus Winch's attack on a 'Weberian' conception of social explanation (Winch 1958) and Kuhn's conventionalist account of the dynamics of scientific change (Kuhn 1962) are taken from their original contexts and marshalled in support of rather different objectives.

In the case of organizational studies, the clearest and most elegant presentation of the case for an 'alternative' organizational analysis was to be found in the work of Silverman. His book, *The Theory of Organizations* (1970), is of pivotal significance in the development of an action frame of reference in organizational analysis for a number of reasons. First, it identified the need for a 'paradigm shift' within organizational studies away from the systems orthodoxy which had largely structured intellectual work within the field since the 1930s. Second, it provided a coherent conceptual framework in which the diverse intellectual strands which constituted the embryonic action tradition could be brought to intellectual maturity. Third, the theoretical synthesis which it attempted was incomplete in that it failed to resolve the tensions between a 'Weberian' and 'ethnomethodological' reading of organizational analysis's intellectual aims and resources.

Silverman's justification for rejecting the possibility of a reconciliation between the system and action perspectives relied on a Kuhnian model of paradigm change and the selective emphasis which it gave to intellectual divergence and discontinuity in accounting for the process of scientific development. In his view, the system paradigm had undergone something of an intellectual overhaul during the 1960s. However, this merely illustrated its evident failure to incorporate key social processes such as social conflict or to provide a coherent explanation of the relationship between human agency and social structure. Organizational studies, Silverman suggested, were ripe for takeover by a rival paradigm that entailed a fundamentally different approach to the central issue which faced all social scientists – 'the nature of the social order that sociologists study and of the major characteristics of the social reality thereby implied' (Silverman 1970: 5). Thus the alternative paradigm which Silverman was in the process of outlining reflected a radical discontinuity between an existing orthodoxy and an increasingly vociferous challenger across a wide range of 'domain assumptions' relating to ontology, methodology, and ideology.

Subsequently, Silverman constructed the action frame of reference on the basis of a generalized critique of positivistic social science and the formulation of a hermeneutic or interpretative methodology that drew heavily on the work of philosophers such as Schutz (1967) and Winch (1958). Positivism was rejected on the grounds of its failure to recognize the categorical distinction between the 'natural' and the 'social' worlds. It assumed that the basic conceptual categories informing social research could be constructed and utilized in such a way that the 'subjective' quality of social reality would be subsumed within a methodology that focused exclusively on directly observable externalities. This resulted in a form of explanation that either ignored or denied the internal logic of social processes which, in Silverman's view, had to be understood 'from within' by the sociologist and directly incorporated into his explanatory framework. It simply amputated, in the interest of methodological neatness and theoretical objectivity, the interaction between structural constraints and subjectively meaningful action. All it left was a behaviourist model of social interaction in which observable regularities between environmental stimuli and behavioural responses provided the psychological foundations on which a scientific sociology could be constructed.

In direct contrast, Silverman maintained, the action frame of reference was grounded in an interpretative methodology that recognized, indeed rejoiced in, the 'meaningful' quality of social interaction and the socially constructed nature of social reality. The latter is reproduced through a network of self-constructed subjective meanings which become institutionalized over a period of time. It cannot be described or explained without a detailed knowledge of the subjective logic which informs the construction of these institutional configurations and the dynamics of their historical transformation. The form of explanation which it requires depends on a creative interplay between a sympathetic description and understanding of actors' subjective states of mind and the application of 'ideal-typical' models of rational action in which ends and means are perfectly co-ordinated and to which actual examples of social action can be compared. Such explanation would have to be 'meaningfully adequate' in the sense of tracing out an identifiable link between subjective intentions and situational outcomes. In addition, 'causal adequacy' would be required – that is, subjectively meaningful courses of social action had to be systematically related to the structures of social interaction in which they were undertaken.

This frame of reference provided Silverman with a methodological framework in which a particular mode of analysis for organizational studies could be further developed. The latter, Silverman contended, focused on six interrelated substantive areas: the historical growth and current structure of the organization's role system; the nature and source of ideal-typical actors' involvements in organizational activities; the definitions of the situation which these ideal-typical actors offer and their expectations concerning the actions of others with special regard to the distribution and use of organizational resources; the typical political strategies followed by different groupings to realize their objectives; the intended and unintended consequences of these strategies for the existing pattern of actors' involvements and institutionalized role expectations; changes in actors' involvements and formalized role expectations brought about by internal and external structural transformations.

The unique contribution of this mode of analysis to the study of organizations, Silverman argued, lay in its capacity to explain the impact of extra-organizational factors on intra-organizational structures and processes. It managed to relate internal developments to the broader social context through the application of an approach that systematically interrelates 'macro' and 'micro' variables. In this way, the action approach makes it possible for the researcher:

> 'to move from an examination of the micro problem of particular actors to the macro problem of the systems of expectations that is established as they pursue their ends in the context of the meanings and symbolic resources which they and other actors import from the wider social structure.'

(Silverman 1970: 165)

Having taken account of the influence of external factors, the action approach also has the additional advantage of being able to explain how organizational change emerges from the interaction of the participants rather than from the failure of a reified 'social system' to adapt to the requirements of its environment.

Silverman's characterization of the action frame of reference as a method of analysis – rather than a 'theory of organizations' – grounded in an interpretative philosophy of social science contained a number of internal tensions and ambiguities which were rather thinly disguised under the presupposition of a process of 'paradigm shift' through which all outstanding difficulties would eventually be resolved. These tensions revolved around the crucial difference between a Weberian and phenomenological conception of 'social action' and its implications for the status and role of structural explanations in sociology.

There are successive indications throughout the book of Silverman's unease over a Weberian conception of social action as subjectively meaningful conduct which has to be identified and explained in terms of a method of analysis (the construction and application of ideal-type constructs) which assumes a privileged epistemological status *vis-à-vis* the actor's definition of the situation. At one point he argues that:

> 'The explanation of why people act as they do may not lie in a combination of "objective" and "subjective" factors, but in a network of meanings which take a "world for granted" (Schutz 1964). Indeed, "objective" factors, such as technology and market structure, are literally meaningful only in terms of the sense that is attached to them by those who are concerned and the ends to which they are related.'

(Silverman 1970: 37)

While Weber is cited in support of this argument, it is indicative of Silverman's inclination to limit sociological explanation to the meaning which 'objective' factors have for participants as communicated through their commonsense understanding of social situations. This is further reinforced by his criticism of the failure of approaches ostensibly located within the action perspective 'to make problematic the commonsense knowledge which is used by participant and observer to produce "convincing" accounts of "what really happened"' (Silverman 1970: 186). Such a failure of the sociological imagination is accounted for by Silverman in terms of the intellectual influence which the residue of positivist methodology still exerts over the practices of social scientists who have nominally rejected its embrace.

However, a consideration of social facts only insofar as they are reflected in actors' commonsense stocks of knowledge would seem to weaken an approach striving to provide explanations of social order which 'take account of the range of motives underlying conformity to the expectations of others and pay attention to the possible role of coercion in imposing a normative definition of the situation on others' (Silverman 1970: 137). As a result, the possible gains to be realized through a phenomenological modification of a Weberian conception of social action may have to be paid for at a very high price indeed; a deeper appreciation of the commonsense rationalities which support particular social structures has to be balanced against the risk of emasculating a form of analysis which presumes to explain a range of structural variables regulating social interaction which are not necessarily reflected in participants' accounts (see Goldthorpe 1973, Giddens 1977).

Silverman would subsequently resolve this dilemma by closely opting for an ethnomethodological interpretation of the action frame of reference in his later work (Silverman 1972 and 1975, Silverman and Jones 1973). In this way, he would become one of the central figures in the development of a 'folk sociology' which totally rejected the central presuppositions and preoccupations of mainstream organizational analysis (in either its 'systems' or 'Weberian' guises) during the course of the 1970s. Before we consider this more radical interpretation of the action approach (and its implications for the practice of organizational analysis) in greater depth, it is necessary to provide a more focused appreciation of the analytical implications of the action approach as conveyed in the 'negotiated order' model of organization.

ORGANIZATIONS AS NEGOTIATED SOCIAL ORDERS

The 'negotiated order' model of organization was originally formulated by Strauss *et al.* (1963) in their research on two psychiatric hospitals, although the central components of the model were foreshadowed in the works of Dalton (1959) and Goffman (1959). The model has been subsequently developed and extended to a range of organizational settings by Bucher and Stelling (1969), Elger (1975), Day and Day (1977), and Strauss (1978).

In 1963 Strauss and his co-authors argued that the 'negotiated order' model was well equipped to deal with the most central of all sociological issues concerned with the problem of how social order was maintained in the face of the inevitable disruptions to established social structures caused by an ubiquitous and inexorable process of social change. This problem, they suggested, had been largely ignored by mainstream organization theorists in that they had tended 'to underplay the processes of internal change as well as overestimating the more stable features of organizations – including its rules and hierarchical statuses' (Strauss *et al.* 1963: 147).

The negotiated order approach took its theoretical inspiration from the work of Mead (1936) who had argued that the problem of incorporating participative mechanisms of social change in the prevailing institutional structure of society was the central political and sociological issue confronting modern industrial society. Given this focus on the reproduction of social institutions through interactional processes, Strauss and his colleagues contended that the structural framework in which collective social action was located had to be continually reworked and renewed through a negotiating process involving all the main social groupings constituting a particular social unit, whether at the level of the nation state or the individual organization.

Subsequently, their research in psychiatric hospitals and other forms of organization employing a relatively high ratio of 'professional' groups supported a conceptualization of organizational structure as a continually reconstituted patterning of social interaction. This was most fruitfully characterized in terms of a complex and subtle interactive relationship between a daily negotiating process between all participants and a periodic appraisal review conducted by organizational elites. All social order in complex organizations was negotiated; there could not be any sustained and patterned – that is, 'organizational' – relationships without accompanying negotiating processes.

This suggested a model of organization in which the more stable elements expressed in the concept of formal organization structure – hierarchy, rules, procedures, regulatory codes – were seen as forming a background context against which the more ephemeral working relations constructed out of everyday interaction could be analysed. Such a model would also allow for the possibility that the relationship between formal structure and everyday negotiation could be reversed so that 'structure' was regarded as a temporary patterning of the ebb and flow of interactional processes which was always open to periodic reappraisal and reconstruction through negotiated agreements between participants.

The general inference drawn from these arguments for the study of organizations was a diminution in the explanatory significance attached to formal organization and a theoretical upgrading of the interactional processes through which structural forms are reproduced. Over a period of time, the negotiated order model was further developed with the aim of accommodating a range of theoretical concerns and empirical actualities which had been 'underscored' in the 1963 article. Thus a dynamic analysis of the manner in which structural arrangements are accomplished in particular situations has been complemented by a more systematic conceptualization of power relations and the role which they play in contextualizing negotiating processes. In this way, the concept of 'power' has been interpreted in terms of the relative capacities of participants to regulate the course of social interaction in the face of specific situational contingencies rather than in terms of any fixed pattern of structural attributes which are deemed to determine the direction and outcome of the former (Day and Day 1977).

As a result of these more recent additions and reformulations, organizational structure is conceptually transformed from a neutral instrument of social control into 'an emergent product of processes of negotiation and interpretation enacted by differentially placed participants within the jurisdiction of organizational decision-rules and administrative programmes' (Elger 1975: 97). This reinforces the importance – both theoretical and practical – which is attached to the way in which the negotiating processes through which organizations are reproduced are constrained by the prevailing pattern of power relations and the unequally distributed capacities which it provides for participants to construct the structural forms through which they interact.

However, the reworking of the negotiated-order model to accommodate both processual dynamics and structural constraints could not resolve, or for that matter disguise, the unresolved theoretical tension which lies at the core of the action approach as it had been developed during the course of the late 1960s and through the 1970s. Silverman's specification of the latter indicated that the structural forms which regulate social interaction had no ontological or explanatory significance apart from that communicated through the subjective interpretations offered of them by organizational members. Yet a growing recognition of the severe limitations which this imposes on an action analysis of organizations has prompted several of its practitioners (Elger 1975, Benson 1977a) to engage in a process of conceptual retooling whereby the regulative force of existing structural forms on the course and outcome of social interaction can be admitted. In turn, this has alienated a number of people working within the action tradition who reject the deterministic implications of such a movement in the direction of structural explanation and have attempted to reconstruct the approach in such a way that a much more radical break with the Weberian problematic can be brought about.

THE RISE OF ETHNOMETHODOLOGY

As a general approach to sociological analysis, ethnomethodology developed out of a wide-ranging critique (Cicourel 1964, Garfinkel 1967) of the epistemological and methodological orthodoxies which had dominated mainstream sociology up until the late 1960s (Lassman 1974, Mennell 1975). At the core of this critique lay a firm rejection of the 'absolutist' conception of objectivity which seeks 'knowledge of man completely independent of, and in opposition to, commonsense by imposing experimental, quantitative, "thing-like" ideas on all scientific studies of man' (Douglas 1971: 25). While the positivistic conception of sociological enquiry logically presupposed a categorical distinction between man as an object of and as a participant in the process of social research, the ethnomethodologists attempted to dismantle the barriers between everyday scientific modes of discourse by focusing on the principles and operation of 'practical reasoning' – that is, the methods and procedures which actors rely on to provide coherent accounts of the social interaction in which they are engaged.

It has been suggested (Attwell 1974) that, in its earlier stages of development, ethnomethodology constituted a logical extension of symbolic interactionism – both in relation to the latter's negotiated conception of social order and its rejection of rationalistic models of social action which had informed a great deal of mainstream organizational analysis. However, over time it came to signify a much more radical and traumatic break with all 'traditional' or 'conventional' sociological perspectives in its single-minded focus on the structure of everyday social interaction itself, rather than viewing the latter as a medium through which various aspects of collective social life are conveyed. This resulted in a drastic limitation being imposed on the theoretical scope of sociological analysis from an ethnomethodological viewpoint; the interpretative procedures and methods through which social interaction becomes meaningfully organized totally occupied the frame of sociological analysis to the virtual exclusion of any interest in social interaction as the strategic process or medium through which social institutions are reproduced. The more radical implications of the 'ethnomethodological revolution' are clearly expressed in the form of the interventions which its adherents made in the field of organizational studies beginning with Bittner's paper, first published in 1965 (Bittner 1965). Conventional organizational analysis, Bittner maintained, was committed to a conception of 'organization' as a goal-attaining social unit in which members' activities are formally programmed. Within this broad conception, the central managerial problem is to ensure that the unintended consequences of informal behaviour do not threaten the 'effectiveness' with which formal organization is applied to the pursuit of organizational goals. This 'programmatic construction', Bittner contended, enabled organization theorists to equate formal organization with human rationality and to treat it as a predictive device whereby observed behavioural patterns and the structure of social relations which they generate can be theoretically explained.

However, this abstract theoretical rationalization is part of the theorist's subject matter – it is a commonsense construct employed by organizational members in their everyday lives which has been unreflectively appropriated for the purpose of secondary analysis. This appropriation, in Bittner's view, contains a theoretical short cut which allows the researcher to treat a managerial definition of organization as an objective analytical construct without any consideration of how it is used by participants in everyday interaction. Insofar as the concept of 'formal organization' is a refined and purified version of the actor's theorizing, it is at the same time a corrupt and incomplete interpretation of that primary process. It simply distils commonsense discourse in such a way that it satisfies the technical requirements of a theoretical framework and ignores the complex network of background assumptions or 'tacit knowledge' in which it is embedded. As a result, it is unable to account for the way in which theoretical discourse is parasitic on practical discourse; the theoretical rationalization which it achieves can only be brought off as the result of the 'collusion' between the theorist and the actor (as theorist) to retain its conceptual integrity.

Bittner outlines three possible research strategies as alternative ways of dealing with this problem: retain unexplicated commonsense meanings of formal organizations as a basis for theorizing, while recognizing their in-built limitations; define theoretical terms by way of sophisticated operational techniques and their supporting statistical procedures; decide that the meaning of analytical constructs and the social facts which they subsume must be uncovered by explicating their use in everyday life by persons who are competent to apply them. Only the last of these strategies, Bittner maintains, 'yields entirely to the rule specifying the relevance of the perspective of the actor in sociological inquiry' (Bittner 1965: 270). This latter strategy clearly sets out the programme of organizational research on which the ethnomethodologists subsequently embarked and its focus upon the actor's methodical use of rational constructions subsumed under the concept of 'formal organization' which 'seeks to describe the mechanisms of sustained and sanctional relevance of the rational constructions to a variety of objects, events and occasions relative to which they are invoked' (Bittner 1965: 271).

Such a programme clearly implied a firm rejection of the key

assumptions underlying mainstream organizational studies, particularly the presupposition that managerial conceptions of organization
enjoyed a privileged epistemological status in proving an authorit-
ative account of social reality. It also implied that a too-easy acceptance
of the most obvious or conspicuous meanings of 'formal organization' invoked in typical cases was to be superseded by a reading of the
concept as a generalized scheme of interpretation through which
a very wide range of practical problems could be managed by
participants.

This programme and its underlying rationale were very evident in
the case-study research of a number of ethnomethodologists working within the field of organizational studies during the course of the
1960s and 1970s: Bittner's research on police-keeping routines on
'skid row' (1967); Cicourel's analysis of the way in which 'juvenile
delinquents' are processed by various social-control agencies (1968);
Sudnow's study of the day-to-day operation of 'plea-bargaining' in
the American courts (1965); Zimmerman's investigation into the
dynamics of bureaucratic processing in welfare agencies (1971); and
Silverman's exposé of the selection procedures relied upon by a
public-sector corporation in Britain (Silverman and Jones 1973, 1976).

Collectively, these studies elaborated and extended the original
mandate for ethnomethodological research in organizational analysis originally set out by Bittner. The dissolution of the concept of
'formal organization' (as conveyed in conventional analyses of
organizations relying on systems theory) was finally achieved and
replaced by a conception of 'organization' as a social construct which
requires continual renewal through the subtle application of interpretative skills and procedures on the part of members in their
everyday lives (see Jehenson 1973). The assumption that formal
organization structures provided 'objective' and indisputable representations of social reality is suspended. In its place, the ethnomethodologists offer a commitment to reveal the shared schemes of
reference and accounting procedures whereby participants attempt
to comprehend and organize the social order of which they are a part.
The interpretation of social reality represented by the commonsense
schemes of typifications characteristic of formal or complex organization is redefined as the existential outcome of human activity which
remains extremely precarious and highly unstable in terms of its
internal coherence and practical relevance for everyday situations
(see Silverman 1975).

At the same time, they gave a highly selective interpretation to a belief which remained firmly locked into the domain assumptions on which the action frame of reference had been articulated; that is, the belief that the meaning and validity of sociological analysis must always be ultimately determined by its 'faithfulness' to 'the ways in which members themselves decide adequacy in everyday terms' (Phillipson 1972: 151). This belief provided the grounds on which ethnomethodology could resolve the traditional analytical dichotomy between 'action' and 'structure' which exponents of an action approach had previously attempted to overcome through their reworking of Weber's conceptualization of 'social action'. Ethnomethodologists achieved a resolution of this problem by restricting the theoretical meaningfulness of structural concepts to those procedural mechanisms through which members achieved coherent accounts of social situations. The analytical and explanatory 'gap' between theoretical accounts of social structure and practical accounts of everyday life was removed by dissolving the former into the latter so that no conceptual residue remained. The need for bridging concepts (such as 'role') or methodological devices (such as statistical operationalization) was expunged by the assumption that:

> 'Knowledge of human reality boils down to continuous self-reflection, open to everybody sharing everyday life and open only insofar as he does share in everyday life without attempting to transcend it and to adopt an outsider's perspective.'
>
> (Bauman 1973: 15)

This placed very tight limitations on the scope and nature of sociological analysis which were unacceptable to many working within the action tradition. In its most extreme form (as conveyed in a number of papers in Filmer, et al 1972), it also implied a denial of the conventional sociological presupposition that institutionalized structures of social relations possessed any significance as meaningful social facts apart from that given to them through the practical reasoning engaged in by participants. It seemed that the latter had been raised to the epistemological status of absolute sociological truth, immune to challenge from or correction by the application of theoretical reason (on this point see Emmet and Macintyre 1970). The relativistic leanings of the action perspective had been taken to their logical conclusion and produced a form of organizational analysis in which the concept of 'organization' – as conveying any interest in or knowledge of the institutional structures through which actors' accounting is facilitated – is completely tied to the usage which it receives in the accounting practices of its members.

Such a drastic weakening of the explanatory power of sociological analysis was hotly disputed by a number of theorists closely associated with the action approach as it had been developed during the course of the 1970s (Goldthorpe 1973, Giddens 1976, Worsley 1974). The 'retreat from institutional analysis' (Giddens 1973) which the ethnomethodological intervention seemed to imply was considered too drastic a limitation to impose, even accepting the contribution that it had undoubtedly made to a much improved understanding of the methods whereby everyday social order is constructed and maintained (Gidlow 1972). The calm indifference which it displayed in relation to the structuring imposed by powerful social institutions, as well as the fundamental political and ethical questions which this raised, was regarded as the logical outcome of an approach to organizational analysis which had at best minimized, and at worst ignored, the fact that 'the construction of realities may be more influenced by power relations, socialization processes and class struggles than by the creative interpretations of the actors engaged in interaction' (Dreitzel 1970: xvi). Whether this range of factors could be systematically incorporated within a theoretical framework which was recognizably related to the action frame of reference was a question which an increasing number of organization theorists were to answer in the negative as the 1970s progressed.

Summary

At the beginning of the 1960s, organizational analysis looked set to provide a general theory of organizations which held out the promise of rational control over the large-scale collective human projects through which the 'second wave' of industrialization (Burns 1963) in the developed countries was to be advanced. Ten years later, this promise looked more like a hollow boast than a youthful aspiration which had been temporarily postponed, but which still remained a realistic and attractive disciplinary aspiration. The field seemed to be in a state of intellectual disarray and ideological confusion concerning both its academic aims and the contribution which their realization was likely to make in improving the quality of human interventions – whatever their objectives or institutional character – in the course of human history. Indeed, Albrow's call for a sociology

of organizations 'untramelled by the needs of "men of affairs"'
(Albrow 1973: 412) sounded passé by the mid-1970s when the field
had become so influenced by an approach which expressed little, if
any, interest in the social needs and aspirations of any social group –
apart, that is, from those conveyed in the intricate transactions of
everyday life. Systems theorists had located the human drive to
organize in the primary need for institutional certainty and order in a
society threatened by unregulated egotistical desire and the endemic
social conflict which it generated. Ethnomethodologists treated
organizational structures and symbols as the fictional devices
through which members warded off the constant threat of localized
anomie arising out of the breakdown in normative consensus in their
immediate social milieu. Both subscribed to a conception of organizational analysis which severely fractured, if not totally sundered,
the historical link between organization theory and social theory
through their common insistence that it was no longer equipped (if it
ever had been!) to address the fundamental questions which had
puzzled the classical theorists in their overriding concern with the
interaction between bureaucratic organization and social structure.

By the time we reach the mid-1970s, any claim to intellectual
coherence and broader social purpose within the field of organizational studies was very difficult, if not impossible, to maintain in the
face of a situation in which practitioners could no longer identify any
common intellectual interests, much less a shared intellectual ances-
try. Organizational theorists had settled for a bifurcated intellectual
practice in which those who continued to trade in what was left of the
systems orthodoxy which had dominated the field for thirty years
merely shrugged their shoulders and sold their intellectual wares to
the highest bidder, while those who had opted for a myopic focus on
the social minutiae of everyday life immersed themselves in the detail
of particular organizational settings and absolved themselves of any
involvement in the larger ideological and moral debates which
swirled around them.

The 'dual vision' which had originated in Barnard's attempt to
combine the competing claims of rationalism and naturalism within
a functionalist framework had eventually produced a situation in
which the unresolved tensions which it contained could not be
embraced within the same intellectual practice. Organizational
analysis seemed no longer able to cope with the underlying contradictions between a rationalistic conception of organization stressing
manipulative control and a naturalistic model emphasizing spon-

taneous co-operation through shared understandings. Students of organization were being forced to choose between a badly damaged orthodoxy that seemed destined to stultify into an even narrower technical exercise and an intellectual heresy which also showed signs of degenerating into a highly specialized and arcane technique aimed at identifying the universal properties of face-to-face interaction. The intellectual and social space available to writers and researchers who rejected both of these options and attempted to preserve and develop something of the intellectual inheritance of the classical theorists was visibly narrowing.

However, at the same time that the field of organizational studies looked set to be dissipated into a number of warring factions holding somewhat tenuous allegiance to one or other of the broad theoretical perspectives which had structured its development up to that date, a number of publications began to appear which suggested that one tradition, which had almost been totally neglected, provided a possible way out of the impasse which had been created – that is, the recovery of the Marxist perspective on the organizational dynamics of the capitalist mode of production. As the 1970s progressed, this body of research and writing would indicate the need to transform previous conceptions of organizational analysis and bring about its rebirth as one element of a total approach focused on the 'inner workings' of modern capitalism and the structural mechanisms which it fosters in contemporary work organizations. In time, this recasting of organizational studies within a theoretical tradition which it had largely ignored would prove that the aspiration to provide a general theory of organizations was far from being regarded as an intellectual anachronism. A rejuvenated Marxist perspective, its advocates maintained, would breathe new theoretical life into the decaying body of organizational studies and would relocate them in their 'proper' place within the political economy of modern capitalism.

2
The rediscovery of critique

Introduction

The development of an action frame of reference in organizational studies emerged out of the methodological critique which its advocates offered of systems theory. In particular, the latter's neglect of the processes whereby human agents – including organization theorists – reflect on and rationalize their actions provided an opening which was exploited to formulate an alternative theoretical framework that challenged both the model of organization and the conception of organizational analysis which systems theorists had constructed. The failure of systems theorists to provide a coherent 'theory of action', and the internal problems which this created when they attempted to accommodate a concern with actors' 'practical reasoning' within their established theoretical structure, provided the central area of weakness which critics would make full use of as the 1970s progressed.

However, the other major failing of structural–functionalist sociology (and the behaviourist social psychology which usually went with it) – that is, its failure to provide, even the theoretical beginnings of, a satisfactory 'theory of power' – did not receive quite the same degree of attention from action theorists (on this point, see Clegg and Dunkerley 1980). This is not surprising given the sort of difficulties which the latter had encountered in attempting to combine an interest in the complexities of transient social encounters with the constraining influence of institutionalized power relations. The nearer they got to a deeper understanding of everyday life, the further away they seemed to get from providing an adequate explanation of the institutional context in which it was carried on.

It is this second problem, and its, at best, partial resolution by action theorists, which provided the initial entry point for the development of a critical theory of organizations in the second half of the 1970s and early 1980s. The critique which critical theorists offered of a systems conception of 'power' as a generalized resource or capacity maintaining normative consensus (Parsons 1967) focused on the link between conceptual limitations and ideological commitments. The failings of action theorists on this score were related to their predilection for a form of methodological individualism which allowed them to avoid the more unpleasant aspects of structurally determined class exploitation and control in a capitalist society (on this see Burrell and Morgan 1979).

In both cases, the intellectual products of organizational analysis, as it had been practised over a period of four decades, were seen to be partially determined by the mode of production in which they had been produced (Salaman 1981). The capacity of critical theory to resist the ideologically distorting effects of the dominant mode of production, its advocates contended, provided it with the degree of intellectual and social autonomy necessary to achieve a more incisive and realistic interpretation of organizational phenomena. This, in turn, could provide an emancipatory guide to the forms of human action and intervention in the contemporary world necessary to bring about a radical transformation in existing social and political structures (Benson 1977a).

This chapter will offer an analysis of the re-emergence and subsequent growth of a critical perspective in organizational studies over the last ten years or so. This will require an appreciation of its key conceptual components, the sort of problems and questions to which they are directed, and the conclusions which are drawn from their operationalization in specific organizational contexts. It will also demand an understanding of the various strains and tensions which can be identified within critical theory's intellectual and ideological parameters, and of the way in which these internal problems are related to the wider body of Marxist social theory on which critical organization theorists have drawn.

The beginnings of this analysis are to be found in the next section which examines the critique which critical theorists provided of 'mainstream' organizational analysis and of the important, but limited, advances which had been made possible through the interventions of those committed to the principles and practices of an interpretative sociology.

The critique of mainstream organization theory

The critique which critical theorists offered of mainstream organizational studies crystallized around three central themes: first, the theoretical orthodoxy which was deemed to have dominated the field's development since the 1930s; second, the methodological principles on which this theoretical approach had been constructed and implemented; and third, the grounding of both of these in an ideological framework which attempted to obscure the logical status and social significance of organization theory as a normative doctrine serving the interests of the dominant class grouping within capitalism.

In the view of most critical theorists, organization theory had been intellectually dominated by a functionalist paradigm since the 1930s to the virtual exclusion of alternative meta-theoretical frameworks until the 1970s (Clegg and Dunkerley 1977, Benson 1977a, Salaman 1979, Burrell and Morgan 1979, Clegg and Dunkerley 1980). The functionalist paradigm, in their view, had achieved the status of a 'hegemonic' intellectual frame of reference to the extent that it had managed to exclude or emasculate alternative approaches so that they became 'satellites which take their principal point of reference from the orthodoxy itself' (Burrell and Morgan 1979: 396). During the late 1960s and early 1970s a number of 'deviant' perspectives had been developed, but these had been compromised by their historical and intellectual associations with the 'functionalist problematic' and had not been strong enough to resist incorporation within its philosophical and ideological parameters.

The position of the functionalist paradigm was seen to have been seriously weakened as a result of a deepening intellectual crisis within its supporting intellectual community brought about by internal disagreement over methodological and theoretical difficulties (Benson 1977b). In turn, this was reinforced by the perceived failure of systems theorists to provide a coherent and valid account of major structural transformations taking place in both capitalist and socialist industrial societies since the early 1960s (Gouldner 1971, Benson 1977a, Clegg and Dunkerley 1980). At the same time, the increasing prominence afforded to approaches developed within an interpretative paradigm (which offered a very different assessment of the Weberian legacy to that provided by orthodox functionalists) had degenerated into a form of sociological idealism in which the structural 'cutting edge' of sociology was completely obscured by the obsession with actors' accounting practices. This also encouraged a quiescent attitude to contemporary political issues which denied any interest in or contribution to the central themes that structured ideological debate over the current state and future prospects of mankind. In this sense, critical theorists were highly conscious of the intellectual conservatism which they perceived as being deeply implanted within the subterranean reaches of the metaphysical substructure on which conventional organizational theory had been constructed since the early decades of the twentieth century. This ingrained conservatism was so strong that previous attempts to formulate alternative perspectives (which rejected orthodoxy and aspired to initiate a clear and radical 'epistemological break' with the status quo) had been severely handicapped by their failure to recognize the pervasive influence which functionalism continued to exert on the manner in which fundamental questions relating to definition of subject matter, characterization of research methods, and specification of explanatory theories were decided.

Functionalist orthodoxy had not only succeeded in determining the formal agenda on which the technical debates between exponents of different approaches was to be structured, it had also managed to retain control over the 'hidden agenda' concerning the philosophical foundations which continued to inform the practice of organizational analysis in either its conventional or deviant forms. If anxiety or uncertainty over the domain assumptions that gave organizational analysis a minimum degree of coherence and continuity threatened to spill over into, or even worse to supersede, discussion on technical adjustments to existing conceptual and methodological equipment, then a range of 'damage limitation' strategies were available to the guardians of orthodoxy. These 'heretical' tendencies could be marginalized as being outside the 'proper' purview of organization theorists or they could be redefined and reincorporated within the main line of intellectual development as this was laid down by leading members of the functionalist community. Thus, for the critical theorists:

'the majority of existing theories tend to be located within a relatively narrow range of academic territory. Despite the apparent diversity reflected in current debate, the issues which separate the parties in academic controversy often tend to be of minor rather than of major significance. The really big issues are rarely discussed, lying hidden beneath the commonality of perspective which induces organization theorists to get together and to talk to each other in the first place.'

(Burrell and Morgan 1979: 120)

The stultifying influence which functionalist orthodoxy continued to exert over contemporary developments was seen to be expressed in terms both of the theoretical conception of 'organization' to which most contemporary organization theorists adhered and of the philosophy of social science in which this conceptualization was grounded. The 'negotiated order' model of organization which action theorists had advocated merely elaborated and enriched the functionalist model of organization as an instrument of impersonal rational control to the extent that it reinforced an 'uncritical acceptance of the conceptions of organizational structure shared by participants' (Benson 1977a: 1). While substantially extending the range of interest groups and coalitions which were deemed to exert some influence over the negotiating process whereby structural forms were reproduced, it simply reinforced the conventional model by deflecting attention away from the dominant social interests and social forces which determined the institutional parameters within which bargaining behaviour was regulated. The exclusive concern with the universal properties of social interaction in everyday situations exhibited by more radical interpreters of the action approach simply reaffirmed the perception of the organizational structure as a symbolic fiction which was beyond the control of any particular social interest or determination by any set of economic imperatives, but which served a useful social purpose in maintaining a precarious sense of order and discipline in the face of multifarious threats to its continued preservation.

The theoretical construction of 'organization' as an institutionalized *modus vivendi* between rational control and natural co-operation rested on a positivist conception of scientific method and an empiricist social ontology (Burrell and Morgan 1979). The latter provided for a conceptualization of formal or complex organizations in terms of commonsense categories derived from an idealized analytical representation of the 'typical' manager or administrator. An un-reflective and uncritical appropriation of these categorizations by organizational theorists legitimized the application of a research methodology whereby conceptual indicies or dimensions consti-tutive of 'formal organization' were operationally defined and stat-istically manipulated to identify significant correlations between selected variables. These statistical relationships were subsequently 'explained' either in terms of their logical derivation from a network of higher-level laws or principles (as in Blau and Schoenherr 1971) or in terms of middle-range theoretical generalizations which can be inductively inferred from research data (as in Pugh and Hickson 1976). In this fashion, critical theorists contend, the combination of empiricist ontology and positivist methodology established the epistemological justification for the belief that unmediated com-monsense categories, distilling the empirical essence of formal organ-ization from a privileged cognitive position (on this point see Whitely 1977a), could be methodologically processed in such a way as to permit the construction of a general theory of organizations.

While the ethnomethodological reading of the action approach to organizational analysis had formulated a methodological critique of functionalist organization theory which ran along similar lines, critical theorists have argued that it falls into the self-same trap of 'taking for granted' a background framework of institutional struc-tures and ideological assumptions which shapes the negotiation of shared meanings in particular organizational settings (Burrell and Morgan 1979: 264). Once again, the pervasive, not to say malignant, influence which the dominant paradigm had exercised is seen to be reflected in the failure of successive challengers to break free from its philosophical conventions and the tendency to reproduce its theor-etical limitations in a different conceptual idiom.

However, both the theoretical and methodological components of the critique of mainstream organizational studies which critical theorists have mounted are subsidiary to the third component of their critique – that is, the weaknesses which they have identified in these areas have to be ultimately accounted for in terms of the ideologically mediated material interests which organizational analysis has served in the form of 'capital' and those who act as its agents. Clegg and Dunkerley express this point in the most direct terms:

'Class relations are fundamentally and inherently antagonistic. These antagonisms can be made opaque through economic, political and ideological interventions on the part of one class interest against another. We shall argue that organization theory is such an intervention.'

(Clegg and Dunkerley 1980: 58)

Taken together, functionalist social theory and positivist methodology are said to produce static descriptions and explanations of organizational phenomena which directly reinforce a one-dimensional representation of the existing pattern of social institutions and the prevailing direction of social change as unalterable and irreversible (Salaman 1978). As a result, organizational participants, especially those excluded from formal positions of command and control, are denied the opportunity to formulate more imaginative visions of the social reality of which they are a part by a form of organizational analysis that prevents any significance being attached to the broader economic and social structure in which particular organizational units are located.

Some academic work is seen to have escaped the more restrictive confines of an ideological framework which transforms the historically specific and politically biased organizational structures of capitalist production into universal and functional instruments of a rationalized industrial society. Yet these deviations are deemed to be of marginal social significance in that they do not threaten the material interests of that ruling class which controls the ends of organizational action and the institutional means through which they are realized in a capitalist mode of production. At the very least, large chunks of the theoretical structure and descriptive generalizations which constitute mainstream organization theory are now reinterpreted as an ideological gloss on the inner dynamics of the material based within a capitalist mode of production. Organization theory becomes a 'superstructural manifestation of the workings of the economic base of capitalist societies' (Burrell and Morgan 1979: 381).

The substantive content of the dominant ideology which mainstream organization theory simultaneously confirms and obscures is represented by critical theorists in the form of a subtle combination of 'instrumental' or 'technical' reason on the one hand (Habermas 1974) and managerialism on the other (Nichols 1969, Blackburn 1972). The former defines the goal of organizational analysis as one of establishing a systematic body of knowledge concerning the structure and function of bureaucratic organizations which will provide the basis for rational decision-making over technical problems of organizational design and control (Salaman 1979). The latter identifies that category of organizational personnel – the members of the managerial and administrative 'technostructure' (see Galbraith 1967) – which will utilize such knowledge in the interests of the organizational community as a whole because of the comparative political autonomy which they enjoy in a situation where ownership and control of the means of production have been institutionally differentiated (on this point see Dahrendorf 1959 and Zeitlin 1974).

In combination, critical theorists argue, technicism and managerialism provide a relatively sophisticated 'scientific gloss' on the normative foundations of organizational analysis and the class interests through which it is socially generated and sustained. While recognizing a caricaturizing element in the following description, Clegg clearly feels that there is a great deal of truth in the contention that:

'Much of the produce of organization theory has been developed at the interface of capitalist theory and capitalist practice in the academic institutions of business. Here it provides both a market and a meeting place for theoreticians and organizers. For these organizers it functions as part of the rhetoric of rule, encapsulated in O & M, work study, job evaluation and the rest. As such, it is assuredly a theory for the organizers of the organized.'

(Clegg 1977: 22)

Considered in these terms, the intellectual trajectory of organization theory's historical development is seen to be largely determined by the administrative and ideological requirements of an emerging managerial cadre from the end of the nineteenth century onwards. It is these needs, admittedly in more sophisticated form, which continue to shape the form and direction of contemporary organizational analysis, whether in the guise of a more subtle appreciation of the internal political processes that regulate the course and outcome of organizational decision-making (Pettigrew 1973) or in the provision of a more advanced organizational technology through which social and ideological control can be maintained in the face of increased social conflict over the terms and conditions of the employment relationship in contemporary capitalist work organizations (Storey 1983). The most strategically important of the managerial needs which are seen to have directed the development of organizational analysis is the continuing requirement to design and implement the most effective forms of organizational control over the labour process in the capitalist mode of production so as to maximize surplus value and the continuous capital accumulation which it makes possible (Goldman and Van Houten 1980). While organization theory had gradually acquired the intellectual and institutional trappings of a social scientific discipline in the course of its historical evolution, its parasitic dependence upon the managerial requirements of monopoly capitalism had largely determined both the character of its central problematic and the quality of the intellectual resources through which it had been pursued.

From the perspective of critical theory, mainstream organization theory remains a distorted form of social knowledge in the sense that it intentionally obscures the material determinants of its development and the strict intellectual limitations which they have imposed. Far from constituting a general body of scientific knowledge and instrumental techniques that can be applied in a wide range of organizational settings, organizational analysis, once it has been 'decoded', can be seen for what it really is – an intellectual framework which helps to sustain the prevailing structure of power relations through which a range of increasingly sophisticated organizational control mechanisms are developed and implemented in capitalist societies (Benson 1977a).

It is in relation to this latter issue – that is, the process whereby the social reality of power relations within a capitalist mode of production is obscured by mainstream, or for that matter interpretative, theorizing – that the distorting impact of conventional organizational theory is seen to be most pronounced (on this point see Whitley 1977a, Clegg 1977, Benson 1977b, Salaman 1978, Burrell and Morgan 1979, Clegg and Dunkerley 1980). Critical theorists recognize that there has been some move away from a conception of power as a 'neutral resource which oils the wheels of the system as a whole' (Burrell and Morgan 1979: 203) towards a view that focuses on the sectional interests which are served as a result of unequal access to and control over the decision-making process whereby economic and technical resources are allocated. However, they maintain that both functionalist and interpretist forms of organizational analysis remain wedded to a view of power as a deviation from a formal system of control which is isolated from the broader structure of social relations of production prevailing under capitalism:

'Thus this structural framework cannot enter into any explanation of how the "exercise" of power can create a variance from

"authority". . . . Power relations are only the visible tip of a
structure of control, rule and domination which maintains its
effectiveness not so much through overt action, as through its
ability to appear to be the natural convention. It is only when
taken-for-grantedness fails, routine lapses, and "problems"
appear, that the overt exercise of power is necessary.'

(Clegg 1977: 31–5)

Critical theorists see their main task as rediscovering that link
between the exercise of intra-organizational power and the 'taken-
for-granted' structure of social relations of production in which it is
located which provided the motivating force for Marx's interest in
the organizational means through which surplus-value extraction
and capital accumulation are made possible on a continuous basis.
The precondition for a recovery of a critical perspective in organizational analysis which is focused on the 'organizational processes of
capitalist employment relations' (Storey 1983: 4) was a demystification of the ideological opacity which overlay orthodox accounts
of organizations and the methodological principles on which it had
traded. Having achieved this exercise in demystification, critical
theorists see themselves as being in a position to offer a more
'objective' analysis of the core structural forms and dynamics which
constitute contemporary work organizations within the capitalist
mode of production.

A critical theory of organizations

The general analytical framework which critical theorists have
formulated for the study of organizations consists of four central
components: a model of work organization derived from a model of
the structure of social relations of production in which it is situated; a
set of methodological conventions or procedures which determine
how each of these theoretical constructs are to be developed and
interrelated; a substantive theory of 'organizational change' based on
the conceptual framework previously outlined; and, finally, a network of normative assumptions specifying the contribution which
the critical theorist can make to a transformation of the dominant
pattern of organized social relations prevailing under capitalism.

The general analytical framework which has been constructed out
of these elements has been based upon a detailed reworking of
Marx's analysis of the way in which the 'labour process' is structured

by the social relations of capitalist production and, to a lesser extent, Weber's analysis of the intensification of the process of bureaucratic rationalization generated by the move to large-scale capitalist production in the late nineteenth and early twentieth centuries. Marx has remained the dominant intellectual influence in relation to both the underlying conception of 'organization' on which critical theory has been developed and the methodological conventions through which it has been derived. However, Weber has proved to be invaluable to the extent that his work has provided the conceptual means for relating administrative structures and ideological systems to the developments in economic organization brought about by the evolution in the capitalist mode of production which lies at the heart of Marx's analysis (on this point see Burrell and Morgan 1979 and Salaman 1979).

Critical theorists conceptualize formal or complex organizations as structured systems of social relations and practices determined by the mode of production and corresponding framework of socio-political institutions which it generates (Burrell 1980). The particular administrative form characterized by the label 'bureaucratic' or 'complex' organization is treated as a product of the general economic structure of that social formation of which it is a constituent unit – that is, of 'the framework of relations between the collective classes based on control of the means of production and labour' (Whitely 1977a: 180). Conventional organization theory treats organizations as relatively passive socio-technical systems reacting to external pressure emanating from an environmental context consisting of a 'loose coupling' of a range of socio-economic elements. Critical theory offers a model of organization as that functionally necessary administrative apparatus through which control over productive activity for the maximization of economic surplus and its appropriation by the capitalist class is regularly achieved. In this way, the concept of organization is theoretically transformed from a social unit fulfilling the key operational objectives of a social order based on economic rationality and ideological consensus into an instrument of class power and domination in a society founded on material exploitation and ideological deception.

This model of organization also requires a fundamental reconceptualization of its key analytical components as they have been normally formulated within the orthodox frame of reference in which the bulk of organizational research had been carried out. Consequently, the defining characteristics of 'organization structure' (hierarchy, division of labour, managerial control systems, etc.) are redefined in terms of the political function which they fulfil in maintaining the administrative means of class domination within the productive system (Marglin 1980) rather than their technical function in ensuring the appropriate response to a shifting pattern of environmental demands. 'Organizational process' is transformed from a range of behavioural responses to a formal configuration of structural relations into the pattern of 'informal rules and relations which workers adapt and transform as a means of coming to terms with their working lives' (Thompson 1983: 152). The interaction between 'structure' and 'process' is relocated from a framework of 'stimulus'/'response' relationships grounded in the behavioural patterns emerging out of atomized interpersonal transactions or exchanges into a historically mediated relationship in which the determining force of institutional constraint and the liberating impact of collective action varies over time and place (Benson 1977a).

This conception of 'organization', as both an institutional means of class domination and as a symbolic expression of the material priorities which it embodies, is based on a specific methodological position which is sharply contrasted with the empiricist and instrumentalist bias implicit in mainstream work. Critical methodology rests on the assumption that the goal of social analysis is to identify the underlying 'mechanisms' which regulate social behaviour by 'going beyond the immediate "surface reality" and explicating structural processes which could account for it, such as fundamental relations of productive activity' (Whitely 1977a: 170). This follows Marx's methodological injunction to reject interpretations of observable social reality offered by bourgeois social scientists and to specify the causal mechanisms that reproduce the particular configuration of social relations (that is, 'the market') which they attempt to universalize as a necessary feature of all socio-economic systems.

Saunders has recently argued that this mode of analysis is most accurately represented as an example of 'retroductive method' which 'involves the attempt to explain observable phenomena by developing hypotheses about underlying causes' (Saunders 1981: 17). It begins from a position in which hypothetical conjectures concerning the underlying mechanisms and conditions which are assumed to generate their corresponding phenomenal form are formulated. Such conjectures are then subjected to a process of empirical demonstration through the detailed examination of individual cases and subsequently recombined within the logical structure of the general theoretical framework from which they were originally derived. As Keat and Urry note:

'It thus follows that social analysis (for Marx) consists of at least two stages: first, the elucidation of the internal structure of each mode of production, a theoretical activity involving the positing of models of the relevant causal structures and mechanisms; second, the analysis of the ways in which different modes of production are co-present within a given society and the social and political consequences that follow.'

(Keat and Urry 1975: 97)

Such a methodological strategy can only be carried through if it is assumed that the underlying or 'hidden' causal mechanisms which generate observable patterns of social behaviour can be systematically explicated by means of a set of analytical categories which distinguish those aspects of social reality (the 'deep structures') which are causally determining as opposed to those that are regarded as corresponding secondary effects of the primary factors (Bhaskar 1978). Keat and Urry summarize the logic of explanation which informs a realist philosophy of science which critical organization theorists tend to adopt in one form or another:[9]

'For the realist, adequate causal explanations require the discovery both of regular relations between phenomena, and of some kind of mechanism that links them. So, in explaining any particular phenomenon, we must not only make reference to those events which initiate the process of change: we must also give a description of that process itself. To do this, we need knowledge of the underlying mechanisms and structures that are present, and of the manner in which they generate or produce the phenomenon we are trying to explain.'

(Keat and Urry 1975: 30)

---

9 The extent to which members of the critical theory tradition in organizational analysis have been committed to a realist epistemology may be questioned by some commentators. However, I would argue that it does provide the epistemological core of the dominant strand of philosophical thinking within the critical theory tradition, even if it has been modified by some exponents of a neo-Marxist approach to organizational analysis.

To the extent that it relies on some version of a realist philosophy of science and the explanatory logic that it specifies, a critical-theory perspective in organizational analysis is committed to the 'base'/'superstructure' conceptual distinction which has characterized Marxist analysis in a number of substantive areas (on this point see Jessop 1982) and the assignment of causal primacy to elements contained within the former (for an elaboration of this point see Cohen 1978).

The base or economic structure consists of that set of production relations (social relations between productive agents such as 'manager' and 'worker') necessary to realize the full productive potential of the forces of production (raw materials, technical instrumentation, labour power possessed by producing agents, etc.). The 'superstructure' consists of that pattern of non-economic institutions and practices (such as the state, the social welfare system, legal system, and mass communications) which supports the continued functioning of the economic system. Consequently, the economic base is assumed to generate and sustain the administrative superstructure in the sense that both the organizational shape and the substantive operation of the latter are seen to be subservient to the functional requirements of the former, given the overriding aim of maximizing the productive potential of the productive forces in any mode of production (Cohen 1978).

Within the capitalist mode of production – as the dominant economic form in the world economic system (Wallerstein 1974) – particular units of work organization (that is, units based on the employment relationship) can be categorized as belonging to the base or superstructure. However, business corporations (analytically located within the economic base) are usually seen to be of primary explanatory significance to the extent that they constitute the strategic organizational units through which surplus value is extracted by the capitalist class in an economic system where productive activity is geared to the appropriation of economic surplus by property-owners (Burrell and Morgan 1979: 379). Thus, at the level of inter-organizational analysis, critical theorists contend that the business corporation is the key organizational unit in that it directly reflects the determinant economic mechanism or structure (the accumulation and appropriation of surplus value by the dominant class) within the capitalist mode of production. It also establishes the institutional core around which networks of inter-organizational relations develop in both the 'private' and 'public' spheres of social consumption (Benson 1975).

The general implications of this 'retroductive' methodology for the conduct of intra-organizational analysis are also reasonably clear. Work organizations (whether formally located in the base or super-structure) reproduce the relation between the economic base and administrative superstructure that prevails within the capitalist mode of production as a whole. As such, work organizations must develop their own superstructure of administrative controls in pro-viding the appropriate institutional framework through which the social relations of production in a capitalist system can be geared to the forces of production on which it depends to generate the economic surplus that is the material 'life-blood' of the dominant class. They constitute 'historically and temporally complex sedimented structures . . . the purpose of the sedimented rules, it will be argued, is to maintain control of the labour process . . . power in organizations derives from control of the means and methods of production' (Clegg and Dunkerley 1980: 509).

In this way, the implications of the 'base'/'superstructure' distinc-tion, and of the relation between them required by the causal mechanism of the process of capital accumulation, for intra- and inter-organizational analysis can be elaborated. Economic organiz-ations constitute the dominant organizational units in the sense that the requirements which they fulfil – the extraction and appropriation of surplus value – condition the nature and role of those organiz-ational units which develop within the superstructure. The latter produce the administrative supports and ideological legitimations necessary to the continued performance of the former. However, critical theorists also maintain that *all* work organizations in a capitalist mode of production (whatever their structural location) have their own material bases and administrative superstructures to facilitate control over the labour process by property-owners and their agents. The intra-organizational base conditions the way in which the internal administrative control system can develop.

However, critical theorists have usually qualified the somewhat over-deterministic implications of this method of analysis, both in relation to the explanatory primacy which it affords to productive units within the economic base and the derivative status that it assigns to administrative superstructures within all forms of work organization within the capitalist mode of production. This is so to the extent that they have allowed that superstructural elements – both within the mode of production as a whole and within its constituent organizational units – can attain and retain some degree of 'relative autonomy' from the economic base in certain situations and over defined historical periods (Allen 1975, Miliband 1977, Burrell and Morgan 1979).

The ability of superstructural components (at the societal or organizational level of analysis) to resist the determining force of economic structures is traced to the internal contradictions – within and between both base and superstructure – that inevitably emerge and intensify as a particular mode of production develops. Consequently, the tight 'functional fit' between base and superstructure posited by the logic of economic determinism is substantially modified by the explicit recognition that the historical evolution of any mode of production must reproduce a range of opposing principles and forces that have to be 'managed' by superstructural elements. The latter consequently assume a strategic role in the maintenance of social order as a precondition for large-scale productive activity and a maximization of the economic surplus that it generates.

In this way, the causal primacy afforded to a structural mechanism analytically located within the economic base is reinterpreted in terms of its role in shaping the broad parameters within which political, administrative, and legal institutions have to function and develop. In addition, the contradictory principles and forces at work in any mode of production also establish the theoretical starting point for the explanation of organizational change, insofar as work organization provide relatively contained social units in which the detail of macro-level conflict and disruption can be more easily identified and analysed.

The concept of 'contradiction' provides critical theorists with the principal means of explaining structural change within complex organizations, both as an expression of and as a medium for opposing forces at work within the inclusive social formation of which it is a constituent element (Allen 1975, Benson 1977a, Heydebrand 1977, Burrell and Morgan 1979). Burrell and Morgan argue that:

'Organizations, particularly economic organizations, are viewed as the stage upon which the deep-seated cleavages within the social formation as a whole are most visible. It is in the workshop and the factory, for example, that the contradictions between the relations and means of production, capital and labour, the measure and use of labour time, and the fundamental problem of over-production, are seen as working themselves out. It is in the empirical facets of this organizational life that contradictions are seen as taking their most visible form.'

(Burrell and Morgan 1979: 368)

While a range of interpretative nuances can be detected in the way in which critical organization theorists have developed the concept of 'contradiction', most of them invoke it to refer to an opposition or disjunction between structural principles that govern the historical reproduction of the social formation as a whole (on this point see Giddens 1979). In the case of the capitalist mode of production, the major structural contradiction within the economic base is between the socialization of production on a collective basis and the private appropriation of the economic surplus which it generates. The opposition between these two overarching, or 'axial' (see Bell 1973), principles necessary to reproduce the capitalist mode of production (that is, collective production and private appropriation) is reproduced at the level of the individual organizational unit which has to struggle to contain and cope with its potentially disruptive consequences. At one and the same time, business corporations are complex organizational mechanisms which further the collective structuring of large-scale productive activity, while facilitating the extraction and appropriation of the economic surplus arising out of production for one powerful sectional interest. As such, they embody the opposition between the very structural principles on which the capitalist mode of production is constructed and maintained. Non-economic organizations which provide the supporting administrative, legal, and welfare machinery necessary to sustained capital accumulation experience similar oppositions as well as the tensions which they create (Heydebrand 1977).

Benson (Benson 1977a) suggests that major structural contradictions of this type can lead to dislocations and crises at the organizational level which engender counter-measures aimed are restoring social equilibrium. On the other hand, he continues, they can also produce social movements and more fragmented forms of collective social action which threaten and undermine the prevailing institutional order. In either case, organizational change within the capitalist mode of production may be analysed in terms of successive attempts to respond to the periodic intra-organizational crises engendered by the dynamic forces released by this fundamental structural opposition between collective production and private

appropriation. Each of these exercises in organizational containment, Benson suggests, will only prove to be of limited success and
will inevitably set off unintended consequences of an unpredictable
and uncontrollable nature, reinforcing the severity of the underlying
problem. In this sense, 'organizational change' within a capitalist
mode of production is analysed as a series of limited institutional
adjustments and marginal reforms aimed at containing the side-
effects of fundamental structural contradictions which are likely to
prove ineffective in the long term and to give rise to more severe
contradictions and crises out of the very solutions which they
propose (on this point in relation to the 'fiscal crisis of the capitalist
state' see O'Connor 1973).

Benson's outline of a dialectical approach to organizational analysis also offers some guidance on the final ingredient of a critical
theory perspective – that is, the role of the critical theorist in helping
to construct and implement alternative organizational forms to those
prevailing under a capitalist mode of production:

> 'Dialectical analysis must go beyond reflexivity; it has an active as
> well as reflexive moment. It must be concerned with the active
> reconstruction of organizations. This reconstruction is aimed
> towards the realization of human potentialities by the removal of
> constraints, limitations upon praxis. This task involves both the
> critique of existing organizational forms and the search for alter-
> natives. . . . The larger objective is the realization of a social
> situation in which people freely and collectively control the
> direction of change on the basis of a rational understanding of
> social process.'
>
> (Benson 1977a: 210)

Benson's interpretation of the role of the critical theorist in acting
as an 'intellectual midwife' for an organizational reconstruction
aimed at the reassertion of social control over institutional development is based upon the distinction which critical theorists have
drawn between 'scientific theories' on the one hand and 'critical
theories' on the other.

Geuss (Geuss 1981) has provided a general characterization of the
way in which this distinction has been drawn, following on from
Habermas's original specification (Habermas 1972, 1974).

> 'Scientific theories have as their aim or goal successful manipu-
> lation of the external world; they have "instrumental use". . . .

Critical theories aim at emancipation and enlightenment, at making agents aware of hidden coercion, thereby freeing them from that coercion and putting them in a position to determine where their true interests lie. . . . Scientific theories are "objectifying". That means that, at least in typical cases, one can distinguish clearly between the theory and the "objects" to which the theory refers: the theory isn't itself part of the object domain it describes. . . . Critical theories, on the other hand, are claimed to be "reflective" or "self-referential": a critical theory is itself always part of the object domain which it describes; critical theories are always in part about themselves. . . . Scientific theories require empirical confirmation through observation and experiment; critical theories are cognitively acceptable only if they survive a more complicated process of evaluation; the central part of which is demonstration that they are "reflectively acceptable".'

(Geuss 1981: 55–6)

Considered in these terms, the strategic aim of a critical theory of organizations is to induce greater self-reflection on the part of those agents to which it is directed so that they will be in a better position to understand the limitations imposed on their thought and action by the complex web of social institutions in which they are implicated. The 'false consciousness' which necessarily results from unreflective participation within an existing structure of social relations can only be combated by making participants much more aware of this 'unconscious determinant' to which their social action is subjected. By making them more knowledgeable of the cognitive constraints implicit in the prevailing pattern of institutional mechanisms and their ideological supports, critical theory, its exponents argue, will provide agents with the opportunity to determine their 'true interests' and the manner in which they may be realized.

Once the structural determinants of conventional thought and action which lie outside the conscious understanding of individual actors have been identified, it will be possible for participants to construct more accurate analyses of the obstacles that stand in the way of realizing the universal human desire for greater self-control over their environment. In this way, critical theory will also reveal the ontological status of existing institutions and practices as social phenomena which are reproduced through the interventions of powerful social groups, rather than as the universal, natural, and objective outcomes of immutable socio-economic laws. As a result of both of these exercises in 'demystification', critical theorists believe that the scope for purposeful social change is dramatically broadened as agents come to see that they have the capacity to transform and manage the social conditions under which they act through various forms of socio-political action. They will no longer be in the grip of repressive status quo ideology that legitimizes existing structures of social, political, and economic domination as immutable features of the human condition.

Thus Clegg contrasts the 'naturalist and ahistorical tendencies that find expression in current versions of the organization as a natural system' with an approach that 'poses an understanding of the organization as the locus of the domination of a specific form of life' (Clegg 1977: 32). This deeper understanding of the organization as an instrument of domination under a capitalist form of life can only be facilitated through a form of theoretical analysis that breaks through the borrowed language of mainstream organization theory and formulates an alternative conception based on the assumption that 'if organization theory is to have any relevance for our liberation from existing forms of domination, then it must begin by offering the basis for a theoretical understanding of this domination' (Clegg 1977: 38).

Critical theory and organizational studies

The four interrelated components of a critical theory perspective on organizations outlined in the previous section provide the framework in which its exponents have conducted substantive analyses of organizational change within a capitalist mode of production. These studies have developed along two main lines: first, a political economy of organizational change focused on key structural transformations in socio-economic relations initiated by the move from 'industrial' to 'technological' capitalism (Karpik 1977, 1978); second, the restructuring of those organizational forms whereby the labour process in a capitalist mode of production is managed as brought about by the shift from small-scale to large-scale productive activity based on the application of modern science and technology (Braverman 1974). To some extent, these separate lines of development have been brought together in an attempt to construct a general theory of production relations which aspires to make 'the politics of the capitalist division of labour more transparent and subject to rational criticism and change' (quoted in Thompson 1983: 213).

Attempts to develop a political economy of organizations based on a critical theory perspective aim to achieve 'a comparative analysis of the political, ideological and economic processes which inter-connect organizations' (Clegg and Dunkerley 1980: 484). This comparative analysis has usually been focused on the key inter-organizational relation within the contemporary capitalist mode of production between large-scale multinational corporations and the state apparatus (Mandel 1975). In 'late capitalist societies' the state is seen to provide a measure of protection for those business organizations unable to face the full rigours of competition between competing corporate giants. It also acts as a guarantor for those large-scale projects requiring substantial amounts of technical, financial, and manpower resources on a continuous basis in 'high risk' areas of business activity. This is so to the extent that the state intervenes in the productive process through the 'socialization of costs, risks and losses, in an increasing number of organizations' (Clegg and Dunkerley 1980: 541). Yet these protective and interventionist state strategies simply generate unintended consequences of 'fiscal crisis' (O'Connor 1973) and 'ideological crisis' (Habermas 1976) that produce severe internal contradictions which cannot be contained within existing state structures. Thus the state becomes a:

'site of a constant battle between different organizations of capital and labour, for control of resources it has available to it. This leads us to adopt a perspective on the state as a formal organization which focuses on its structure, as that of other organizations, as an object of class struggle.'

(Clegg and Dunkerley 1980: 543)

In the face of increasing structural crises generated by the failure of the state to cope with intensified organized conflict over a declining resource base, the possibility of a general move towards a more repressive administrative and ideological state apparatus in the closing decades of the twentieth century is countenanced by a number of critical theorists (Clegg and Dunkerley 1980, Jessop 1982).

The analysis of 'organizations in crisis' has proved to be a fruitful area for a number of researchers attempting to develop a political economy of organizations within a critical theory perspective. This is a central feature of Burrell and Morgan's characterization of a radical organization theory which focuses on extreme structural contradictions and dislocations within the social formation as a whole and their impact on established organizational forms:

> 'If there is a change in totality there is necessarily a change in organizational forms. . . . Organizations monitor and reflect the movement of totality from one crisis to another. . . . Crises of ownership and control, factory occupations, Wall Street crashes and large-scale redundancies are of particular significance . . . as episodes yielding considerable insights insofar as the understanding of the nature of the social formation is concerned.'
>
> (Burrell and Morgan 1979: 369)

Considered in these terms, the study of 'middle-range' organizational change in a particular economic sector or within a specific unit in that sector is justified more in terms of what it can tell us about the dynamics of 'macro-level' social structural change within society as a whole, and less in terms of the substantive detail which it provides on the internal operation of sectors or organizational units within those sectors. 'Organizations' *per se* are no longer the central focus of theoretical attention and deserve our interest only insofar as they can be reconceptualized as middle-range 'social laboratories' within which long-term structural transformations can be more easily identified and their impact on existing institutional arrangements more systematically mapped.

This focus on the organizational implications of structural dislocation and crisis within contemporary capitalism has reinforced critical theorists' abiding concern with the link between class relations and organizational structures. Salaman argues this point most forcefully:

> 'A theory of organizations must include reference to a theory of class . . . without the clear recognition that the design of work, the distribution of work rewards, the process of organizational control and legitimation and relations between grades of employee within the plant reflect the class relations of the wider society our understanding of organizational process and structures can at best be partial, at worst hopelessly unreal.'
>
> (Salaman 1981: 229–30)

This leads him to argue that the theme of 'organizational control' is central to any understanding of the interaction between changes to the structure of production relations under capitalism and developments in internal control mechanisms such as technology, employment practices, and authority systems. In his view, increasing state intervention within capitalist economies aimed at shoring up and supporting the existing structure of class relations is having a profound effect on internal organizational arrangements to the extent that it has intensified the drive to rationalize work designs and related control systems.

Salaman is also keen to emphasize the strategic 'mediating role' played by corporate management in bringing about a technical, organizational, and ideological symmetry between social and organizational structures within contemporary capitalist societies. However, the extent to which this can be achieved is seen to be limited both by the capacities and knowledge of corporate management, and by the ability of the rank-and-file workforce to resist further managerial encroachment on their areas of self-control:

> 'To argue for the continuing relationship between capitalism as a form of economic system based on class conflict and class interest and organizational structure and the design of work is not to assert that this relationship will be automatically achieved. It is mediated through what at any time stands for management and expert knowledge of what constitutes the most efficient form of organizational structure. . . . Such "knowledge" is always incomplete and, in "pure" terms, relatively defective. It can always be argued over by specialists of differing schools. It is always capable of generating precisely the effect that was most feared.'
>
> (Salaman 1981: 249)

This theme of changing structures of organizational control in advanced capitalist societies has provided the second line of intellectual development for a critical theory of organizations during the second half of the 1970s and early 1980s. During this period a number of works have been published on this theme which collectively constitute an attempt to construct a general theoretical framework for analysing changes to the labour process within the capitalist mode of production (Braverman 1974, Friedman 1977, Burawoy 1979, Edwards 1979, Nichols 1980, Wood 1982, Zimblast 1979, Littler 1982, Littler and Salaman 1982, Storey 1983, Thompson 1983).

While Braverman's work on the deskilling process engendered by increasing reliance on Taylorite methods of work rationalization and control has been the dominant intellectual influence, recent work has been much more critical of the theoretical limitations and empirical inadequacies of his study and has turned towards 'an understanding of the combinations of control structures in the context of the specific economic location of the company or industry' (Thompson 1983: 152). This has encouraged a growing number of labour-process theorists to recast the original theoretical framework through which Braverman analysed the process whereby forms of work organization and control have been restructured in line with the move from 'competitive' to 'monopoly capitalism'. The theoretical recasting has focused on the range of managerial strategies which have been designed and implemented to ensure control over the labour process, as well as the modes of worker resistance which they have generated. As a result, labour-process theory has attempted to provide a synthesis of both the Marxian and Weberian perspectives on work organization as establishing an analytical framework for studying the process whereby human labour transforms objects into commodities to be exchanged on the market within a capitalist mode of production (Thompson 1983).

Littler's book (Littler 1982) is an excellent example of recent work within this area and of the contribution which it has made to a more sophisticated and empirically grounded critical theory of organizations. His analysis of the forms of managerial control structures implemented within a number of capitalist societies at different stages of their economic development is based on a detailed critique of Braverman and a theoretical synthesis of the contribution which Marx has made to our understanding of the labour process and Weber's analysis of the dynamics of bureaucratization in work organizations.

The analytical components which Littler derives from Marx relate to three areas: the relative autonomy of the labour process; the conceptual differentiation between labour and labour power; and the structural dynamics of capitalism as a distinctive mode of production. In relation to the first of these, Littler argues that there is a continuing interdeterminacy to the labour process such that the socio-economic conditions prevailing within any particular historical period will rarely provide a detailed specification of the form of work organization adopted. In this sense, he continues, employers will be faced with a choice of organizational means whereby they attempt to control and exploit labour (Littler 1982: 30). This clearly rules out any complete structural determination of the form and content of work organization in specific socio-historical circumstances.

The labour/labour-power distinction indicates that: 'The commodity which the worker sells is not a fixed amount of labour embodied in a completed product but "labour power" – that is, the capacity to work' (Littler 1982: 31). Consequently, there is also a recurring historical indeterminacy of the effectiveness with which this potential is fully realized. Within the capitalist mode of production, the employer must develop and implement structures of control over the labour process so that this potential capacity is maximized. However, these control systems have contradictory implications in that they bind both the capitalist and the worker into an employment relationship in which they are forced to adopt strategies that are inimical to their 'true' interests. Capitalists are forced to co-operate with their workers rather than simply and directly exploit the latter's potential through coercive means of one form or another; workers are forced to maintain the employment relationship to meet their immediate economic needs rather than simply resist its encroachment to the point of destruction.

At the level of the individual capitalist enterprise, Littler continues, the centrality of control over the labour process for the capitalist and his agents will also be subject to historical variation – in some firms the realization of surplus value and capital accumulation through financial, marketing, and commercial strategies may be more significant than the realization of surplus value through transformation of the labour process in the direction of more effective exploitation. This will depend upon the level of technological and economic development reached by any particular capitalist economy and by specific industrial sectors within the mode of production as a whole. In this way, Littler concludes, a single-minded focus on the realization of surplus value through the application of more systematic and sophisticated control systems at the point of production may lead researchers to neglect the significance of accumulation strategies which bear no direct relationship to the labour process itself.

Taken together, Littler maintains that these three arguments indicate that 'the linkage between the logic of capital accumulation and transformations of the labour process is an indirect and varying one' (Littler 1982: 34). What is required to accommodate this potentially wide-ranging empirical variation is a theoretical approach that distinguishes between managerial strategies aimed at controlling work behaviour at the point of production and those directed at the employment relationship. It is at this point that Weber enters the argument to the extent that Littler reworks his ideal-type model of rational bureaucracy into two broad conceptual categories

– those structural items relating to the structure of work control (such as hierarchy) and those relating to the official's link with the employing organization (such as the contractual employment of formally free labour).

This modified Weberian ideal-type of rational bureaucracy is then combined with the neo-Marxian model of the labour process to provide the analytical basis for constructing a complex typology of employer strategies of control and the socio-historical conditions in which one type (or combination of types) is likely to prevail over any others. For Littler, there are three distinct levels of analysis at which the process whereby forms of work organization are determined can be understood – the division of labour, the structure of control over task performance, and the employment relationship. He suggests that there may be an empirical tendency for these three levels of 'work structuration' to be interrelated, but it is always possible that they can develop in a relatively independent way. Consequently, 'it is possible to conceive of the bureaucratization of the structure of control and the bureaucratization of the employment relationship as two separate processes' (Littler 1982: 43).

This distinction, Littler contends, is fundamental to the explanation of Taylorism as the most significant form of employer-control strategy developed and implemented in America between 1900 and 1920, and in Britain during the inter-war years. However, Taylorism involved the bureaucratization of the structure of work control at the point of production, but not of the employment relationship. The distinction also helps Littler to highlight a second employer-control strategy which was followed much more closely in Japan than in either America or Britain – that is, a form of ideological control relying on human relations techniques of work group integration and solidarity infused with the same culturally derived values of the formal organization (Littler 1982: 55 and 186–95). In the Japanese situation, the bureaucratization of the employment relationship provided an absolutely crucial structural precondition for the successful implementation of a strategy of ideological control. This facilitated the development of a form of corporate paternalism into which Taylorite ideas and methods could be subsequently inserted without threatening the culturally established pattern of work values and institutions.

The need to integrate the political economy and labour-process perspectives within a critical theory of organizations has been recognized by a number of writers and researchers operating within its parameters who wish to combine an interest in workplace control with a focus on the ideological means through which it is institutionalized within the capitalist mode of production (Burawoy 1979, Thompson 1983). This has reinforced a concern with the interconnections between workers' interpretations of workplace behaviour and the production of consent within the wider structure of social relations in which the workplace is embedded. While serving to re-emphasize one of the central propositions of a political economy perspective which suggests that the structure of production relations under capitalism reproduces the material and social conditions necessary for class conflict, it also warns against assuming that it provides the sufficient conditions for such conflict to be realized. In short, it cautions against a too-easy acceptance of the structural determinism which is an important aspect of more orthodox interpretations of critical theory and calls for a renewal of the theoretical commitment to analyse the dynamics of class action as the outcome of a complex interaction between the objective structure of work control and the subjective interpretations of those who daily experience the fact of subordination at work. This refocusing of critical theory, its advocates contend, may provide the theoretical foundations for a form of 'production politics' which bridges the gap between workplace and national action, as well as stressing the vital significance of 'practices, demands and forms of organization that are transitional between factory and state, and between immediate and long-term goals' (Thompson 1983: 238).

As such, the resurgence of a labour-process perspective within a critical theory of capitalist work organization as the institutional terrain on which the conflict between capital and labour is most visibly fought out has highlighted three central areas of debate around which the tension between a 'structuralist' and 'voluntarist' reading of the critical tradition is most apparent. First, an empirical debate concerning the short-term impact and long-term effects of Taylorite forms of work organization and control in industrial capitalist societies. Second, a theoretical debate crystallizing around the relative strengths and weaknesses of a structuralist interpretation of the critical tradition which downgrades the explanatory significance of social practices in the reproduction and transformation of structural relations (see Giddens 1981). Third, an ideological debate focused on the 'terms and conditions' on which the critical theorist should accept his involvement in political debate and action as a necessary component of his intellectual practice.

In each of these areas a revived labour-process perspective has questioned the more deterministic leanings of structuralist interpreters of the critical tradition. It has provided a much more theoretically sophisticated and historically informed account of Taylorism and alternative forms of employer strategies of labour subordination and control. Second, it has managed to resist the functionalist predilections of structuralist analyses by emphasizing the range of alternative control strategies and structures which employers may choose and the contrasting forms of worker resistance which they are likely to elicit. Consequently, contemporary patterns of work organization and control within capitalist societies are analysed as the often precarious products of 'the dialectical interplay of employer structures of control and forms of resistance' (Littler 1982: 158) rather than as the necessary outcomes of the functional imperatives lodged within the capitalist mode of production. Third, it has reopened the fundamental question of the relationship between 'theory' and 'praxis' for those who see organizational analyses as an exercise in 'demystification' (on this point see Bradley and Wilkie 1980) in that it has resisted any attempt to deal with this issue in terms of ritual genuflections in the direction of a 'fusion' of theory and praxis or a categorical denial of any link whatsoever between engagement in an intellectual practice and an interest in practical affairs (on this latter point see Burrell 1980).

However, a deeper understanding of these internal tensions and their implications for the further development of critical organization theory requires an appreciation of the broader framework of social theory from which it draws inspiration – that is, Marxism.

Internal strains and contradictions

Gouldner (1980) maintains that Marxism, as a constituent element of Western social theory, contains a fundamental analytical contradiction between a voluntarist and a determinist interpretation of social analysis and its philosophical base:

> 'Marxism and theorists of the Marxist community have been divided, it has long been noticed, into roughly two tendencies: one conceiving of Marxism as "critique" and the other conceiving of it as some kind of "science". . . . Critical Marxism leads towards a perspective in which human decisions can make an important

difference, towards a voluntarism in which human courage and determination count, while Scientific Marxism stresses the lawful regularities that inhere in things and set limits on human will, counterposing determinism to voluntarism. . . . Critical Marxism is more disposed towards an historicism in which each different social plane of society is seen as operating according to unique and different requirements, and it stresses society's organic character as a special totality. Scientific Marxism is more disposed towards structuralism in which the social totality is viewed as a configuration of abiding elements which transcend its boundaries in time and space, and thus has an atomistic and mechanistic character.'

(Gouldner 1980: 32–59)

He also makes the point that each of these interpretations of Marxist social theory can be seen as a response to the internal weaknesses and difficulties identified in the other: 'Thus, though they are in tension, the Two Marxisms constitute a "dialectical unity of oppositites", each contributing to the development of its adversary' (Gouldner 1980: 54). In this way, Critical Marxism sets out to repair the ambiguous consequences of Scientific Marxism's stress on structural determination and its in-built predilection for a passive political Utopianism. It achieves this by providing a clearly articulated theory of political praxis in which human action plays a strategic historical role in shaping the dynamic processes whereby economic structures are reproduced and transformed.

This underlying creative tension between voluntarism and determinism is clearly evident in the contributions of those who have attempted to develop a critical theory of organizations out of the basic intellectual ingredients of Marxist social theory. Thus Burrell and Morgan's formulation of a 'radical structuralism' in which the economic structure is viewed as the key determinant of organizational power relations and processes (Burrell and Morgan 1979) is counter-balanced by Benson's dialectical approach which involves a search for 'dominant forces or components' that account for the emergence and dissolution of social structures without resort to deterministic argument (Benson 1977a).

This basic analytical contradiction within critical organization theory has to be related to the perceived failure of structuralism to provide a systematic account of key aspects of contemporary work organization – organizational hierarchies, new technologies and working practices, more sophisticated forms of ideological appeal,

information-control systems, accounting methods, and other related managerial practices – insofar as these are 'sociologized' away
into the encompassing social formation and subsequently 'hived off'
into general discourses on the nature of class structure, power, and
ideology. As Tomlinson suggests, this leaves 'the enterprise as little
more than a relay for forces constructed and battling elsewhere; that
is, little in particular is said about the enterprise' (Tomlinson 1982:
8). In turn, this has encouraged the further development of a
voluntaristically inclined concern with the social processes through
which specific patterns of organizational control are designed, implemented, and monitored which proceeds by way of a much more
coherent theoretical synthesis of Marx and Weber (Littler 1982,
Thompson 1983).

Nevertheless, as is the case with each of the theoretical traditions
surveyed so far in this book, the underlying tension between structuralism and voluntarism is likely to weaken the internal logical
coherence and explanatory power of a critical theory of organizations. In particular, it has produced a theoretical frame of reference
which is somewhat uneasily suspended between a highly abstract
and generalized account of macro-level forces or 'tendencies' in
capitalist political economies and the organizational forms which
they generate and a much more limited empirical analysis of transformations in existing patterns of work organization which can only
be accepted if many of the key presuppositions contained within the
former are rejected. To this extent, Littler's plea that the link
between the logic of capital accumulation and the historical transformation of the labour process be rethought in terms of an indirect
and variable relationship mediated through human action rather than
in terms of structural necessity is indicative of the unresolved
theoretical tensions which this contradiction produces.

Consequently, critical organization theorists seemed doomed to
live with very similar internal conflicts and stresses to those experienced within the systems and action traditions. The theoretical
idioms in which these are expressed take a very different form in each
case – economic determinism and political voluntarism as opposed
to rationalism and naturalism or objectivism and subjectivism – but
they each express the unresolved tensions which lie at the heart of an
intellectual practice which has always been more prone to internal
disagreement and fragmentation than either its 'conservatives' or
'radicals' have been prepared to admit.

The extent to which these internal intellectual problems have shaped the overall historical development of organizational analysis, and the degree to which they have to be related to the particular socio-economic contexts in which each tradition or approach has been formulated, are questions that are considered in greater detail in the next chapter which focuses on the general condition of 'post-interregnum' organizational studies in the 1970s and 1980s.

Summary

This chapter has provided an exposition of the rediscovery of a critical theory perspective within organizational analysis and the substantive analyses of organizational change within the capitalist mode of production which its advocates have offered. It has also highlighted the fundamental intellectual contradiction between voluntarism and determinism contained within such a perspective and the roots of this problem (and the tensions it produces) within the general body of Marxist scholarship developed in the Western world.

In turn, it has suggested that the resurgence of a critical theory perspective within organizational analysis simply reproduces, in a different theoretical form, an intellectual contradiction which is embedded deep within the domain assumptions of both the systems and action traditions – that is, between a model of organization as both the necessary outcome and the required instrument of imma-nent structural principles or laws and a model of organization as the contingent product and optional tool of transitory social groups or interests. Each of the perspectives or traditions surveyed in these opening chapters has attempted to contain both of these concep-tions of organization within a single and unified theoretical struc-ture. Each has been forced to pay the price for this attempt by way of internal tension and conflict which have both creative and debilitat-ing moments.

The general implications of this analysis for an assessment of the present state of contemporary organizational analysis are considered in the following chapter.

3
Post-interregnum organizational studies

Introduction

The dominant theme in organization theory's historical development has been the construction of a general theory of organizations which approximates as closely as possible to the logical structure and methodological conventions which are assumed to prevail within the natural sciences. The social purpose which has informed this intellectual characterization of the subject's disciplinary aims and logical structure was the full realization of that potential for rational control over human beings which a new organizational technology seemed to offer; that is, the development of bureaucratic organization and its associated structural mechanisms of functional differentiation and hierarchical co-ordination.

It is this aspiration to construct a body of factual law-like generalizations concerning formal organization which will provide the 'stock of knowledge' from which the bureaucrat or manager can control and manipulate the social environment in which he operates which has recently moved MacIntyre to argue that:

> 'we can now see in bare skeletal outline a progress first from the Enlightenment's ideal for a social science to the aspirations of social reformers, next from the aspirations of social reformers to the ideals of practice and justification of civil servants and managers, then from the practices of management to the theoretical codification of these practices and of the norms governing them by

sociologists and organization theorists, and finally from the employment of textbooks written by those theorists in schools of management and business schools to the theoretically-informed practice of the contemporary technocratic expert . . . in every case the rise of managerial expertise would have to be the same central theme, and such expertise, as we have already seen, has two sides to it: there is the aspiration to value neutrality and the claim to manipulative power.'

(MacIntyre 1981: 83)

Considered in these terms, organization theory has presented management with a stock of 'moral fictions' (such as 'managerial effectiveness') that disguise the social reality of contemporary management practice and the institutional structures through which it is carried on; that is, as an activity through which certain groups (non-managers) are persuaded to act in the furtherance of particular interests which are conveyed in the form of general interests or technical imperatives, or are coerced into following these precepts in a situation where they might begin to question the technocratic vision which provides the normative foundations of the institution-alized relations in which they are implicated.

However, MacIntyre's characterization of organization theory's intellectual development and its contemporary social function ignores the sub-plot of the historical drama which has been narrated in previous chapters; that is, the aspiration to found a new theory and a corresponding morality which would help regulate the more unsavoury and dangerous consequences of the aggressive and rampant individualism that industrial capitalism has let loose on the world. He is not alone in being far too impressed by the public relations exercise in which organization theorists have been systematically engaged during the better part of this century and insufficiently sensitive to the highly fragmented and divided condition of their intellectual practice. Their role as 'merchants of morality' – as creators and pedlars of symbolic fictions on which modern managers and bureaucrats have relied to legitimate activities that are pervaded by fundamental moral dilemmas and conflicts of one sort or another – has simply provided a useful ideological gloss on their engagement in an intellectual practice which is riddled with deep-seated ambiguity and uncertainty over its philosophical foundations, disciplinary aims, and social purpose.

As we have already seen, the extent to which this inner tension is explicitly articulated and discussed tends to vary in relation to the wider socio-historical context in which organization theory has been developed and practised. The relatively successful containment of these underlying problems during the heyday of the systems approach as compared to the internecine conflict which has prevailed for the last fifteen years or so has to be related to the encouragement of and receptivity to debate over philosophical fundamentals which the prevailing contextual conditions provide.

The aim of this chapter is to chart the interaction between intellectual innovation and contextual change which has already been sketched in the previous chapters. It begins with an interpretation of the relative intellectual dominance achieved by exponents of a systems approach between the 1940s and mid-1960s as one manifestation of the interregnum in Western social and political thought experienced during this period (Haddon 1973). This leads to further reflection on the contextual changes which facilitated a breakdown of the systems orthodoxy in the post-interregnum period and their implications for the present condition of contemporary organizational studies. The chapter concludes with the argument that it is the 'problematic of human agency' (Dawe 1979) which provides the key to understanding the unresolved tensions which lie at the philosophical and theoretical core of organizational studies. It also indicates that there is a need to construct an alternative conception of 'organization' and 'organizational analysis' which is better equipped to make sense of the wide diversity of experience made available through a changing pattern of organizational forms as these have been transformed over time.

The interregnum and organizational studies

In the early 1970s Crozier ventured to provide a retrospective assessment of the achievements made within the field of organizational studies since the beginning of the twentieth century. He identified two overarching themes which had dominated work during this time: first, the meaning of and limits to 'organizational rationality'; and second, the desire to intervene in the process of organizational change so as to improve the effectiveness of collective social action and the quality of social life which it achieved for the mass of the population (Crozier 1974).

In relation to both of these issues, Crozier maintained that the systems approach had provided the dominant intellectual frame of reference in which reflection over the nature and function of complex organizations in a modern industrial society had proceeded. As a result, it had largely succeeded in pushing problems associated with what Crozier labelled 'the logic of struggle' endemic in all organizations on to the margins of the intellectual agenda or had managed to sublimate them within a conceptual vocabulary in which they became unrecognizable. In this way, the issues of organizational rationality and institutional change had been approached in an excessively formalistic and abstract manner which completely failed to make any contact with the everyday experiences of organizational participants and the problems they confronted.

The analysis provided in previous chapters of this book has also attempted to indicated the costs which had been incurred in achieving the limited successes which had been made possible under the integrative push provided by the systems framework. The institutionalization of organization theory as an accredited academic enterprise with its technical concerns, body of theoretical knowledge, and practical contributions to make to problems of 'organizational government' (Pugh and Hickson 1976) had been largely achieved by the end of the 1960s. However, these long-term academic objectives and institutional needs had been secured on the back of an intellectual edifice which had been continually patched up and modified so as to avoid serious evaluation of its philosophical foundations and substantive theoretical core.

This intellectual negligence had been further encouraged by a marked inclination on the part of most organization theorists to ignore the historical roots of their intellectual practice in the social and political upheavals occasioned by the industrial and political revolutions of the late eighteenth and early nineteenth centuries (Wolin 1961, Burns 1974). In turn, this collective intellectual myopia facilitated a truncated reinterpretation of past developments which suggested an unbroken line of linear intellectual ascent which had culminated in the general theoretical synthesis made possible by modern systems thinking (Scott 1961, Pugh 1966, Blau 1974). This lack of historical imagination and vision had encouraged many organization theorists to sever their links with the broader Western tradition of socio-political thought of which they were a part – whether they liked it or not. For them, organization theory had no intellectual history, merely a somewhat confused and fragmented past which could only be made sense of as a series of staging posts on the way to the intellectual order and analytical purity offered by systems theory. They were more than happy to make do with a series of second-hand regurgitations of poorly digested lumps of intellectual fat which stressed the underlying coherence and continuity of the historical tale they were telling.

It is impossible to understand or explain these internal developments unless they are set within the wider social context of which they were an integral element. That is to say, they were merely one expression of a much wider and more pervasive intellectual ethos dominating Western social thought and analysis during the 1950s and early 1960s which Haddon has interpreted as a relatively brief intellectual interregnum that reflected prevailing socio-economic conditons:

> 'The optimism which pervaded so much of the writing and reflection on industrial society and industrial man in the late 1950s and early 1960s can be seen now, with the benefit of hindsight, to have been a reflection of a brief interregnum in Western social thought. . . . A number of theses were advanced in an effort to explain and interpret what was taking place. Amongst the most popular of these theses were embourgeoisement, various versions of managerialism and the end of ideology. In sum, they amounted to a theory of the incorporation of the working class into the mainstream of affluent capitalism, both a political and an economic incorporation. . . . The interregnum marked a point of discontinuity between the old political and theoretical discourse and the new phenomena of social reality and social consciousness.'
>
> (Haddon 1973: 1–3)

A similar characterization of broad developments in socio-political thought occurring during this period and their resonance with an overriding confidence in the capacity of modern industrial societies to eradicate deep-seated social and economic problems previously regarded as endemic to industrial capitalism is also reflected in Kumar's argument that:

> 'Western industrial societies, and to a good extent those of Eastern Europe too, found in the post-war period a first point of rest and reflection in the late 1950s. Looking back on the decade some twenty years later, it has increasingly the look of a watershed. It seems to mark the climax of industrialism, both as a social system and as an ideology. Certainly in the consciousness of the time is

clearly revealed the view that, after a period of "un-natural" disturbances, deflections and retardations, the long-term tendencies of industrialism had re-asserted themselves and reached a point of maturity. It is true that there were many deceptive aspects to this position, particularly in the extent to which the theorists seemed to think that the industrial societies could freeze the flow of history at the date of their theorizing. But in many ways it was also a fair reflection of the actual course of development since the beginning of the century.'

(Kumar 1978: 174–75)

Goldthorpe's analysis (Goldthorpe 1971) of the historicist leanings and technocratic quality of 'convergence theory' (Kerr *et al*. 1960) also highlights the conservative implications which were drawn from the concept of 'industrial society' as a way of combating the radical implications of Marxist social thought with its unremitting focus on revolutionary social change through class conflict. The thesis that all societies were converging, at different speeds, towards a shared institutional configuration of industrial and political organization reinforced the in-built predilections of a form of social analysis that neglected the 'way in which social action can impinge upon processes to speed, check, divert them etc. . . . the expression of values and to changes in values conceivably determining the course of social development tends in fact to be often minimized' (Goldthorpe 1971: 280–82).

In this way, the intellectual and operational convergence between academic and managerial interests in 'complex organizations' to form a seemingly coherent and viable 'theory of organizations' in the early 1960s was facilitated by the comparative socio–economic stability prevailing during the period and the support which it provided for a type of social analysis which assumed that the flow of history could be frozen in the institutional structures which a century and a half of industrialization had produced. The 'orthodox consensus' (Giddens 1979) dominating social analysis and reflection during much of the 1950s and early 1960s merely gave academic expression to the popular belief that the major institutional landmarks of modern industrial society – the factory, the welfare state, the business corporation, representative democracy, an independent civil service, universal education, and medical care – were firmly set in place and equipped to manage any new problems which were likely to emerge in the foreseeable future. Institutional fine-tuning and technical adjustment were all that was necessary to maintain social stability and economic development.

The three central substantive components of this *Weltanschauung* – embourgeoisement, managerialism, and the end of ideology – received considerable intellectual sustenance from a conception of organizational analysis as an applied administrative science which would provide the theoretical and instrumental means necessary to rationalize the authority structures and control systems of complex work organizations as permanent features of industrial society. Organizations were to be the key social units in which the incorporation of the working class or 'lower organizational participants' (Etzioni 1961), under the benevolent control of an enlightened and expert managerial elite freed from the material constraints of ownership and the ideological tributes which it demanded, could be realized and maintained.

By the beginning of the 1960s, further refinements had been introduced to the basic outlines of the systems model of organization as constituting a complex socio-technical system in which the central relationship between production technology and the structure of work roles which it required became the focal point for academic reflection and managerial manipulation (Woodward 1958, Trist *et al.* 1963). Subsequent modifications were carried out to accommodate a broader conception of 'technology' as a transformative process requiring a variety of material resources and cognitive mechanisms, as well as highlighting the range of organizational control systems available to management in any particular situation (Burns and Stalker 1961, Woodward 1965, Perrow 1967, Thompson 1967). Eventually, the theoretical developments taking place within the systems tradition culminated in a 'contingency theory' of organizations which attempted to specify the appropriate 'functional fit' between environmental settings and the internal organizational structures which they required (Lawrence and Lorsch 1967, Pugh, Hickson, and Hinnings 1969).

Each of these approaches and their subsequent incorporation within more sophisticated analytical models was based on what Child has called a 'logic of effectiveness' (Child 1973b) – that is, a commitment to rationalize the organization and control of work tasks through the application of scientific knowledge about the structure and function of organizations which is uncontaminated by conflicting material interests and the ideological distortions they produce. Yet, as Child argued, this 'logic of effectiveness' is itself an ideological rationalization for a form of analysis which accepts certain institutional characteristics of complex organizations as functionally necessary and socially given – as beyond the conscious choice and evaluation of human agents holding conflicting views as to the desirable aims which ought to inform collective social action. As a result, the possible connections between the authority structures and administrative control systems of work organizations and the structure of class relations and political power in the wider society are obscured by a theoretical frame of reference which assumes and reinforces ideological consensus over the fundamental characteristics of established institutional arrangements.

Indeed, the 'logic of effectiveness' which informed the work of mainstream organization theorists in the 1950s and early 1960s can be related to the 'logic of industrialization' promulgated by convergence theorists such as Kerr (1960) and Parsons (1960, 1967) over the same period. Each is based on a belief in the 'homogenizing' impact of basic technology upon the core social and organizational structures which it demands to function effectively. Each removes fundamental issues concerned with the distribution of political power and its impact on the allocation and utilization of economic resources from the realm of public discourse and judgement by relocating them within a technical context in which human decisions are made subservient to the dictates of inexorable and irreversible structural change. Both rest on the underlying domain assumption that the social and political conflicts which characterized previous historical epochs are no longer meaningful in a society which has provided sufficient economic wealth, social well-being, and technical expertise to regulate the occasional frictional disagreements over the distribution of material and social goods. Both are directed to the expanding section of managerial, administrative, and technical experts within industrial societies which would play a prominent role in helping to implement the detailed institutional reforms demanded by the long-term direction of social and organizational development. Taken together, they reduce the 'stuff of politics', to use Goldthorpe's phrase, to questions of an instrumental kind:

'to questions, that is, of a kind which may be appropriately determined by the "technocracy" without their discussion in public or even their full communication to the public. . . . Questions of quite a different order which concern the ends of political action – the nature of the good society, the good life etc. – tend, in

this perspective, to be given only a minor residual role or indeed to
more or less disappear: for within advanced industrial society "real
ideological alternatives" cannot exist.'

(Goldthorpe 1971: 275–77)

Post-interregnum organizational studies

By the mid-1960s, Haddon argues, the interregnum in social and
political thought was coming to an end as a new series of severe and
deep-seated social conflicts affecting both the internal and external
relations of Western industrial societies became more prominent.
The model of industrial society as a relatively stable social system
based on the theoretical knowledge and technical expertise of a
managerial elite more or less in control of the direction and course of
social change became increasingly difficult to sustain in the face of a
destabilizing series of events which, in the fullness of time,
threatened to destroy the ideological and material foundations of
'pluralistic industrialism'.

In general terms, it is possible to characterize the period from the
mid-1960s onwards as one in which the economic, political, and
ideological conflicts which had once been presumed to be 'dead' or
'dying' were resumed with renewed vigour and intensity. The 'end
of ideology' movement, the 'convergence thesis', and the 'collapse
of class politics' confidently identified and expounded during the
interregnum were all subject to trenchant criticism issuing from a
number of sources.

The announcement of the 'end of ideology' by commentators such
as Bell (1960) and Lipset (1960) seemed presumptive, to say the least,
given the ideological and political impact of the Vietnam war within
Western industrial societies, as well as the intensification of class
conflict experienced in these societies as a result of increasing industrial militance during a period of economic prosperity and the
response which this elicited from dominant interests within their
political economies (on this point see Crouch and Pizzorne 1978).
The 'convergence thesis' confidently propounded by writers such as
Kerr (Kerr *et al.* 1960) and Parsons (1960) looked increasingly suspect
from the vantage point of the early 1970s as it had seemed to have
translated the 'opportunities' of technology into the 'imperatives' of
technology (on this point see Dore 1973 and Abrams 1982) and
ignored the social values and practices which necessarily inform the

construction and implementaton of such a human artifact (Gold-thorpe 1971). Not only was the 'convergence thesis' seen to be theoretically suspect on the grounds of technological determinism and sociological historicism, but its empirical foundations looked increasingly shaky as comparative institutional research – particularly on Eastern-bloc countries – illustrated the considerable divergences which still remained (Goldthorpe 1964, Feldman and Moore 1969, Weinberg 1969, Lane 1977, Abrams 1982). Associated arguments concerning the institutional separation and isolation of industrial and political conflict (Dahrendorf 1959), the withering away of the strike weapon as a traditional method and symbol of industrial conflict (Ross and Hartman 1960), and the growing 'maturity' of collective bargaining procedures and processes as a means of regulating distributional conflicts (Kerr 1960), all seemed in need of radical revision as the structural changes and social movements of the late 1960s and early 1970s gathered pace. Other 'pseudo-facts' (to use Zeitlin's term), such as the 'separation of ownership from control' and its implications for the characterization of corporate management as the neutral guardians of a new ideological consensus around the theme of 'meritocracy', were also found wanting in terms of their theoretical grounding and empirical veracity (on this see Zeitlin 1974).

By the middle of the 1970s, one of the foremost contributors to the 'orthodox consensus' of the interregnum was calling for the 'new liberty' of maximizing individual 'life chances' by the regulation of distributional conflict through a social market economy, but in a contemporary social context characterized by 'falling incomes, a new distribution of power and impotence, threats of war and starvation, crime and disorder, and declining confidence in the capacity of those who govern, or even the institutions of government' (Dahrendorf 1975: 5).

In particular, the long-term impact of large-scale organizational action upon the lives of millions of people, as reflected in the 'discovery' of the transnational corporation (Vernon 1973, Radice 1973, Tugenhadt 1973, Said and Simmons 1975), provided a focus of concern which had been conspicuous by its absence under the interregnum when interest in the technicalities of organizational design and control precluded the explicit recognition and pursuit of such questions. The proposition that organizational structure and behaviour were very largely determined by environmental factors had consolidated into an academic orthodoxy which remained impervious to a systematic consideration of a broader range of 'environmental contingencies' which might impinge upon decision about organizational design. However, growing political and social concern with the environmental consequences of organizational activity (Dickson 1974) – evidenced in such developments as consumerism, popular ecology, critical appraisals of national and local planning systems, the social audit movement – helped to prise this orthodoxy open and to establish the relevance of moral and social issues in the analysis of complex organizations. As Perrow maintained, the impact of organizations on society may be as important as their impact on members (if not more so), because organizations are multi-purpose tools which can be directed at a wide range of social practices:

> 'They provide the means of imposing one's definition of the proper affairs of men upon other men. The man who controls an organization has power that goes far beyond that of those who do not have any such control. . . . organizations are tools; they mobilize resources that can be used for a variety of ends. These resources and goals of the organization are up for grabs and people grab for them continually.'
>
> (Perrow 1972: 14–16)

Thus, in a number of respects, the 'technocratic paradigm' which had dominated social thought and analysis in the West during the 1940s, 1950s, and for much of the 1960s was proving to be much less resilient in the face of a series of often disparate socio-economic upheavals which it could not accommodate within its conceptual parameters and related terms of rational discourse. As Gouldner reflected in 1971:

> 'With respect to its theoretical and intellectual dispositions, then, as well as with regard to its ideological ramifications, the structure of academic sociology promises to become much more polycentric than it has been. It will, also, become more ideologically resonant than it has been. . . . one may conjecture that there will increasingly emerge a tensionful polarization between this development and the growth of an instrumental orientation. . . . In short, all schools of sociology will face the common problem of eluding the confining perspectives of the Welfare State, though some will do so more than others.'
>
> (Gouldner 1971: 444–46)

The intellectual impact of escalating economic, social, and political crisis in Western industrial societies on the development of organization theory in America and Europe was expressed in a variety of ways. In the case of America, Mintzberg, one of the more sophisticated advocates of 'administrative science' in the late 1960s and early 1970s, has recently argued that:

'Vietnam represented a critical turning point in the perceptions of many of us concerned with analysis. It would be trite to say that a reading of Halberstram's "The Best and the Brightest" signalled that the honeymoon with analysis was over. Its relationship with management, which began in the factory with Frederick Taylor, flourished in the office with the introduction of Operations Research, and culminated in Robert McNammara's application of the Hitch and McKeen proposals for PPBS and cost-benefit analysis at the policy level, started to come apart in the rice paddies of Vietnam.'

(Mintzberg 1977: 351)

At a less anecdotal level, Lammers's personal survey of the perceptions of a number of prominent American organization theorists concerning the present condition and future prospects of their field in the early 1970s revealed a collective mood of restiveness and uncertainty in relation to the perceived need to enlarge and enrich the scope and potential of the area in response to a changing set of social conditions which resisted incorporation within established categories (Lammers 1974). However, Lammers concluded that this prevailing mood of eclecticism and openness indicated not an imminent revolutionary change in theoretical paradigm but a change of focus in terms of three major themes: a shift to multi-level analysis (societal, inter-organizational, and internal); a trend towards more dynamic theoretical approaches; and a movement towards a more 'political', as opposed to 'scientific', ideological stance. While Lammers would maintain this perception of contained theoretical refocusing and incremental ideological adjustment to changed social circumstances in later evaluations of the 'state of the art' (Lammers 1981), subsequent developments within the field suggested that his analysis had understated the significant 'change of problematic' and associated theoretical and ideological fragmentation which was well under way by the middle of the 1970s both in America (Benson 1977b, Pfeffer 1982) and to an even greater extent in Europe (Crozier and Frieberg 1980).

In Europe, the break-up of the systems orthodoxy in organizational analysis was signalled by a number of publications which indicated that the constraints imposed by the former on the questions which could be asked and the manner in which they were to be approached were no longer acceptable to a growing body of scholarly opinion (Mouzelis 1967, Silverman 1968 and 1970, Child 1973a and 1973b, Crozier 1974, Clegg 1975). Many of the critical assessments of the dominance of systems theory within the field were brought together in Child's critique of contingency theory and his attempt to develop an alternative approach based on the concept of 'strategic choice' (Child 1973a, 1973b). His critique accused contingency theorists of sociological naivety and ideological bad faith; they had simply modified the systems approach to accommodate a broader range of factors without considering the deterministic logic of explanation on which it traded and the implicit ideological support which this gave to powerful supporters of the institutional status quo. His alternative approach drew attention to the range of strategic choices available to participants in the areas of organizational design and environmental enactment, as well as theoretically situating the fact of organizational choice within a political process in which the interpretation of constraints and opportunities is shaped by the power exercised by organizational elites in the light of their ideological preferences.

However, Child's contribution to the widening debate taking place within the field in the 1970s over the 'proper' concerns and approaches of an organizational analysis subject to the fragmentary impact of competing schools of thought and warring factions was of greater significance than is conveyed in the notion of 'strategic choice'. It also provided an excellent illustration of the continuing tensions and strains which beset organizational studies at a time when the social setting in which it was practised positively encouraged a more open and explicit questioning of domain assumptions that had largely remained unchallenged since the 1930s. Child stands at the intellectual crossroads between a systems-derived approach which is struggling to retain its intellectual grip on organizational studies through a strategy of containment and an action-derived approach which is intent on freeing organizational analysis from the restrictive confines which it imposes. He attempts to take them in the direction of a much more radical stance in relation to both theoretical commitments and ideological appeal. Nevertheless, Child seems unsure as to whether 'strategic choice' is to be regarded as a supplement to the functionalist analysis inherent in contingency theory (Child 1973a: 102) or as a radical alternative to the conservative assumptions in which the latter is necessarily embedded (Child 1973a: 247–48). The language of 'strategic choice' would seem to suggest a radical theoretical and ideological break with functionalism, but the implementation of the approach indicated a more modest aim of extending the theoretical scope and empirical range of an established orthodoxy which still had its uses.

This underlying uncertainty and tension between opting for a strategy of contained reformulation or one of total reconstruction is maintained in the 'Babel of theoretical voices' (Giddens 1979: 238) which have clamoured for attention during the course of the late 1970s and early 1980s. Some continue to fight a rearguard action against the increasing clamour of the critics (see Pugh and Hickson 1976, and the exchange between Donaldson and Schreyogg 1982), while others demand a complete reconstruction of the philosophical and ideological foundations of organization theory which rejoices in the political struggles in which the latter is necessarily implicated (see chapter 2).

A range of themes (organizational politics, inter-organizational relations, macro-level comparative studies, organizational culture and symbolism) and approaches (political economy, population ecology, neo-Marxism, negotiated order, ethnomethodology) have been developed within the intellectual and institutional space made available by the gradual dissolution of the systems orthodoxy. These developments will be discussed in greater detail in the final chapter of this work. At this point it is necessary to reflect on the major internal structural outcome of this dissolution which many commentators saw as gathering pace as the 1970s progressed – that is, the putative intellectual bifurcation of organizational analysis into two distinctive traditions as conveyed in the categorical distinction between the 'sociology of organizations' on one hand and 'organization theory' on the other.

As we have already seen, the anticipated bifurcation of organization studies into two distinctive and radically opposed forms of intellectual practice labelled 'the sociology of organizations' and 'organization theory' had been identified in the early 1960s by commentators such as Mayntz (1964) and later by critics of systems theory such as Albrow (1968). The latter insisted that there was a need to draw a clear analytical distinction between a non-prescriptive sociology of organizations 'which had no concern with the applications of its results' (Albrow 1968), and an administrative theory pandering to the strategic and operational requirements of the practising manager or administrator. While these two spheres of interest may at times overlap and may have something to say to each other, this must not divert the sociology of organizations from its mission of discovering the causes and consequences of various organizational forms: 'The organizational theorist is concerned to help managers and administrators. By contrast, the perspective of the sociologist is "impracticable". His is the search for understanding untrammelled by the needs of "men of affairs"' (Albrow 1968: 167).

However, Albrow does not suggest that this position logically implies a 'value-free' sociology of organizations as opposed to a 'value-less' organization theory, even though the case for a policy of 'intellectual apartheid' based on this distinction is one interpretation which could be, and has been, drawn from his analysis (Bradley and Reed 1980). Indeed, in later publications he explicitly argues for this division on the basis of a clear recognition, not to say celebration, of the fact that the sociology of organizations – in terms of assumptions, substantive problems, conceptual frameworks, theoretical explanations, and research methods – is necessarily implicated in those moral and political dilemmas which face all organizational participants whatever their structural location and ideological motivation (Albrow 1974).

Nevertheless, what is clearly implied in this distinction is the contention that the 'sociology of organizations' can transcend the technocratic foundations and aspirations of 'organization theory'. The former can claim some kind of objectivity (relative to the ideological bias necessarily built into the concerns and concepts of organization theory) to the extent that it is not directly implicated in engineering a particular form of social technology within modern industrial society – which usually requires the acceptance of an unqualified managerial conception of organizational problems – and it struggles to analyse ideological and political conflicts characteristic of bureaucratic organizations without accepting the vocabulary and language of one particular interest group within that conflict. Organization theory, in sharp contrast, is logically and practically implicated in this conflict to the extent that it identifies with and is pervaded by the managerial interests of improved organizational efficiency and effectiveness. These valued-ends are unreflectively assimilated within organization theory and provide the domain assumptions for a form of intellectual practice which is unable to examine its own philosophical and ideological foundations.

Subsequently, some version or another (often a caricature) of Albrow's distinction was uncritically accepted by a number of commentators who wished to speed the demise of a technocratically conceived systems orthodoxy and to promote their alternative brand of theorizing, whatever the design and colour of its intellectual packaging (Silverman 1970, Salaman 1978). Yet in their haste to advance the claims of a radical sociology of organizations, as against those of a conservative organization theory, Albrow's interpreters failed to assess the historical, sociological, and philosophical support for this presumed segregation or to perceive the 'positivist twist' which his argument could be given by those who wished to deny the relevance of ethical conflict and moral choice for the practice of organizational analysis.

The analysis already provided in this book suggests that Albrow tended to underestimate the complexity of the field which he was surveying and to impose a categorical distinction which was very difficult to maintain in practice. In short, he substantially underestimated the continuing interest of the sociology of organizations in social engineering of one sort or another, and overestimated its capacity to incorporate a sufficient plurality of perspectives within the terms of its theoretical discourse. He may also have been guilty of presenting an over-simplified analysis of the historical development and conceptual resources of 'organization theory' which neglected the contradictory implications of declared ideological commitments and substantive intellectual practice. There may be some evidence to support the contention that organizational sociologists have been prepared to include a broader range of variables and levels of analysis within their studies than has conventionally been the case with organization theorists (Eldridge and Crombie 1977). However, it has also been true that their work may be informed by assumptions which are as 'conservative' (if not more) in their operational implications as is the case with organization theorists.

In addition to this over-simplification of the complexity of those substantive interests and moral values which have informed the practice and history of organizational analysis, the manner in which Albrow formulated his case also gave a 'hostage to fortune' to those who wished to smuggle positivism in through the back door. This was so to the extent that his generalized distinction between a technocratic organization theory and an impractical sociology of organizations which took nobody's side gave support to those who wished to empty organization studies of their constitutive moral dilemmas and replace them with an 'ethical instrumentalism' of one kind or another. This moral denudation would be achieved by making organizational analysis serve the interests of an identifiable group, class, or category (the 'technocrats', 'proletariat', or 'people') which was presumed to embody the universal needs of society as a whole.

In this way, organization studies would be made subservient to a form of ethical instrumentalism which denied, implicitly if not explicitly, the inevitability of ethical conflict and the inseparability of intellectual practice and moral choice. It would also threaten to obscure a deeper problem which lay at the heart of those fundamental intellectual contradictions (naturalism/rationalism, functionalism/actionism, determinism/voluntarism, instrumentalism/relativism) which have previously been discussed within this book – that is, the problematic of human agency and its implications for the manner in which we understand and interpret the historical development of organizational analysis as an intellectual practice rooted in the 'positivist' social thought of mid-nineteenth-century Europe.

Organization studies and the problematic of human agency

Haddon argues that the end of the 'interregnum' in Western social thought and analysis by the concluding years of the 1960s was symbolized by a rediscovery of what Dawe (1970) had called the 'problem of control', as opposed to the 'problem of order' which had dominated sociology in Western capitalist societies since the Second World War:

'In the modern world, the problem of control has a dual meaning. Firstly, there is the modern thrust to dominate nature in which science and technology has played a vital role, and which has expressed itself in the industrial system of production and distribution. . . . Secondly, however, the problem of control has to do with men's (collective) control over their own institutions and relationships. . . . The most difficult issue which confronts us, both in theory and practice, is the link between these two mean-

ings or aspects of the problem of control. . . . the effort to
subjugate nature is a collective effort, and since this is so it is also
essentially political. The organization of this collective effort
involves relationships of power and class between men. . . .
Control, in the sense of seeking to increase the domination of
nature, is therefore not separable from the control of human action
and social institutions.'

(Haddon 1973: 21–3)

Haddon's characterization of the problem of control, in terms of the
ambiguous, not to say contradictory, relationship between the drive
for power over the natural environment and the reassertion of social
control in societies increasingly subject to technocratic domination,
led him to advocate a view of 'society in terms of structures of power
and decision-making, and to examine empirically in any given
society which groups and agencies have an interest in promoting
(their subjective definition of) structural consistency; and what
sanctions they have at their disposal to implement it' (Haddon 1973:
26). This call for a 'sociology of control' which resisted the technocratic determinism inherent in functionalist analyses of social
change and re-emphasized the centrality of human action and its
unintended structural consequences for an understanding of socio-
political development was echoed in the works of several prominent
sociologists in the early 1970s such as Dreitzel (1970), Friedrichs
(1970), Gouldner (1971, 1973), Giddens (1973), Habermas (1972,
1974), and Touraine (1974).

However, Dawe's more recent (1979) analysis of the nature and
scope of the 'problematic of human agency', based on his earlier interpretation (Dawe 1970), indicates the continuing significance of a
far more complex dilemma than was admitted in influential works
published during the initial aftermath of the interregnum and the
intellectual vitality and imagination which its eventual break-up
released; that is, his identification of the underlying 'dismal paradox'
that 'human agency becomes human bondage because of the very
nature of human agency' (Dawe 1979: 398), and the continuing
relevance of this fundamental contradiction to an understanding of
contemporary social thought and analysis.

In an extremely rich and sensitive interpretation, Dawe traces the
historical career of the concept of social action from its roots in the
political philosophy of Hobbes and Rousseau, through the sociology
of Marx, Durkheim, and Weber, to the contemporary sociological

systems of theorists such as Parsons. His analysis is based on the premise that:

> 'the idea of social action has been central to sociological thought less as a theory or set of theories in any formal sense, than as a fundamental moral and analytical preoccupation. Indeed, sociology has no "theories" of social action. What it does have is a vast body of theorizing about social action: its nature, its sources, its consequences. And this theorizing around a single idea, has . . . been decisive for and definitive of the entire history and nature of sociological analysis from its very inception.'
>
> (Dawe 1979: 363)

His account of successive attempts to theorize the concept of social action as the central and active mediating process between institutional constraints and social agency reveals a consistent incapacity on the part of social theorists and sociologists to tolerate and cope with the 'one genuine necessity inherent in human agency and social action . . . the necessity of ambiguity' (Dawe 1979: 389). Thus, unable to accept the necessary ambiguities and contradictions of social action, particularly in relation to the unavoidable and unsolvable conflict between instrumental and moral action within all forms of social experience and practice, the history of sociology becomes the story of repeated denials or negations of the goal of extending individual freedom through communal action in which it was originally grounded in the Enlightenment philosophy of eighteenth-century Western Europe. In Dawe's opinion, it is the continued intellectual domination of a scientistic conception of sociology since the mid-nineteenth century which has facilitated the transformation of the concept of social action as exemplifying the essential autonomy, contingency, creativity, and inconsistency of human agency into the rationalized, mechanistic, deterministic, and predictable concept of social system, and the 'unworldly imperatives of certainty and necessity which it conveys'.

The resort of scientific metaphor may have led to the denial of human agency, but the alternative metaphor of 'conversation' – as an open-ended, contingent practice of intellectual argument and enquiry which is sensitive to the diversity of human experience and the alternative opportunities and directions that it conveys –

> 'retains the enduring vision of human agency as moral action and moral experience. It also retains its grounding in an articulation of

human social experience. . . . For ambiguity remains essential to any serious conception of the self- and socially creative capacities and possibilities of human agency. . . . Only by virtue of the ambiguity is it possible to envision a community of moral caring being created out of a community where "none can care". So it is the prime imperative of the sociology of the conversation that we ceaselessly listen to and converse with the voices from everyday life, whenever and however they are to be heard, including our own.'

(Dawe 1979: 414)

The significance of Dawe's interpretation for the analysis of organizational studies' historical development and current condition which has been offered in this book is clear; it illuminates the process whereby the intellectual conflicts and oppositions which have informed that history come to signify a deeper failure to understand and come to terms with the paradoxical character of human agency and its implications for the scope, nature, and claims of organizational analysis. Repeatedly we have witnessed the same transition from creative human action and co-operation to imposed institutional order and control. Barnard's conception of the organization as a spontaneous expression and articulation of the human need and facility for communal action gives way to a model of the organization as a mechanism for maintaining the political domination of one interest group over others who cannot be trusted to recognize their 'true interests'. Selznick's belief in the creative challenge which grass-roots democracy presents to the stultifying effects of bureaucratic structures of control is transformed into a pessimistic evaluation of the marginal adjustments made possible to the institutional status quo by the organizational politicking that contains and channels potentially recalcitrant action. Silverman's commitment to the dialectical interplay between the liberating potential of social action and the restraining influence of organizational structure is superseded by a myopic focus on the minutiae of everyday life and the universal accounting procedures through which it takes on an ordered and stable character. Clegg's demand for a critical theory of organizations which is sensitive to the contradictory implications of organizational membership within capitalist work organizations becomes trapped in a reductionist methodology which ensures the subservience of human agents to the logical imperatives of a particular mode of production.

Viewed in these terms, the history of organizational analysis – in either its pre- or post-interregnum phases – can be seen in terms of a recurring failure to recognize and appreciate the full meaning of the theoretical and practical dilemma of human agency which cannot be resolved or transcended by recourse to a scientistic or instrumental reading of its intellectual aims and practical significance. On the contrary, organization theorists need to reconsider the contribution which they have made and can continue to make to improving our understanding of the terms and conditions of this dilemma by examining the practical forms and contexts in which it takes on a definite institutional shape for human beings participating in specific socio-historical locations.

Abrams has recently argued that:

'the most promising move I can envisage from that point of view so far as the dilemma of human agency is concerned is to insist on the need to conceive of that dilemma historically: to insist on the way in which and the extent to which the relationship of action and structure is to be understood as a matter of process in time. I would almost say that it is a question of trying to build a sociology of process as an alternative to our tried, worn and inadequate sociologies of action and system.'

(Abrams 1982: xv)

There have been times when this need for a complete reworking of the terms within which the dilemma of human action has been discussed within the field of organizational studies has been clearly recognized. As long ago as 1966, Burns was calling for an approach to the study of organizations which recognized the fact that:

'We are, I believe, closer to the study of the social world as a process, instead of an anatomy frozen into "structured" immobility; closer to the identification of the abstraction, society, with the empirical fact, behaviour, if we accept the essential ambiguity of social experience and organized interpretation of it in dynamic rather than structural terms. In this way, by perceiving behaviour as a medium of the constant interplay and mutual redefinition of individual identities and social institutions, it is possible to begin to grasp the nature of the changes, developments, and historical processes through which we move and which we help to create.'

(Burns 1966: xvi)

While Burns has consistently pursued this 'sociology or process' in his research and writing on organizations (Burns 1974, 1977), the challenge which he presents has not been followed with the same enthusiasm by fellow organization theorists who have opted for the presumed certainties of structural explanation (of one sort or another) and the 'homogenizing' influence which it has exerted over their thinking and analysis.

Nevertheless, if Dawe's metaphor of 'conversation' provides a basis for the wider conceptual frame of reference in which his (and Abrams's) 'sociology of process' must be constituted, then the next chapter of this book offers a conception of organizational analysis as an intellectual practice focused on the shifting patterns of administrative practices that have given expression to the necessary tensions and conflicts between instrumental and moral action which lie at the core of the modern condition.

Summary

This chapter has attempted to provide a general assessment of the development of organizational studies since the 1950s in relation to the changing patterns of socio-economic conditions and structures in which it has been practised. This analysis has identified a growing appreciation of the characteristic dilemmas, tensions, and contradictions which have been contained within this developmental process on the part of a number of prominent contributors to the field. However, it has also highlighted a consistent failure on the part of succeeding generations of organization theorists to focus on the problematic of human agency and its fundamental significance for the manner in which the study of organizations has been practised.

The following two chapters of this book attempt to rectify this situation by offering a systematic conception of organizational analysis as an intellectual practice which is sensitive to the problematic of human agency and its implications for the way in which such a practice is carried on.

4
The practice framework and organizational analysis

Introduction

The analysis provided in the three previous chapters of this book has identified a number of fundamental problems in contemporary organizational analysis which require a different kind of theoretical response to that which has conventionally been provided by its practitioners.

In general terms, the analysis provided so far has indicated the need for a 'sociology of process' which is sensitive to the necessary tension, not to say contradiction, between instrumental and moral action or formal association and natural community which is constitutive of 'complex organizations'. This general failure to provide a form of organizational analysis which can make a major contribution to our understanding of the characteristic institutional dilemmas of the 'advanced industrial societies' (Giddens 1973) has been broken down into its constituent components.

First, there has been the repeated failure to come to terms with the paradoxical quality of human agency and the problems which this creates for both actor and observer. Second, there has been a successive series of transitions from the conception of organization as embodying the creative and co-operative potential of human action to one of imposed institutional order and control without any explicit recognition of these theoretical elisions and the severe limitations which they place on any attempt to improve our understanding of the conflicting principles and practices which contemporary work organizations contain. Third, and as a consequence of the two previous failures, the majority of organizational analysts have been unable to maintain sufficient theoretical space for the essential ambiguity of organizational life and the need to construct interpretations of it in dynamic rather than structural terms.

The aim of this chapter is to develop a conceptual framework for the analysis of work organizations which may go some of the way to meeting the problems which have been identified above. The following chapter will 'rework' a number of major studies of work organizations carried out since the 1940s as a way of illustrating the insight which the practice framework can provide into the organizational forms which express the necessarily ambiguous and paradoxical quality of human agency.

This chapter opens with a consideration of the way in which the concept of 'practice' has figured in recent social theory and analysis. It is followed by a detailed specification of the analytical framework which is on offer within this book as providing the basis for a more subtle and sophisticated appreciation of the problematical nature of human agency and the changing organizational forms through which it is expressed. The chapter concludes with a discussion of the implications of this framework for the conduct of organizational analysis and the status of the knowledge which is produced as a result of engaging in such an intellectual practice.

The concept of social practice

The concept of social practice has figured prominently in the works of a number of contemporary social and political theorists who have attempted to develop a more systematic appreciation of the problematic of human agency and its implications for the analysis of institutional change (Bordieu 1977, Harré 1979, Giddens 1979, Pettit 1979, McDonald and Pettit 1981, MacIntyre 1981, Bernier 1983, Bernstein 1983). It has also informed substantive empirical research and analysis in a number of fields ranging from family units to class structures (Donzelot 1980, Burns 1981, Parkin 1981, Tomlinson 1982).

Within this body of writing and research, three themes have predominated. First, the desire to develop a philosophical anthropology – as a basis for substantive analysis – which offers an alternative conception of human agency to that entailed in more deterministically inclined approaches, while at the same time resisting the theoretical embrace of rational individualism and its reductionist predilections (Hollis 1977). Second, the attempt to construct a systematic conceptual framework which can overcome the traditional duality between 'structure' and 'process' which has informed so many of the philosophical and theoretical debates between competing schools of social theory. Third, the intention to use this conceptual framework for the purpose of providing studies of institutional change that focus on the sources which generate and the mechanisms that direct transformations in the organized social practices in which human beings are necessarily engaged as members of a population involved in transforming the natural and social environment in which they are situated.

These three themes are brought together in Harris's book *Fundamental Concepts and the Sociological Enterprise* (Harris 1980). An exposition and elaboration of his theoretical contribution will be followed by a consideration of its implications for a general reconceptualization of the notion of 'work organization'.

Harris's aim is to construct a conceptual framework which synthesizes key theoretical components drawn from both the action and structural frames of reference to form a more adequate approach for realizing the disciplinary aims of sociology as an intellectual practice; this is, 'to exhibit the relation between social situations and their outcomes' (Harris 1980: 22). Both the action and structural frames of reference are seen to be essential for this enterprise to the extent that the former focuses on the description and interpretation of human actions, while the latter attempts to link actions and outcomes by specifying the pattern of interrelations between elements of the social situation in which action takes place. Nevertheless, taken in isolation from each other both are theoretically defective in the sense that they have forced sociologists to develop 'linking concepts' that relate action and structure (such as 'role', 'institution', and 'relationship') in such a way that any reference to the intentional character of actions and the situational outcomes it generates are omitted (Harris 1980: 25). In turn, this has encouraged a corresponding 'decoupling' of what is necessarily assumed to be the 'individual' character of intentions, purposes, and motives on the one hand and the 'collective' nature of values, norms, and institutions on the other.

Harris maintains that the major theoretical requirement in contemporary sociology is 'some conception which will carry back reference to the constituent categories of action, but at the same time be of such a nature as to constitute an element of structure' (Harris 1980: 29). Consequently, he recommends the concept of 'social practice' as fulfilling this dual need in that:

'While it retains reference to the concepts constitutive of action, it does not refer to individual actions but to actions typical within the population studied. To engage in a form of practice is not to engage in individual action in the sense of an action which is only intelligible in terms of the meaning structure peculiar to a unique individual. Nor is it necessarily to engage in a form of collective action, that is, to act in association with others. It does involve acting in a way similar to others, with a view to achieving states of affairs which others also attempt to achieve, and using the same type of resource as they do to achieve that type of end.'

(Harris 1980: 29)

In this way, the concept of practice integrates three conceptually distinct aspects of human existence and action – the animal, the culture, and the social; practices are 'the outcome of the social life of animals who have developed symbolic systems of communication' (Harris 1980: 31). It allows us to focus on those forms of distinctively human activity whereby men maintain themselves through their characteristic life activities and transform their relationship to their natural and social environment.

In Harris's view, it is this self-transforming capability and skill which provides the distinguishing characteristic of human, as opposed to animal, populations, as well as making the subject matter of the social sciences different in kind from that of the natural sciences:

'The primary characteristic of human life which makes it distinctively human is not that men engage in animal activity or in thought, but in activity which engenders and embodies thought, and in thought which arises out of and is in turn embodied in practice. Without activity there would be no thought; without thought there would be no practice, only activity. If this view of the human condition is correct, it is small wonder that the attempt to analyse the forms of men's common life in terms of unchanging categories of activity, or thought, or individual action, have met with so little success.'

(Harris 1980: 31)

Having established the anthropological foundations which inform his theoretical work, Harris proceeds to a more detailed specification of the concept of 'social practice' as the *a priori* synthetic constituting category of social life. Thus to engage in a social practice involves:

'engaging in a class of actions which are intelligible in and through the concepts which inform them, which have to be understood as directed towards ends which all members of the community of practitioners share, and is defined through the means adopted to the attainment of those ends which are to be understood as determined by the conditions under which the practice is undertaken.'

(Harris 1980: 29)

Considered in these terms, any social practice can be seen to consist of the following conceptual components:

1 the class of actions in which the community of practitioners are engaged as members of that community;
2 the network of concepts which inform their actions and which endow them with a shared meaning and symbolic significance for the community of practitioners as a whole;
3 the common aims or purposes which are generated and developed through the acceptance and communication of conceptual communality;
4 the resources, both material and symbolic, which are utilized by practitioners in the performance of their activities;
5 the situational conditions or constraints under which these communal activities, the resources they require, and the relationships which they engender between individual members of the community of practitioners are shaped and directed.

Harris argues that all social situations are constituted through communities of practitioners related to each other through the concepts internal to the practices in which they are engaged and by virtue of the shared resources and conditions under which they are undertaken. However, these practices have to be 'assembled' in various ways through a process of institutional construction and reconstruction to form social formations which prevail over time and exhibit a minimally acceptable degree of structural continuity and cultural homogeneity. Consequently, Harris introduces the distinction between 'primary' and 'secondary' social practices as a way of theorizing the process whereby practices are assembled to form distinctive and recognizable institutional configurations. Primary practices are aimed at transforming the environmental circumstances under which human life is carried on through the production of goods and services and the concepts which inform our conceptions of them. Secondary practices are directed at achieving overall integration and regulation of the former through the design, implementation, monitoring, and redesigning of various administrative, political, and judicial mechanisms which combine the multifarious primary practices in which human populations are necessarily engaged. They are imposed with the aim of co-ordinating the diverse and complex array of primary 'productive' practices in which communities of human populations are engaged into institutional structures which provide the required degree of normative coherence, social control, and stability necessary to sustained continued productive activity.

In a situation where primary productive practices are diverse and the resources necessary for their performance are technically advanced and exclusively owned and/or controlled by a particular group or community within the population, then there will be conflicts of interest between members over the allocation of productive resources and the distribution of the communal product which will have to be regulated and redirected in various ways. Secondary, or 'integrative', social practices provide the institutional means and mechanisms whereby the regulation and mediation of the conflicts generated by primary productive practices of this kind can be achieved. As such, the necessity of institutionalized practices of regulation and co-ordination arises from the range and complexity of the primary productive practices exhibited by a population, the patterns of resource ownership and control under which they are undertaken, and the existence of a natural and social environment in which its members need to act together to achieve their aims.

The form of integrative practice which is likely to predominate in populations where productive practice is diverse, takes place between associated producers, and depends on exclusive possession and/or control of productive resources is 'imperative co-ordination'. The existence of the latter indicates that the assembly and regulation of primary productive practices are being achieved through the exercise of legitimate domination and its supporting institutional mechanism – rational bureaucratic administration.

This leads us to the final part of Harris's conceptual framework – that is, the identification of the sources of institutional change and the mechanisms through which it is shaped and directed. Previous discussion has indicated that any social formation will be constituted through the assemblage of the primary productive practices in which its members are engaged, as this is facilitated through the institutional mechanisms whereby the co-ordination and regulation of productive activity can be achieved. For Harris, the advantage of conceptualizing social formations in this way – that is, as assemblages of primary productive practices achieved through the construction and implementation of various political, judicial, and administrative mechanisms – is that its basic elements are treated as processes rather than entities, activities rather than structures. Consequently, the sources of social change:

'must be located in the practices which constitute the elements of formations rather than in the natural environment or an isolated individual. . . . It is therefore necessary to consider what account may be given of the endogenous transformation of practices.'

(Harris 1980: 176)

Approached in this manner, the most significant source of the endogenous transformation of practices lies in the conceptual and symbolic means through which they are socially constructed and maintained. Yet this conceptual innovation has to be analysed in relation to the changing relationship between the concepts which are internal to a practice and the material resources and tools which practitioners rely on in the course of consciously engaging in the social activity appropriate to that practice:

'To attempt to explain social change requires the prior identification of the sources of change. It has been argued that the source of change lies in the relation between the concepts and tools constitutive of a practice and the consciousness which reflects the experience which is a by-product of engaging in that practice under specific conditions, changes in which arise from the activity of practitioners.'

(Harris 1980: 189)

However, this focus on the source of social change in the interaction between the conceptual and material activities of practitioners does not provide an account of how social formations, seen as assemblages of practices, are transformed. For this, an understanding of the 'mechanisms', as opposed to the 'sources', of social transformation is essential:

'When we shift our attention from the attempt to locate the causes of change to an attempt to elaborate the mechanisms whereby changes in the practices constituting a social formation result in its transformation, then the manner in which these practices are assembled and the resultant ways in which they condition each other become our central concern.'

(Harris 1980: 195)

Harris suggests that the strategic theoretical issue which a concern with the mechanisms directing the process of social change has to deal with is the type of situational conditions which facilitate the spread of new forms of practice throughout the social formation as a whole. In particular, the problem of identifying those innovative conditions which will generate novel forms of integrative and co-ordinative practice through which assembly is made possible becomes central. Here, the notion of 'dominance' and the institutional mechanisms through which it is realized and maintained take on a particular explanatory significance. This is so to the extent that the supersession of one practice by another and the institutional mechanisms through which primary practices are assembled are likely to be determined by:

'Struggles whose outcomes are determined by the relative power of the participants. . . . Hence the establishment of a new formation will require the transformation of the forms of primary practices so that they "fit" the new mode of assembly, a process which must be gradual, since many practices will have to continue without interruption if life is to continue.'

(Harris 1980: 214)

Thus it is transformations in the mode of assembly – that is, the set of secondary social practices through which primary productive practices become organized – which constitute the key mechanisms for understanding and explaining the direction of social change. While the source of social change lies in the continuing dialectical interplay between the conceptual and material components of primary productive practice, the institutional mechanisms by which this process is regulated and directed are to be located in the secondary practices through which social transformation takes on recognizable organizational forms. Changes in the latter are seen to be initiated through the power struggles engaged in by conflicting groups who strive to manage and control the integrative apparatus whereby the assembly of productive activity is achieved. In the modern world, imperatively co-ordinated institutions – rational bureaucratic structures – provide the institutional means through which this struggle is carried on and the mechanism in terms of which it is temporarily resolved in favour of certain interest groups or classes rather than others. Consequently, it is the changing balance of power between conflicting groups and its impact on the administrative mechanism whereby communal production and its outcome are organized and distributed which is the key to explaining the process of social transformation. Bureaucratic structures are interpreted as the strategic institutional mechanisms through which a prevailing pattern of power relationships is maintained and the means whereby that pattern – and its implications for the organization and distribution of communal production and its product – may be transformed.

It is this aspect of Harris's argument and its theoretical implications for the study of complex work organizations which needs further elaboration in the following section.

Organization as a secondary social practice

The implications of Harris's framework for the reconceptualization of complex work organizations attempted here are analysed at two interrelated levels: first, a generic reworking of organizations as integrative practices geared to the assembly of primary productive practices by means of imperative co-ordination and a bureaucratic control mechanism; second, a series of modifications to that generic reconceptualization which focuses on the plurality of additional means and mechanisms which have to be relied on to achieve integrative assembly in specific situations.

The central theme which both of these exercises in reconceptualization will highlight is the unavoidable ambiguities and contradictions which are generated as a result of the inability of explicit principles or mechanisms (such as rational bureaucracy) to facilitate detailed control and the consequent need for implicit assumptions and codes to act as control devices which inevitably generate potential areas of resistance and change. This focus, it will be argued, provides one way of analysing the 'problematic of human agency' at the organizational level without 'reducing' it to an inevitable clash between competing organizational logics or suggesting that it can be 'overcome' through some dramatic synthesis or 'dissolved' through a phased withdrawal into the minutiae of everyday life.

In terms of the practice framework, complex organizations are treated as constituent members of a particular type or category of social practice which is defined in terms of both its function within a social formation and the structural mechanism necessary to realize that objective. Complex organizations provide a pivotal structural mechanism whereby the wide range of primary productive practices in which communities are engaged in the course of transforming the social situations of which they are a part can be systematically assembled so as to constitute coherent and ordered social formations. As specific mechanisms for the assemblage of a range of primary practices necessary to the reproduction and transformation of social existence, they take on a distinctive institutional form as corporate groups with their accompanying administrative systems. To constitute a corporate group, it is necessary that a plurality of practitioners involved in primary productive practice 'possess the means of arriving at common decisions so as to the action they will take and the means of carrying out those decisions' (Harris 1980: 112). This will require a specialized administrative structure made up of 'administrators', 'officers', or 'managers' who achieve integration through the exercise of imperative co-ordination – that is, by securing compliance with their commands through the threat and implementation of coercive sanctions (of one kind or another) which is legitimated by virtue of the positions which they occupy within the administrative system.

In this way, the assembly of primary productive practices necessary to the maintenance and reproduction of a social formation through the exercise of imperative co-ordination is closely related to the distribution of social power within communities of productive practitioners whose interests often come into conflict. Access to and control over the organizational means and mechanisms whereby regulation is secured will provide the critical power resource through which certain groups of practitioners are in a position:

'to ensure that the definition of the ends of the population as a whole and the means to those ends which are adopted serve their interests. . . . A most powerful dominant class will seek to maintain its dominant position by controlling the apparatus of imperative co-ordination.'

(Harris 1980: 115–18)

We can illustrate this general conception of 'organization' as the key secondary social practice through which primary practices are assembled by reference to the average industrial firm in the United States or Western Europe. It is an association of people, through whose combined activities a communal product is produced; it is a community of production. It is within such a population that the capital and technical resources necessary to such a community of production are exclusively owned, and where people are entitled, and more or less constrained, to sell and buy labour potential; that is, where people come to have access to the resources necessary to engage in certain practices through the practice of exchange – labour for wages. Consequently, the form and conditions under which certain productive practices come to be practised are institutionalized in ways which confer the right to decide on these matters to the owners of capital and their agents, even though this right is challengeable in its detailed application. Critical significance is attached to the way in which the general practice of wage labour is divided within the community of production into determinate types of practice, such a determination deriving from the division of labour. Actual patterns of interaction between members of the community of production are only meaningfully understood within the context of the kinds of social and material relations typical of production within that kind of population.

In such a case, the notion of 'organization' may be seen as the mode of assembly of the various types of practice which together constitute the elements which characterize the community of production – exclusive possession of resources, wage labour, and the rights of the agents of capital to 'integrate' the whole. Interests derive not only from the particular exigencies of the division of labour, and the forms of particular primary practices, but also from the fact that the communal product is exclusively owned by the owners of capital resources.

'Organization' may thus be generically reconceptualized in this context as constituting that mechanism which represents the variety of integrating practices and their basis in the form of ownership through which a more or less heterogeneous set of productive practices are assembled into communities of production. It provides the administrative apparatus whereby the diversity of practices in which productive practitioners are engaged can be regulated so as to reproduce the fundamental principles of the wider social formation in which it is located and the distributional outcomes that they generate within the population as a whole. At one and the same time, 'organization' constitutes a mechanism which facilitates the integration of primary productive practices and constrains the manner in which they may be carried on in the interests of certain groups rather than others.

However, it is not a static mechanism; it responds to changes taking place within the general mode of assembly of which it is a component element and it regulates innovations originating within the communities of primary practitioners to which it is directed. Consequently, the study of 'organizational change' from the perspective provided by the practice framework has to be unwrapped into a variety of forms of analysis. Two interrelated levels of analysis in the study of organizational change need to be identified: first, those transformations in the administrative mechanism whereby assembly of production practices is achieved taking place as a result of changes to the conditions and form under which the latter are engaged in; second, specific modifications to particular instances of organization resulting from small-scale changes in the supply and form of conceptual and technical resources or in the conceptions of their practice held by primary practitioners.

This distinction between different levels of analysis in the study of organizational change indicates that the detailed application of a generic conception of organization (as a secondary practice facilitating the assembly of primary practices into social formations by means of imperative co-ordination through a bureaucratic control mechanism) must be qualified by a concern for the additional, often multifarious, and conflicting ways in which co-ordination and regulation may be achieved in particular situations. Imperative co-ordination through a bureaucratic mechanism merely provides the general framework within which a wide range of detailed regulative devices may be operationalized to achieve co-ordinated productive activity. This raises the important issue of the spectrum of regulative devices used by managers in particular contexts and their impact on the day-to-day organizational processes whereby the work tasks of primary producers are routinely performed and controlled. An interest in this problem will also guard against a too-easy acceptance of a 'monolithic' conception of organizational management (Salaman 1981, Tomlinson 1982) which neglects the substantial conflicts of interest which occur within this grouping as they attempt to cope with recalcitrant primary producers and to maintain the underlying integrity of their organization's public persona (Storey 1983).

Recently, Burns has argued that:

'In practice working organizations seem to be assemblies of relationships and activities which operate in accordance with several quite different sets of principles and presumptions – different rationales. They are, to use Lévi-Strauss's useful word "bricolages", composed out of secondhand bits and pieces of rather general notions and traditions of how to go about things, each having its own semblance of logic and its own semblance of legitimacy.'

(Burns 1981: 3)

This model of the working organization is based on the underlying premise that 'there is a pervasive pluralism affecting the organizations we work in and study, a pluralism which affects their make-up and which our perceptions and analytical apparatus have tended to pass over' (Burns 1981: 3). However, Burns's argument should not be taken as implying that he wishes to dissolve the concept of organization into a formless aggregate of assumptions and traditions which have no overall pattern or coherence. Neither should it be interpreted as signifying that the concepts of 'power' or 'structure' have no analytical or explanatory role to play in accounting for the operational systems which are developed out of the plurality of general principles and practices which constitute the working organization.

Rather, Burns's approach needs to be treated as a restatement of the descriptive and analytical virtues of a modified 'negotiated order' model of the working organization in which two key sub-systems can be identified – what he labels the 'collaborative system' and the 'managerial structure'.[10] The former refers to the implicit understandings and values which ensure that the necessary level of overall commitment and personal skill required of personnel in task performance is attained through shared moral values and priorities inculcated through socialization processes of various kinds. It is based on trust and appeals to the moral commitments of members on the basis of values and objectives shared by the community of practitioners as a whole. The 'managerial structure' refers to the various bureaucratic systems and regulations which managers and administrators impose on the collaborative system to secure the

---

10 Burns originally developed this conceptual distinction in relation to hospital organization. I am suggesting that it can be applied, with certain modifications, to a much wider range of organizational types.

required degree of administrative rectitude and political control which their employing organization demands. It is based on mistrust and relies on formal control and coercive sanctions to secure routine compliance with its dictates.

While the collaborative system may be seen as an organizational infrastructure sustained by commitment, trust, and the habits of mind and conduct inculcated through the appropriate socialization processes, the managerial structure incorporates various forms of organizational principles and practices which are imposed on the former with the aim of using and directing the commitment which it generates (Burns 1981: 4–10). This process of imposing the managerial structure on the collaborative system often provokes severe outbreaks of tension and conflict within the work organization which have to be contained and coped with by the managerial practitioners who produced it in the first place.

This is true to the extent that managers are forced, by the very nature of the practice in which they are engaged – imperative co-ordination through bureaucratic control – to impose a series of control mechanisms and supporting rationales which potentially threaten the commitment built up by the collaborative system.[11] They are constrained by their structural location and functional role – as secondary practitioners acting as agents on behalf of the dominant class groupings within the social formation – to initiate and maintain control mechanisms that can undermine the potential source of commitment and stability offered by the collaborative system. The problem from their point of view is to secure that routine control over job performance and work tasks facilitated by the bureaucratic structure without stifling, and possibly destroying, the moral commitment nurtured within the collaborative system.

---

11 Examples of this dilemma are provided in chapter 5. MacIntyre suggests that it is a structurally determined dilemma to the extent that managers, under the ideological and material imperatives presented by modern industrial societies, are forced to construct human institutions which are corrupted by the quest for economic expansion and power. This is so because of the contradictory nature of the social practice in which modern managers are necessarily engaged – building institutions which sustain human communities and at the same time directing them in pursuit of economic and political goals that emasculate, if not totally destroying, their potential for human association based on co-operative values (on this point see MacIntyre 1981).

This problem is likely to become particularly acute when the material and social conditions under which primary productive practices are engaged in within the social formation as a whole seem to demand tighter formal co-ordination and regulation of the activities of primary producers.

It is this theme – the dialectic between commitment and control (or moral and instrumental modes of action) in threatening socio-economic conditions – which forms the central focus for the following chapter of this book which reworks a number of classic case studies in organizational change using the analytical framework developed in this chapter. The latter has provided a conception of organization as a co-ordinative or regulative social practice which assembles primary productive practices through a bureaucratic control mechanism supplemented by an infrastructure of collaborative effort in the interests of the dominant social grouping within the social formation.

This conception of organization has several distinctive advantages compared to the alternative approaches which have been discussed in this book. First of all, it provides the means through which the constituent categories of social action and social structure can be theoretically integrated in a single conceptual framework. As such, it offers one way out of the 'theoretical dualism' that has bedevilled organizational analysis in which the concept of organization is either reduced to a social aggregate of previously scattered and unorganized individual components (March and Simon 1958) or reified to form a structural entity that is unable to carry back reference to social action (Burrell and Morgan 1979). Second, it avoids the 'Lego style' mode of conceptual development that has characterized a great deal of contemporary work by simply adding or 'grafting on' (usually in an *ad hoc* manner) concepts which have either been completely ignored or insufficiently elaborated within conventional frames of reference (for a recent example of this see Ranson, Hinings, and Greenwood 1980). The practice framework deals with this problem by treating 'organizations' as integrative and regulative mechanisms which are developed out of secondary social practices aimed at assembling primary productive practices into coherent social formations. This avoids the conventional theoretical isolation of the concept of organization (that is, treating it as a 'closed system') or the unsuccessful attempts which have been made to break out of this isolationism by unsystematically tacking on notions such as the 'environment', 'political economy', or 'macrostructure' (for example, see Benson 1975). Third, it focuses attention on the dynamic interaction between the subjectively meaningful activities in which pro-active human agents are engaged (as members of particular communities of practice) and the objective relations which emerge out of their practice, as mediated by structures of domination and control that constitute their mode of assembly.

This also facilitates a reworking of the concept of power that overcomes the theoretical and methodological constraints imposed by a forced choice between either an 'actionist' or a 'structuralist' paradigm (Lukes 1977b). In the case of the former, the concept's meaning and explanatory value are translated into an individualized capacity exercised in interpersonal relations and determined by the distribution of material and symbolic resources produced by micro-level processes of socio-economic exchange. In the latter case, the concept is treated as a collective property embedded in an objectified structure of social relations over which actors have little or no control, so that they are reduced to the status of 'supports' or 'cyphers' for structural forces contending elsewhere.

Within the practice framework, the concept of power is redefined as a relational concept which links the capacities of human agents to transform the structure (and hence outcomes) of the social situations in which they are implicated to a differentially distributed access to and control over the institutional mechanisms whereby this structure is assembled and maintained. This connection is forged by construing the concept of organization as a social practice which simultaneously refers to the purposive activities of its practitioners and to the means and mechanisms which they rely on to achieve the objective for which it is performed.

Organizational analysis as an intellectual practice

The concept of organization developed in this chapter rests on a view of organizational analysis as an intellectual practice drawing on a range of disciplines which constitute the social sciences as we know them today. Harris defines an intellectual practice in the following terms:

'Any intellectual practice may be regarded as a human activity whose object or aim is to produce knowledge. Such practices are, however, closely related to other forms of human activity. Indeed, it may be argued that those curious and distinctively human activities which can be termed intellectual practices arise out of men's reflections on their experience of other forms of practice in which they engage unreflectively and to which they are committed by the fact of their existence in human society.'

(Harris 1980: 20)

In this way, the conceptual framework outlined in the previous section is located within an interpretation of organizational analysis as a reflective, knowledge-generating activity which is closely bound up with other forms of human activity which proceed in a relatively unreflective way. For Harris, sociology is an intellectual practice which attempts to identify the relation between social situations and their outcomes through the systematic analysis of those social practices through which the former are constituted. His characterization depends on the argument that the historical development of sociological thought is rooted in the practical need to understand the predicament of others and not in the desire for description and explanation as ends in themselves. The inclination to engage in systematic reflection over the form and content of social arrangements is seen to arise out of the aspiration to illuminate the distinctive predicament of other practitioners who seek to bring about a more satisfactory state of affairs through practical interventions in the social situations in which they are located. This process of illumination requires that we penetrate the conceptual communality of the practitioners we choose to study through the construction and application of 'second order' conceptual frameworks that facilitate general statements of a theoretical kind which are unavailable to the commonsense categories of the practitioner group. As such, intellectual practices (such as sociology and organizational analysis) are to be included in the category of primary productive practices to the extent that their purpose is to produce systematic and reliable knowledge which may change our conceptions of our involvement in the social world and hence alter the manner in which it is constituted.

Considered in analogous terms, organizational analysis may be characterized as an intellectual practice which attempts to identify and account for the relationship between the regulative mechanisms through which primary productive practices are assembled and their impact on the manner in which the latter are carried on. This conception of organizational analysis clearly recognizes the practical grounding of the intellectual activities in which its practitioners have been engaged since the latter half of the nineteenth century as they have been documented and interpreted in previous chapters of this book.

At the same time, it considerably broadens the notion of 'practice' in which organizational analysis has been intellectually grounded and historically developed beyond the 'technocratic', 'interpretative', and 'liberative' modes of human intervention informing the alternative traditions previously discussed. The 'technocratic' vision of organizational analysis conveys the image of an objective, value-free social science of organizational behaviour directed at the solution of technical puzzles which simply require the vastly superior cognitive capacity of a method of analysis facilitating the identification and treatment of 'pathological' organizational phenomena. The 'interpretative' mode treats organizational analysis as an exercise in the recovery of subjective meaning and its situational location within conventional cultural frameworks making possible the construction of a symbolic order that protects the individual actor against the constant threat of cognitive and normative anomie. The 'liberative' mode defines organizational analysis as an exercise in intellectual and ideological demystification through which the material, social, and psychological constraints preventing the realization of a level of conscious self-reflection by which agents' 'true interests' may be rationally ascertained can be resisted and, ideally, eradicated.

The focus for the 'practical' conception of organizational analysis offered in this book is the essential ambiguity of organizational life as it gives particular expression to the unavoidable and unsolvable conflicts between instrumental and moral action characteristic of modern industrial society. As an intellectual practice, organizational analysis can be seen to hold a contingent historical relationship to the development of a particular mode of assembly and the material and social conditions under which it was established – that is, the imperative co-ordination of primary productive practices made possible through the mechanism of rational bureaucracy required by the conditions established under 'rational capitalism' (Collins 1980). Initially, the concept of organization can be treated as an analytical category referring to the form of co-ordinative apparatus through which the assembly of primary productive practices under a capitalist system of production is achieved and sustained. Subsequently, this category became subjected to further intellectual refinement and elaboration as the conditions under which the primary productive practices characteristic of a capitalist mode of production underwent various forms of mutation. In turn, this process of change and development in the conditions under which productive practices are engaged in encouraged the growth of a much wider and more complex range of organizational mechanisms through which 'management' attempt to integrate and regulate the activities of primary producers (Gospel 1983). As a result, organizational analysts have been forced to widen their theoretical focus to incorporate the multiplicity of mechanisms and supporting rationales through which management attempt to integrate and regulate productive practices (Reed 1984). Thus Burns's insistence on the 'pervasive pluralism' of contemporary work organizations and his conceptual distinction between the 'management structure' and the 'collaborative system' as necessary but conflicting mechanisms of organizational control and integration both serve to remind us of the need for theoretical flexibility in the face of empirical diversity and ambiguity:

'However establishment-minded, or radical, that picture [of working organizations] purports to be; whether it represents the assembly of material and human resources and their collective use as an instrument serving the purpose prescribed by an individual entrepreneur, an interest group, or what government interprets as the public good; whether it is presented as one of the principal means whereby the prevailing structure of power in society is both put to use and maintained; and however many anomalous, fictional and irrational elements or confusions and conflicts of interest it may contain, the picture is always one of a system of collective action which is (or, at the very least, should be) rationally ordered according to coherent and unitary principles. It is no such thing.'

(Burns 1981: 30)

The central substantive concern of organizational analysis considered in these terms is the type and range of organizational mechanisms through which management attempt to integrate and regulate productive practices within industrial capitalist societies. However, it is not necessarily restricted simply to providing a more systematic redescription and evaluation of these control mechanisms than that forthcoming from managerial practitioners. Indeed, in establishing a framework of categories that guides the reportage of practitioners' conduct and the theoretical concepts required to account for what is reported, organizational analysis can also undermine the dogmatism often inherent in conventional organizational forms by helping to question our established conceptions of the way in which they are practised.

The latter can be achieved in a number of different ways. First, by improving our knowledge of the general impact on the mass of organizational members and clientele of the various mechanisms through which management attempt to achieve and sustain regulatory control. Second, by facilitating a more informed evaluation of the consequences, both intended and unintended, of such regulatory mechanisms for the extent to which primary practitioners are equipped to realize their preferred aims with reference to a broad range of economic, social, political, and moral objectives. Finally, by enabling a better grounded assessment of the complex interaction between organizational mechanisms, collective aims, and situational outcomes, organizational analysis may also encourage a deeper appreciation of the material and social conditions under which certain 'intervention strategies' aimed at improving the quality of social life are more likely to succeed than others.

Taken as a complete package, these components of a conception of organizational analysis as an intellectual practice provide the opportunity for improving the degree of conscious self-reflection on the part of both the 'organizers' and the 'organized' concerning the organizational mechanisms through which primary productive practices are assembled and their implications for the realization of valued social ends. In a society in which 'ends collide' (Berlin 1966), this necessarily entails that the student of organization will be unavoidably implicated in the economic, political, ideological, and ethical conflicts which shape the mechanisms they are analysing. This means that he or she will have to choose between the competing claims that constitute those belief systems through which social life is made meaningful within any society as providing a basis for making sense of their engagement within such an intellectual practice. These value-related epistemological concerns will help to formulate the basis on which the organizational analyst will attempt to explicate those concepts internal to a particular organized social practice and to explain the outcomes which are produced as a result of engaging in the kind of activity which such a practice requires.

To this extent, a conception of organizational analysis as an intellectual practice logically precludes the 'technocratic' frame of reference in which a great deal of work has been carried on since the closing decades of the nineteenth century. It also helps to attune its practitioners to the range and diversity of technical and moral questions which will be encountered in the process of constructing and pursuing a coherent and defensible intellectual practice. The subtle and complex relationship between the technical and moral aspects of organizational life is also likely to prove a source of continued intellectual challenge for those who conceive of their engagement in organizational analysis in this way.

Summary

This chapter has provided a conception of organization as a secondary social practice directed to the co-ordination and control of primary productive practices through a range of mechanisms and devices in which bureaucratic domination remains the predominant principle and structure. This conception of organization has been relocated within a view of organizational analysis as an intellectual practice which aims to provide a better account of the relationship between organizational mechanisms and social action within a changing socio-economic environment. This relationship is seen to be inherently ambiguous and conflictual, given the inability of general principles and mechanisms to cover every eventuality and the corresponding need for supplementary assumptions and understandings which undermine the consistency and integrity of formal control structures. The resulting tension and conflict generated by this endemic and unavoidable tension between instrumental and moral modes of action within work organizations are seen to become particularly acute in changing socio-economic conditions which demand the imposition of tighter formal control mechanisms by management. The latter's actions are seen to be constrained, but not determined, by the requirement to protect the interests of those dominant groups or classes which own and control the resources necessary for primary productive activity and the communal product which it provides. In this way, the manner in which managerial practitioners interpret these dominant interests in specific circumstances will have a consequential effect on the control strategies and mechanisms which they attempt to implement. The response which they elicit from primary productive practitioners is also likely to have a substantial impact on the courses of action which managers will follow in particular situations over a period of time.

The following chapter reworks a number of classical case studies on the process of organizational change to illustrate these themes and the specific method of analysis through which they may be most fruitfully understood and explained.

5
Studies in organizational practice

Introduction

The purpose of this chapter is to apply the conceptual framework outlined in the previous chapter to three 'classic' case studies in the field of organizational analysis. This reworking of the three case studies is intended to provide further illustration of the more insightful and systematic appreciation of the 'problematic of human agency' in its organizational setting to be derived from the practice framework.

In chapters 3 and 4 of this work I have suggested that the 'problematic of human agency', as exemplified in the unresolved, and unresolvable, conflict between instrumental and moral action, expresses itself through the necessary tensions and contradictions between various aspects of organizational life – such as that identified by Burns between the 'management structure' and the 'collaborative system' (Burns 1981). Succeeding generations of organization theorists have attempted to overcome – if not to deny – this endemic tension between instrumental and moral modes of social action by reasserting the deterministic claims of their intellectual practice and its implications for organizational practice. However, the unintended consequence of this strategy of theoretical containment and filtering has been to deny – implicitly if not explicitly – the essentially ambiguous and paradoxical quality of social action and of the organizational forms which it generates. At the same time, its perpetrators have managed to convey an image of complex organizations as 'an anatomy frozen in "structured" immobility' (Burns 1966: xvi) and a conception of organizational studies as a generalized science focused on instrumental issues which are beyond the purview of ethical discourse and debate.

The previous chapter provided a concept of organization and a conception of organizational analysis which may be better equipped to come to terms with the 'problematic of human agency' and to provide a more sensitive understanding and coherent explanation of its intellectual and practical implications. In this chapter that framework will be utilized for a reinterpretation of three case studies which have focused on this theme, but have done so in a conceptual vocabulary and an explanatory logic that often seem to deny the very dilemmas which the research had revealed. In this way, succeeding analysis will attempt to recover the 'problematic of human agency' which lies at the heart of each of these case studies and to reinterpret that theme and its implications within the terms of reference provided by the practice framework.

However, before that task is carried out it is necessary to develop in more detail the sort of analytical focus which the practice framework can bring to bear on this issue and the research orientation through which it is best pursued.

Analytical focus

The previous chapter suggested that complex organizations be treated as secondary integrative practices which are geared to the assembly of the primary productive practices in which human populations are engaged to form coherent social formations. This assembly is achieved through the design, implementation, and revision of various forms of control mechanisms, as well as the acquiring and allocation of the various material and symbolic resources required for their construction and maintenance.

The predominant institutional structure through which assembly has been attempted in modern society is rational bureaucracy. The material and ideological resources normally depended upon for its maintenance have been contained in the notion of 'imperative co-ordination' (see chapters 1 and 3). However, it has also been pointed out that practical control exigencies also demand the supplementation of the bureaucratic mechanism by various forms of socialization processes and technical devices which often conflict with the ideological imperatives implicit in the structure of bureaucratic authority. This is particularly true at a time when changes to the material, social, and technological conditions in which bureaucratic control is imposed erode and gradually undermine the legitimacy of 'superior competence' as providing a reliable and defendable ideological foundation for that set of practices associated with such a control mechanism (Offe 1976, Burns 1980).

Reference has already been made to Burns's characterization of the endemic tension between the 'managerial structure' and the 'collaborative system' as providing an organizational expression of the conflict between instrumental and moral modes of social action embedded in the institutional fabric of working organizations as integrative practices. This reveals the ingrained 'dualism' of working organizations as essential social instruments for the realization of socially valued objectives and as structures of control and domination by which the moral commitments generated through communal action are expropriated for the achievement of sectional interests. Yet at the same time it also shows that engagement in the process of organizational practice unavoidably reinforces the underlying ambiguity of the structures and mechanisms which it produces. This is so to the extent that they constitute hierarchies of commitments and controls which provide a focus for co-operative action and sectional conflict which vary in strength and intensity as the material and social conditions under which they are experienced are transformed (Burns 1977). In this way, the dualistic quality of complex organizations (considered as social institutions) merely reflects the underlying ambiguities contained within the social process whereby they are constructed, maintained, and redeveloped.

As we shall see from the re-analysis of the case studies, more uncertain and unstable conditions which seem to threaten organizational survival are likely to produce a tightening of the bureaucratic control structure and a corresponding stifling of the moral trust and commitment nurtured by the collaborative system. In turn, this can lead to further 'alienation' from the official system and an intensification of the sectional conflicts which are already facilitated by existing structural segmentation and occupational specialization within the organization. In this situation, the dilemma for management is whether they chance complete destruction of the collaborative system through the imposition of further restraints and controls or whether they attempt to realize their objectives by means of a more sophisticated manipulation of the socialization processes on which the former depends. In either case they risk revealing the structure of power relations and control mechanisms to which the collaborative system is subordinated and endangering the growth of a more reflective awareness on the part of primary producers concerning the structural constraints to which they are routinely subjected. Whether this risk is perceived, and what form of strategic action is undertaken, largely depends upon the internal political machinations taking place within the managerial group during this period and their impact on how the situation and its long-term prospects are assessed.

However, it is important to remember that, from the perspective provided by the practice framework, the source of organizational change is to be located within the broader pattern of material and social conditions under which the structures and mechanisms required to assemble productive activity are implemented. The practice of assembly – as the outcome of a complex bargaining process taking place within and between a range of managerial and producer groups – establishes the organizational mechanisms through which those changes are filtered and interpreted to form seemingly coherent and rational responses to a changing situation. It channels the process of organizational response to situational changes in certain directions rather than others.

Thus the central problem for organizational analysis considered in these terms is to identify the dynamic relationship between situational conditions and the mode of organizational assembly as it reveals the underlying tensions and contradictions embedded in institutions which are at one and the same time exercises in co-operative endeavour and structures of sectional domination.

The details of the research orientation in terms of which this task may be carried out are discussed in the following section.

Research orientation

The previous section has suggested that the main intellectual challenge for organizational analysis is to trace the link between situational conditions and the mode of organizational assembly, and the effect which it has on the outcomes which are realized for various groups of organizational participants.

The achievement of this intellectual objective in any particular research setting can be formally broken down into four interrelated modes of analysis which call for considerable interpretative and analytical skills on the part of the individual researcher. These can be respectively labelled as 'cognitive mapping', 'interpretative understanding', 'structural analysis', and 'historical reconstruction'. For methodological purposes, these activities can be logically distinguished in this manner. However, in the actual conduct of organizational research they are likely to overlap and intermingle as the researcher attempts to come to terms with the complexities of the situation in which he or she may be operating.[12]

'Cognitive mapping' indicates a concern with explicating the concepts which practitioners rely on to make sense of the practice in which they are engaged – that is, with describing and reporting the framework of assumptions, beliefs, and ideas which practitioners develop to communicate the purpose of their engagement in the range of activities which their practice requires. The focus for cognitive mapping is the reconstruction of practitioners' accounts of their practice insofar as they endow the latter with a symbolic and communal significance in which all members can participate. While it looks for emerging patterns of belief and the conceptual models in terms of which these patterns can be extended and generalized to the community of practitioners as a whole, it also sensitizes the researcher to points of divergence and disagreement which may be crucial in understanding and explaining potential sources of conflict within the community as they are expressed through the activity of symbolic communication.

The underlying assumptions, concepts, and research methods most closely associated with a phenomenological level of analysis would seem to be most appropriate to this exercise in cognitive mapping. However, the need to develop an 'insider's' view of the social practice or practices in which one is interested should not be taken as implying an acceptance of the epistemological and theoretical limitations often imposed by exponents of the phenomenological method or approach in organizational analysis (see chapter 1). In particular, the propositions that the latter should be restricted to a 'cultural redescription' of the practitioners' organizational world is firmly rejected to the extent that cognitive mapping is simply seen as

---

12 This point is brilliantly illustrated in the methodological appendix to *Patterns of Industrial Bureaucracy* (Gouldner 1954a).

one element within a total research strategy which is aimed at developing a better theoretical grasp of the interrelationships between situational conditions, organizational assembly, and historical outcomes.

'Interpretative understanding' suggests a focus on the relationship between practitioners' cognitive maps and the social activities in which they are routinely engaged as a result of performing that practice with which they are associated. This interest in the range of conduct associated with a particular practice or set of practices and the conceptual categories and models in terms of which it takes on social meaning for the community of practitioners is best facilitated by the research tradition conventionally linked to the action frame of reference (see chapter 1). Insofar as the latter has been focused on the social interaction taking place between organizational members over a series of encounters which are shaped by the situational context in which they are located, it has helped to enrich our understanding of the often tenuous link between actors' interpretations and organizational outcomes. At the same time, it has tended to degenerate into a method or approach which single-mindedly concerns itself with subjective meaning to the virtual exclusion of any interest in the structural forms or mechanisms that both enable and constrain the process of social interaction.

To the extent that this limitation of the action approach has been recognized, it indicates the need for a form of 'structural analysis' which complements the interpretative benefits to be derived from the former. Structural analysis attempts to link the understanding of practitioners' conduct to the structural configurations which are established and reproduced as a result of engaging in the range of activities associated with their practice. It conveys the desire most closely expressed by advocates of a 'Weberian' tradition in organizational analysis (see chapters 1 and 2) to identify the structural mechanisms whereby the distribution and allocation of material and symbolic resources are more favourable to certain 'definitions of the situation' (within and between different communities of practitioners) rather than others (Willmott 1981). In this way, the integrative practices whereby productive activity is assembled and co-ordinated are seen to be necessarily implicated in the struggle for control over resources and the capacity which it affords to determine the outcomes which are produced through organized social action. Thus the exercise of power facilitated by access to and control over the structural mechanisms and resources through which social action is organized is a regular and routine feature of social life rather than a temporary aberration which only appears when conflicting interests have to be settled in some way or another. Giddens has provided the most succinct interpretation of power as a relational concept linking structures of domination and the transformative capacity of agents:

'Power intervenes conceptually between the broader notions of transformative capacity on the one side, and of domination on the other: power is a relational concept, but only operates as such through the utilization of transformative capacity as generated by structures of domination. . . . Power, in this relational sense, concerns the capability of actors to secure outcomes where the realization of these outcomes depends on the agency of others. The use of power in interaction thus can be understood in terms of the facilities that participants bring to and mobilize as elements of the production of that interaction, thereby influencing its course.'

(Giddens 1979: 92–3)

In this sense, the engagement in structural analysis affords a better understanding of the way in which the specific mechanisms and resources through which the assembly of productive activity is achieved both shape the exercise of power by organizational members in particular situations and reinforce the generalized structures of domination from which this transformative capacity is derived. The conceptual tools and analytical apparatus usually related to this conception of structural analysis are to be found in the 'critical school' of organization theory reviewed in chapter 2 of this book. However, this approach needs to be tempered by a concern with the underlying constraints and opportunities highlighted by the historical reconstruction of organizational development that substantially moderates the more deterministically inclined predilections of critical theorists.

This brings us to the final component of the research orientation which has been outlined in this section – that is, 'historical reconstruction'. It is worth returning to Abrams at this point to provide an insightful exposition of the subtle relationship between 'narrative' and 'analysis' to be discovered within any attempt to provide a coherent and systematic historical reconstruction of social change. Abrams concludes his book with the thought that:

'The prospect of historical sociology involves us in superimposing structure on history with a view to recovering the way history superimposes structure on us. It crystallizes as a negotiation of concept and evidence in the concrete study of structuring.'

(Abrams 1982: 335)

This conclusion is supported by his detailed and sympathetic discussion of a wealth of sociological and historical studies which focus on 'the problematic of structuring' and the shared theoretical strategies and methodological procedures which they exhibit.

As we have already seen, this problematic is conveyed through Abrams's exploration of the process whereby a 'working apprehension' of the complex interaction between action and structure 'has emerged from successive attempts by sociologists to explain relatively specific historical transitions and master specific problems within the traditional domain of the historian' (Abrams 1982: xxiii). In tracing this dialectic between action and structure in the analysis of particular historical transitions, Abrams suggests that the intellectual core of historical sociology is to be found in the concept of 'cumulative causation' which frames explanatory accounts in terms of the concatenation and phasing of actions and conditions. This conveys a conception of an intellectual activity in which 'knowledge is achieved by an intellectual estrangement from phenomena as well as intimate contact with them' (Abrams 1982: 316). The sociological analysis of historical transition requires a continual shifting of focus between specific detail and general context with the aim of demonstrating a clear relationship between the chronological order of events in the historical case and a formal model of the causes which generated them and the mechanisms which produced one set of outcomes rather than another (Abrams 1982: 206).

The implications of Abrams's characterization of historical sociology for the historical reconstruction of particular cases of organizational change and development can now be discussed. Each of the case studies analysed in the following section are primarily concerned with the transition from one mode of assembly to another under the pressure exerted by a changing pattern of social and material conditions. Each of them focuses on the strategic role played by managerial practitioners in affecting this transition in the organizational mechanisms whereby productive practices are co-ordinated as they respond to threatening developments in their external conditions and their impact on internal circumstances. Each attempts to link this transaction in the mode of assembly to the changing patterns of power relations discovered within the organization and its overall impact on the position of various sectional interests and groupings in the wider institutional setting.

The realization of these objectives requires a form of analysis in which historical narrative is interwoven with theoretical interpretations with the aim of identifying the conditions which generated certain forms of structuring and their consequences for the relative positions of organizational groupings. In this interweaving of narrative and analysis the 'negotiation of concept and evidence in the concrete study of structuring' becomes clearer as the researcher is involved in:

'a continuous dialectical tacking between the most local of local detail and the most global of global structure in such a way as to bring both into view simultaneously. . . . Hopping back and forth between the whole conceived through the parts which actualize it and the parts conceived through the whole which motivates them, we seek to turn them, by a sort of intellectual perpetual motion, into explications of each other.'

(Geertz 1979: 239)

This 'dialectical tacking' is evident in each of the case studies discussed in the following section when the individual researchers move between the analysis of institutional context and the explication of organizational milieu in the search for an historical reconstruction of the move from one mode of assembly to another which is sensitive to the points of intersection between structural trend and situational detail. While none of the case studies is entirely successful in the quest to integrate historical narrative with formal analysis, their attempts have produced studies which are rich in the particular ambiguities and dilemmas faced by organizational participants that convey a general significance beyond the confines of the specific situations on which they are focused.

It is possible to apply Giddens's distinction between 'strategic' and 'institutional' analysis (Giddens 1979) to the components of the research orientation which have been sketched in this section. Both 'cognitive mapping' and 'interpretative understanding' clearly fall within the category of strategic analysis to the extent that they are focused on the transactions between agents which generate the social structures that are drawn on to provide the resources and rules necessary for social interaction as a skilled and knowledgeable accomplishment. 'Structural analysis' and 'historical reconstruction' are located within the category of institutional analysis in that they concentrate on the structural configurations which facilitate and constrain the reproduction of social systems through social interaction (Giddens 1979: 81–95).

However, Giddens's 'methodological bracketing' of these two forms of analysis is dissolved in his conception of the duality of structure which maintains that 'the structural properties of social systems are both the medium and the outcome of the practices that constitute those systems' (Giddens 1979: 69). In this sense structure is considered to be both enabling and constraining in that it is essentially implicated in the production of social systems as a resource to be used by actors which necessarily limits the strategies which the latter are able to follow. The discussion of general research orientation developed in this section does not explicitly draw on Giddens's formal conceptual apparatus. Nevertheless, it has assumed the theoretical validity of the duality thesis in its attempt to integrate the analysis of strategic conduct and institutional constraint through the conception of organization as a secondary social practice geared to the assembly of primary productive practices.[13]

The four components of the research orientation outlined in this section are represented in diagrammatic form in *Figure 1*.

Figure 1   Research orientation

Mode of analysis	*Level of analysis*	
1 Cognitive mapping	phenomenological	⎫
		strategic analysis
2 Interpretative understanding	interactional	⎭
3 Structural analysis	organizational	⎫
		institutional analysis
4 Historical reconstruction	institutional	⎭

Case studies

The reworking of the case studies provided in this section is divided into two parts: first, each case study will be reworked separately

---

13 A more explicit application of Giddens's framework to the field of organizational analysis is to be found in Willmott (1981).

using the conceptual apparatus and research orientation developed in this and the preceding chapter; second, the common themes which emerge out of the previous discussion will be highlighted and subjected to a form of theoretical analysis derived from the practice framework. The purpose in each case is to reclaim the 'problematic of human agency' which lies at the centre of each of these studies from the functionalist straitjacket in which it was previously imprisoned.

THE CASE STUDIES

Three case studies have been selected for reworking within the parameters provided by the practice framework: Selznick's *TVA and the Grass Roots* (1949, second edition 1966); Gouldner's *Patterns of Industrial Bureaucracy* and its sequel *Wildcat Strikes* (Gouldner 1954a, 1954b); and Crozier's *The Bureaucratic Phenomenon* (1964). The status of these studies as classics in the field of organizational analysis remains unchallenged and they have been referred to time and time again by various authors to provide theoretical inspiration and empirical insight. The purpose of the following discussion is to provide a brief résumé of each case study and then to extend the analysis by recourse to the conceptual resources and research orientation facilitated by the practice framework. In each case, the latter will demand:

1 a description of the changing material and social conditions in which the organizations operated;
2 an exposition of the transition from one mode of assembly to another in partial response to the pressures and demands generated by (1), as interpreted and mediated by powerful organizational groups;
3 an analysis of the range of mechanisms and resources which were relied upon by managerial practitioners to realize the transition in modes of assembly and to sustain the new mode of assembly in the face of novel pressures and demands which it may have helped to generate;
4 an explanation of the overall impact of the change in the mode of assembly on the prevailing pattern of power relationships within the organization and its implications for the realization of conflicting sectional interests;
5 an assessment of the implications of these internal developments

for the wider structure of institutional relations in which the organization is located and their possible effects on future organizational change and development;

6 an evaluation of the unresolved problems and dilemmas that still remain and which will provide a focus for subsequent phases of organizational development.

Selznick's study examines the development of the Tennessee Valley Authority (TVA) which was created by Congress in 1933 to plan the proper use, conservation, and development of the natural resources of the Tennessee River drainage and its adjoining territory. It traces the process whereby the Tennessee Valley Authority's administrative leadership adapted the agency's programme and structure to meet the demands of local interest groups through skilful use of the official 'grass roots' ideology which had promoted its foundation and the mechanism of 'informal co-optation' that ensured the representation of these interests by way of internally reorganized 'administrative constituencies'.[14] The theoretical apparatus relied on to carry through this analysis was a synthesis of the 'elitist' strain found within bureaucratic theory and a particular interpretation of structural-functionalist theory which traces the behaviour of individuals 'to the needs and structure of the organization as a living social institution' (Selznick 1966: 14).

The central focus of Selznick's analysis is the subtle process of administrative and political manipulation whereby the doctrines and practices initially associated with a radical philosophy of 'grass roots' control over policy implementation were reinterpreted so as to ensure policy outcomes of a much more conservative nature as the necessary, and acceptable, price to pay for organizational survival. The key organizational mechanism through which the agency's senior management achieved this objective was the process of 'co-optation' – that is, 'the process of absorbing new elements into the leadership or policy-determining structure of an organization as a means of averting threats to its stability or existence' (Selznick 1966: 13). Two forms of organizational co-optation are highlighted: formal co-optation which publicly absorbs new elements into the

---

14 There is a close analytical parallel between Selznick's concept of 'administrative constituency' and Child's notion of 'dominant coalition' (Child 1973a) in that they both refer to tightly coupled clusters of interest groups which direct and control organizational policy.

policy-determining structure as a way of protecting and enhancing the legitimacy of the agency's role; informal co-optation which is a response to the political pressures exerted by specific power groupings within the wider community and involves an actual sharing of power through unofficial channels of representation and involvement (Selznick 1966: 13–16). The latter involves an actual sharing of power, while the former simply provides accessibility and legitimacy through formal devices.

For Selznick, informal co-optation is the more theoretically and politically significant mechanism to the extent that it produced a dramatic shift in the character and the role of the Tennessee Valley Authority in a direction which protected and enhanced the power of large-scale farming interests, and correspondingly weakened the position of conservation groups and those representing small-scale farmers and ethnic minorities within the local agricultural community:

'My conclusion was not merely that the TVA trimmed its sails in the face of hostile pressure. More important is the fact that a right wing was built inside the TVA. The agricultural programme of the agency was simply turned over to a group that had strong commitments, not only to a distinct ideology but to a specific constituency.'

(Selznick 1966: xiii)

Having provided a brief outline of the study, it is now necessary to rework it relying on the conceptual framework and research orientation provided by the practice perspective. This will be developed in six phases corresponding to the logic of analysis discussed at the beginning of this section.

The establishment of the TVA in 1933 with the general support and guidance of the federal government in Washington was promoted by President Roosevelt in terms of a form of integral planning in regional areas which were suffering from the ravages of rural neglect and decay intensified by the catastrophic economic recession which America was suffering during this period. To achieve this objective of national planning for many States and for the future lives and welfare of millions of people, the central government recommended the passing of legislation to create 'a corporation clothed with the power of central government but possessed of the flexibility and initiative of private enterprise' (Selznick 1966: 5). Consequently, a government agency was established that had a special responsibility (which was neither national nor State-wide in scope) for the resource development of a whole region. As Selznick notes:

'The TVA act, and more fully the message of President Roosevelt requesting the legislation, represented a political challenge, even if it was not an entirely new departure in the exercise of federal authority for general welfare objectives. . . . This represented a model of positive government which could not be put forward for the federal government as a whole but rather, for reasons of strategy, as an experiment to be extended as conditions might warrant. . . . the special administrative form of TVA was derived from the circumstances of its inception rather than from general principles.'

(Selznick 1966: 53-4)

Yet Selznick also argues that the TVA, while symbolizing central effort and planning, had little direct authority to engage in large-scale regional planning. Its delegated powers were very specific in nature and scope relating to the primary problems of flood control, navigation, fertilizer and power production and distribution. Nevertheless, it was given the administrative discretion to devise a range of policies and programmes dealing with local people and institutions reflecting the 'grass roots' ideology on which it was founded. As a result, the agency's leadership very quickly developed policies and programmes adapted to the views and demands of local interest groups and institutions which were originally hostile to its existence as a mechanism of central control over regional affairs. This local institutional environment supported the 'grass roots' ideology and the demand for managerial autonomy and discretion which went with it as long as the agency's programme mirrored its interpretation of the region's needs and problems. The freedom from centralized control and the discretion afforded to officials to make significant decisions on their own account concerning key areas such as personnel recruitment and financial planning was legitimated in terms of a working partnership with existing agencies and institutions in the region. This was seen as an indispensable prerequisite for the effective development of regional resources and as a political expression of the 'grass roots' ideology of local involvement and participation in day-to-day operations and long-term strategy.

In political terms, the most significant of these local interests were those represented by the land-grant colleges[15] which bolstered the position of the existing farm leadership in the area. As such, senior managerial and administrative practitioners within the agency elected to adjust their policies, programmes, and structures to the existing pattern of State and local power groupings rather than adjust to the prevailing pattern of national government as represented by agencies such as the Department of Agriculture or various federal bureaus such as the Bureau of Agricultural Economics and the Social Conservation Service.

Considered in these terms, the TVA found adjustment to its local area of operation a prior necessity and consequently committed itself to a theory and structure of 'grass roots' control which would generate its own tensions and conflicts. Thus the transition in mode of assembly from a 'formal' bureaucratic machine under central direction and control by national government to a 'strategic' administrative agency penetrated and dominated by local interest groups was carried through by a managerial group (particularly a younger group of officials whose careers were bound up with the fate of the TVA) determined to make 'realistic adjustments' to the prejudices of the locality in which they operated. The interpretations which senior managers and administrators constructed of the prevailing pattern of power relations and positions between various interest groupings within the region became the key factor in determining the agency's programme and the administrative structures utilized to carry it through. In this way, they skilfully manipulated the doctrine of 'grass roots' control as an ideological justification for maximizing their managerial autonomy in decision-making and using it to incorporate – either directly or indirectly – 'administrative constituencies' within the organization's decision-making structure which represented the views of the dominant local groupings.

The organizational mechanism whereby the managerial leadership of the TVA achieved this transition was 'informal co-optation' and its associated administrative practices of constituency-building and interest-group incorporation. The organizational ideology legitimating this mechanism – if public legitimation was deemed to be necessary – was the doctrine of 'grass roots' control that effectively disenfranchised the low-income farmers and reinforced

---

15 Land-grant colleges were educational and research institutions which had a crucial political impact on the direction of the TVA's agricultural programme.

the existing economic and political domination of large-scale land-owning and farming interests. The process of formal co-optation 'represents a mechanism of comprehensive adjustment, permitting a formal organization to enhance its chances of survival by accommodating itself to existing centres of interest and power within its area of operation' (Selznick 1966: 217). It reflected the political priorities embedded in managerial practitioners' interpretation and assessment of the adjustments which were necessary to guarantee the long-term organizational survival and growth required to achieve community development on a regional scale. It facilitated the unofficial and unacknowledged absorption of influential local power groupings into the organization's administrative structure which allowed them to exert a disproportionate control over policy-making and implementation. This was deemed to be an acceptable price to pay for appeasing their potential opposition and established a close, if clandestine, political relationship between big farming interests and the dominant managerial groups within the agency.

In addition, the agency's administrative leadership also used the network of supporting voluntary associations – such as local agricultural associations, land-use planning committees, and tenant-purchase committees – to bolster policy and administrative imperatives as these were perceived and articulated by the former. Thus the specific form of organizational participation selected by the administrative elite within the TVA emphasized the co-ordination of leading local elements on a regular basis so that they would identify with and support the agency's programme. This strategy discouraged direct access by individual citizens through communication channels which offered personal contact between the public and officials. In addition, the network of voluntary associations operating within the area were arranged in such a way as to form an administrative constituency which legitimated the agency's strategy and structure rather than allowing them to participate on an independent basis. Consequently, the voluntary associations became agents of the TVA through their absorption into the corporatist structure of interest-group intermediation which the administrative leadership had carefully constructed over a period of time.

The co-optative mechanism reinforced the existing pattern of power relations within the local institutional environment of which the TVA was a part. Low-income farmers, ethnic minorities, conservation groups, and co-operative associations were relatively disadvantaged in a succession of policy areas where large-scale farming interests (through the land-grant college system) predominated. In particular, control over the TVA's agricultural programme (involving matters such as the production and distribution of fertilizers and land-use policy) was delegated to the big farming interests represented by the land-grant colleges.

Yet there was a political price to be paid for this adjustment in the strategy and structure of the agency under the tutelage of its managerial elite and the network of local groups which supported them. First, the agency became much more exposed to the organizational and political conflicts occurring at national level within and between 'New Deal' agricultural agencies. Eventually, it aligned itself with the local opponents of those agencies and the policies which they represented, so altering its character as a conservation agency utilizing publicly owned land and resources for ecological rather than commercial objectives. Second, this produced an increasingly visible tension between the official doctrine of 'grass roots' control and the operationalization of that doctrine through an organizational strategy and structure which enhanced powerful local interests at the expense of disadvantaged groups. As a result, managerial elites were increasingly forced to provide a public defence of their policy as it became evident that it inhibited the direct participation of local citizenry by forging commitments to sectional interests which were concerned to preserve the status quo. Third, this left managerial practitioners with an organizational structure that found it increasingly difficult to contain the contradictions and ambiguities generated by the uneasy relationship between a formal administrative system which lacked any real power and an unofficial network of coalitions and understandings that secured the collaboration of potential enemies. The undercurrent of critical comment and outright disaffection on the part of 'New Deal' federal agencies with which the TVA should have established an amicable and effective working relationship was merely one expression of an intensifying assault which agency officials had to fend off during the 1940s.

Organizational survival had been secured but at the cost of undermining the moral foundations and political authority of its 'mission' within American society. The 'grass roots' doctrine had been turned to instrumental ends for a mixture of administrative and political motives held by the agency's managerial elite who were then left to cope with the new tensions and dilemmas which their organizational solutions had created.

Gouldner's study focuses on the process of bureaucratization at a plant owned and operated by the General Gypsum Company over a period of three years between 1948 and 1951. The plant was situated in a traditionalistic rural community located in the Great Lakes region, and reflected, in its internal organization and ideology, the customary values and norms associated with the former – that is, a paternalistic managerial attitude and a flexible social organization stressing the importance of toleration and understanding as a basis for stable social relations. There were social cleavages within the plant but these paralleled those found in the community which Gouldner describes as 'gentle tensions, barely rippling the surface' (Gouldner 1954a: 41).

The study opens with a description of the relatively dramatic changes in internal plant organization which were initiated in 1948 and traces them through (in *Wildcat Strikes*, the sequel to *Patterns of Industrial Bureaucracy*) to an industrial conflict which occurred in the plant in 1950 and its eventual resolution through a new labour contract negotiated and operationalized in 1951. In the course of narrating this sequence of organizational changes and their impact on organizational members, Gouldner relies on various theoretical devices drawn from structural–functionalist sociology to provide an overall explanation of the process he had identified. The following discussion of this case study will attempt to extract the material from the structural–functionalist framework in which it was originally developed and relocate it within the theoretical frame of reference provided by the practice framework.

Developments within the structure of material and social relations in which the plant was embedded can be described at two levels: first, changes to the local rural community in which the plant was situated, and second, the broader structure of socio-economic relations prevailing in the post-1945 gypsum industry. Gouldner argues that the local rural community had undergone a series of economic crises which had helped to transform the structure of social relations and values on which it had been constructed and maintained. The countryside became industrialized and the farms mechanized; commercial farming became dominant and generated increasingly evident economic distinctions and divergencies within the community:

'With the transformation of farming into a business, class stratification in the area emerges more clearly, and intimate personalized relationships begin to move. While the community is still very far from being fully urbanized, it is certainly less rural than it used to be.'

(Gouldner 1954a: 44)

The post-1945 gypsum industry was characterized by increased competition following the gradual dismantling of the war-time economy and by a tighter product market in which higher production output and lower labour-unit costs would be crucial to continued economic viability. This was reinforced by a tightening of the local labour market as a number of factories dependent on military contracts located in the area closed down and increased the pool of surplus labour available to management.

This institutional setting of a declining rural community undergoing industrial and agricultural rationalization and an industrial sector characterized by increased competition within its product and labour markets provided the context in which corporate management took the decision to replace the deceased plant management with a successor who had the overall remit to improve operational efficiency by any means at his disposal. This resulted (over a period of three years) in the transition of the mode of assembly through which managers co-ordinated and controlled primary productive practices from a 'mock' to a 'punishment-centred' form of organizational bureaucracy. While the former had relied on a flexible interpretation of rules at the discretion of individual managers and on an implicit consensus between management and workers concerning the particular circumstances in which sanctions were legitimate, the latter assumed that deviation from formal controls was deliberate and required the immediate imposition of coercive sanctions. Mock-bureaucracy had enabled management to achieve the assembly of primary productive activity through the judicious enactment of formal controls. This reinforced the paternalistic ideology on which the plant's social order had been legitimated and maintained. Punishment-centred bureaucracy demanded the consistent and continued implementation of formal controls in response to behaviour on the part of primary producers which was perceived to be inimical to the realization of improved plant productivity as required by senior management located in head office. However, the social cost which management had to pay as a result of the tighter control which this mode of assembly facilitated was a heightening of tension in labour-management relations and an increased potential for 'organized' industrial conflict.[16]

The transition in mode of assembly was facilitated by a process of organizational rationalization and ideological indoctrination which had four major structural elements: strategic replacement within the plant's managerial hierarchy; the introduction of new technology; the operationalization of a formal control system; and finally, the promulgation of an 'economistic' ideology.

Strategic managerial replacement occurred in two phases: one between 1948 and early 1950 and a second in January 1950. The first phase was initiated by the plant manager who took over in 1948 (Peele) and resulted in a number of changes being made in the occupancy of senior management positions within the plant, particularly in the area of personnel management. The second phase was implemented by Peele's successor, Landman, and resulted in an even more traumatic 'shake-out' at both senior- and middle-management levels within the organization. Peele was demoted to a supervisory post in the maintenance department and a number of 'outsiders' were brought in with the objective of tightening managerial control even further. Both phases can be explained in terms of the interaction between the interpretations of the plant situation formulated by both successors and the limitations imposed upon them by the head-office requirement to increase efficiency relatively quickly without having the time to assess the local situation in any depth or detail.[17]

Both phases of managerial succession generated a process of internal bureaucratization whereby a system of formal rules and related sanctions was codified and implemented on a routine basis. This demanded a much more intensive monitoring and sanctioning procedure on the part of first-line supervisors who no longer had the flexibility and discretion enjoyed under the 'indulgency pattern'. In turn, this was reinforced by the introduction of more modern machinery which required greater physical and psychological effort from operators acting under the additional pressures and strains generated by faster machine speeds. Finally, each of the structural

---

16 The distinction between 'organized' and 'unorganized' industrial conflict is further developed in Hyman (1972). However, in the latest edition of his book (Hyman 1984) Hyman has cautioned against making a categorical distinction between these two forms of industrial conflict.
17 Further details on these developments can be found in Gouldner (1954a).

mechanisms through which managerial practitioners attempted to rationalize productive activity was complemented by a company ideology which stressed economic efficiency and the legitimacy of managerial controls aimed in this direction. Pre-existing moral commitments embodied in the indulgency pattern were not allowed to get in the way of the new economic rationality and its bureaucratic correlates. This economic ideology offered some recognition to the material claims and grievances expressed by the workforce over this period of organizational upheaval, but denied legitimacy to any claims which seemed to threaten managerial prerogative in the area of organizational control. Economism also implied the rejection of any claims to special treatment allowed under the old 'indulgency pattern' as this was now seen as a major obstacle to the achievement of increased organizational efficiency. The traditional understandings prevailing under the factory's *ancien régime* were swept aside in a rationalization process which would not be impeded by non-rational considerations. The ethical commitments and moral claims implicitly recognized under the paternalistic ideology supporting the indulgency pattern had been replaced by the ideology of the 'cash nexus' and its treatment of the employment relationship in narrow economic terms shorn of any remaining normative residues.

The more extensive framework of organizational controls prevailing under punishment-centred bureaucracy and its implications for more intensive methods of labour utilization led to a 'wildcat strike' in April 1950 which was finally settled after several weeks of difficult negotiation between the company and the union in the late spring of 1950. Management viewed the strike as a struggle for control between them and the local workforce which had been led astray by more militant elements within the union leadership. As a result, conflict over the structural mechanisms whereby control over the labour process[18] was to be achieved assumed a moral significance

---

18 The concept of 'labour process' has assumed central theoretical significance in a continuing debate over the nature of work organization under a capitalist mode of production originated by Braverman (1974). However, there is some ambiguity, not to say confusion, over the analytical content and purpose of the concept which has not been dispelled by more recent contributions to the debate. For a recent elaboration within an avowedly Marxist perspective see Thompson (1983).

for management quite out of proportion to their instrumental purposes. Workers interpreted their action as a moral or ethical claim on management for the sort of 'fair' treatment which they had received under the implicit understandings and assumptions of the old indulgency pattern. The expression of this moral claim through strike action had been necessary because formal union officials had lost control of the situation as they had moved closer towards the economic ideology which the new managers had been promulgating. This more aggressive behaviour towards management was legitimated in terms of the threat which the latter, in collusion with the existing trade union leadership, posed to their indulgency expectations under the pressure of new economic exigencies. Thus both groups were led to formulate a private interpretation of the conflict in moral terms, while publicly communicating this interpretation in a utilitarian language which was in keeping with the times – that is, when material interests and concerns were predominant.[19]

The agreement settling the strike directly reinforced the bureaucratization of labour–management relations which had been in progress since the beginning of 1949. It produced a centralization of decision-making powers within both organizational hierarchies, extended the range and sophistication of formal rules and strengthened the ideology of impersonal attitudes and rational economic expectations as a basis for future organizational involvement.

Nevertheless, this bureaucratic solution to a conflict which had been generated as a result of destroying the legitimacy of the indulgency pattern through the imposition of a mode of assembly based on 'imperative co-ordination' generated its own tensions and contradictions which would come to haunt participants in the future. A more formalized bureaucratic machine and a supporting economistic ideology provided the mechanisms through which future conflict could be engaged in more successfully by either group of practitioners. This was so to the extent that the underlying stability facilitated by the indulgency patterns had been virtually destroyed and replaced by a more transient and fragile set of understandings and relations which would prove to be extremely brittle when new

---

19 This may be taken as an example of a situation in which the instrumental vocabulary and language of the management structure were superimposed upon the expressive symbolism of the collaborative system.

waves of organizational rationalization became necessary. The shift to punishment-centred bureaucracy as a mode of organizational assembly had provided the mechanisms whereby an outbreak of industrial conflict could be temporarily settled without doing anything about the underlying causes of that conflict. Management would find it increasingly difficult, if not impossible, under these circumstances to make any future demand for moral commitment on the part of the workforce when it had initiated those very structural changes whereby the moral foundations of that normative involvement had been undermined. The underlying fragility of the 'cash nexus' and the relative impotency of formal bureaucracy in the face of behaviour which challenges its ideological rationale provide a source of potential tension and conflict for future phases of organizational change and development.

Crozier's study attempts to provide a theoretical synthesis of Selznick and Gouldner based on an empirical analysis of two French public bureaucracies. This analysis proceeds by way of a structural–functionalist framework which is appropriately modified to account for the general social process which Crozier perceives as underlying all organizational change and development – that is, the unceasing power struggle for control over 'areas of uncertainty' which is inevitably generated by the failure of bureaucracy to provide a universally effective control mechanism (Crozier 1964: 1–9).

One of the case studies in Crozier's analysis examines the hierarchical structure and operating routines found within the Parisian branch of the French giro system; the other case study involves an in-depth analysis of three Parisian plants (and a general survey of twenty provincial plants) of a state-owned tobacco monopoly. Each of these organizations is located within a rigid framework of highly centralized authority relations in which the operational environments of both are closely structured by the state bureaucracy.

The first case study ('The Clerical Agency') concentrates on the formal administrative structure of the organization, the positions of actors within this structure, the relationships which develop between them, and their impact on internal decision-making processes. The central aim of the case study is to describe and explain the generation of a formalized and routinized pattern of decision-making that protects the power and status interests of occupationally based work groups. The latter are socially isolated and politically fragmented in that the formal structure of control prevents the development of any traces of a particularistic primary group network which cuts across formal divisions.[20]

The second case study ('The Industrial Monopoly') focuses on the link between the formal structure of administrative control and the network of power relations that develops between groups within the social system located at both management and shop-floor levels. This focus, argues Crozier, is justified because:

'The behaviour and attitudes of people and groups within an organization cannot be explained without reference to the power relations existing among them. All the lessons of the past fifteen years' research in organization have brought to light more and more the importance of these problems of power and control that the first attempts at understanding leadership had neglected.'

(Crozier 1964: 107)

The main objective of the second case study is to describe and account for a situation in which the tight regulatory system imposed through the organization's formal structure cannot cover every eventuality and power relations between interest groups develop around these loopholes. Thus maintenance tasks, because of their inherent resistance to bureaucratic rationalization and the bargaining skill of these groups performing such tasks, are not readily amenable to formal control and provide a power base from which maintenance workers can ensure the dependence of production workers and senior management. The political dependencies and psychological frustrations initiated by these power struggles generate further pressure on management for increased bureaucratization and the 'vicious circle' which this produces.

This analysis of internal power relations and their structural sources is linked to a discussion of selected institutional characteristics of French society which reinforce the intra-organizational patterns that the individual case studies reveal. In particular, the cultural norms operative in French society concerning the way in

---

20 Crozier eventually traces the institutional origins of this organizational structure to facets of French social and cultural life which are deeply embedded in the historical development of French society since the revolution of 1789. The extent to which his analysis of organizational dynamics can be generalized, without modification, to other cultural contexts is a moot point.

which authority relations and group conflicts should be handled are seen to be especially influential in reproducing a highly centralized and routinized pattern of intra-organizational relations. These norms, which stress the importance of avoiding face-to-face conflicts or the open exercise of authority in transactions between superiors and subordinates, are reinforced by the educational system and the structure of class relations with its emphasis on rigid stratification and strata isolation.

Having provided a brief descriptive outline of Crozier's study, it is now possible to move on to a more detailed theoretical reconstruction relying on the six interrelated areas of analysis informing the previous reinterpretations of Selznick and Gouldner

Both the organizations which provide the empirical basis for Crozier's theoretical analysis were situated in a highly structured institutional environment in which their management teams were continually subjected to the control of senior officials located within the central government bureaucracy. In the case of the Industrial Monopoly, the sale of its products was controlled by another government department which closely followed the fiscal policies of central government and dissuaded the agency's management from engaging in major technological and organizational innovations that would require substantial state investment. In this sense, senior management were not competent to deal with investment decision-making and were forced to concentrate their efforts on internal politics.

While this highly structured institutional environment removed the usual commercial pressures to which most private sector organizations are subjected, it intensified the degree of political uncertainty which both agencies faced and its corresponding effect on internal decision-making processes and patterns of power relations. In both cases, the pattern of intergroup relations was highly stable and centred around those areas of the organization's operations which had not been subjected to the full force of management's rationalization strategies.

However, this highly structured institutional environment was itself coming under increasing pressure from the accelerated evolution of French industrial society during the 1950s.[21] The established pattern of French bureaucracy was finding it more and more difficult

---

21 The arguments are developed further in Crozier (1969).

to cope with the problems which this accelerating process of socio-economic change was producing. The internal rigidities of the system made it virtually impossible for French organizations to adjust gradually to environmental transformation in the direction of decentralized control and a diffusion of political power (Crozier (1964: 224–25). This had resulted in a continuing series of crises in French public life and institutions which was undermining the political and technical foundations of the French bureaucratic system of organization in which central decision-makers were unable to change existing organizational patterns because of their isolation from subordinates. They were located at the apex of a centralized system which maximized the ability of primary producers to resist innovation and minimized the capacity of managerial practitioners to restructure existing arrangements except through crisis management in difficult circumstances.

Yet a gradual transformation in the mode of assembly whereby productive practices are co-ordinated and controlled in French society (under the pressure generated by macro-level socio-economic change) is documented in Crozier's book. This is the transition from 'strategic' to 'mechanistic' bureaucracy; that is, a move towards an organizational structure which more closely approximates to Weber's ideal-type of rational bureaucracy. The latter, Crozier argues, provides a set of more flexible administrative arrangements which makes it easier for organizational members to participate in the standardized and controlled activities of large-scale social units (Crozier 1964: 299). This is so to the extent that the 'mechanistic' structure eliminates some of the factors associated with the 'vicious circle' generated by its strategic counterpart. It achieves this by preventing the degree of 'premature centralization' associated with the strategic model which maximizes the ability of subordinate coalitions of primary producers to resist any element of restructuring which threatens the status quo and the privileges (however minor or insignificant) which they enjoy under such a system. In facilitating a much higher degree of decentralized managerial control, Crozier argues, the mechanistic structure encourages increased subordinate participation across a wider range of organization activities. This also discourages them from becoming locked within their own areas of operation as is the case with the impersonalized centralization associated with the strategic model. The mechanistic system does not eliminate the political struggle over 'areas of uncertainty' and the potential control over decision-making which they offer. However it does provide managers with a much more sophisticated administrative system whereby they can attempt to contain these conflicts and turn them to the organization's long-term advantage. This is true to the extent that the mechanistic model allows a sufficient degree of decentralization to accommodate internal power struggles, while at the same time fostering the required degree of knowledge, skill, and sensitivity on the part of the top-level decision-makers to initiate and maintain incremental change without engendering traumatic crises.

The key mechanisms which managerial practitioners rely upon to achieve this incremental transition in the mode of assembly is a process of rationalization with two main components: greater sophistication in the technical system whereby production is achieved and greater subtlety in the administrative structure through which productive activity is controlled. Technical rationalization facilitates a much more routine performance of the production system which drastically reduces the uncertainties created by machine breakdown and related technical failures. Administrative rationalization encourages self-conformity on the part of primary producers to the organizational discipline which a more advanced technical apparatus normally requires; primary produces are freed from the more constraining aspects of formal rules and procedures only to find themselves much more severely dictated to by the demands of the production cycle. Both the strategies of technical and administrative rationalization are supported by a managerial ideology which extols the virtue of socio-economic progress through increased organizational efficiency and denies the necessity for power struggles which threatens the continuous operation of the productive apparatus. Utilitarian goals and standards are emphasized as universal criteria to which all other particularistic values and prejudices should be subordinated. The managerial stratum is portrayed as the institutional embodiment of this ideology which emphasizes the paramount importance of technical advance and commercial success at the expense of outmoded sectional conflict. The severe intergroup struggles and tensions generated by the highly centralized and impersonal structures of strategic bureaucracy are now reinterpreted as the major obstacles standing in the way of the widespread economic and social benefits to be realized by the steady advance of organizational rationalization. Individual freedom and personal liberty are now associated with the universal flexibility afforded by a more decentralized mode of assembly rather than the particularistic discretions enjoyed under the rigid structures characteristic of centralized control.

The major impact of this shift in mode of assembly has been an increase in the power exercised by senior managerial practitioners at the expense of that control previously enjoyed by 'expert groups' within the ranks of middle management and shop-floor operatives.[22] Thus the discretionary control over decision-making concerning technical and administrative matters afforded to the latter through their skilful manipulation of the 'areas of uncertainty' which the formal system encourages is slowly being rationalized out of existence by the former's strategy of productive rationalization and organizational routinization. However, the victory of the manager over the expert is unlikely to be complete. The rationalization strategies which the former initiates are likely to open up new sources of uncertainty and the potential for control which they offer to subordinate groups quick and skilful enough to maximize that potential. This indicates the probability of a much more dynamic and fluid pattern of intra-organizational power relations under a more decentralized and flexible set of administrative arrangements which facilitates much closer control over day-to-day operations on the part of managerial elites.

The implications of these twin developments of a gradual shift in mode of assembly and the more fluid patterns of intra-organizational power relations associated with it for the prevailing structure of inter-organizational relations in which particular units operate can also be discerned in outline form. They indicate increasing political domination on the part of those class groupings or factions which are seen to carry the managerialist ideology and its institutional supports furthest. This is likely to be realized at the expense in political power and social prestige of those groupings which are seen to have most to lose by this major transformation in institutional machinery and normative structures, such as the traditional bourgeois and bureaucratic cadres who ruled on the basis of a judicious mixture of economic paternalism and political authoritarianism.

As has already been suggested, these gradual shifts in the organiz-

---

22 More detail on the impact of a change in the mode of assembly on middle-level and specialist management within the French organizations studied by Crozier is to be found in chapters 4 and 5 of his book (Crozier 1964).

ational and institutional arrangements of French industrial society create their own problems and dilemmas. The highly centralized and rigid patterns of the orthodox model of bureaucratic organization in French society generate a 'vicious circle' which its constituent groupings help to reproduce in their everyday routine transactions. This 'vicious circle' has four basic elements – centralized decision-making, a framework of rules and procedures emphasizing strict conformity to impersonalized modes of social interaction, the isolation of various social groupings located at different levels within the formal hierarchy, and the development of parallel power relations around those 'areas of uncertainty' which the formal system cannot eliminate (Crozier 1964: 187–94). The shift to a more rational form of bureaucratic organization will alleviate the more excessive features of this self-generating and reinforcing process of intergroup tension and conflict. Yet it is unlikely to remove them altogether and is almost certain to produce novel sources of ambiguity and contradiction around which alternative struggles and patterns of power relations will congeal:

> 'Bureaucratic systems persist and always find new forms. This is the result of two opposite and yet convergent pressures. On the one side each individual, each group and category within an organization will always struggle to prevent rationalization and maintain the unpredictability of their own task and function. . . . On the other side, the constant progress of rationalization offers the possibility and the temptation, to those responsible for it, to push planning and standardization further than is rationally possible. Two kinds of privileges and vicious circles, therefore, tend to develop. The former correspond to the resistance of groups trying to preserve their positions of strength which can be weakened by technical progress, and the latter to the desire of other groups to impose a rationalization which is not yet warranted by this progress.'
>
> (Crozier 1964: 299–300)

Crozier traces this necessary dialectic between rationalization and resistance to the inevitable conflict between universal goals that derive from a form of utilitarian rationality (which is the dominant ideological strain in modern industrial society) and the specific means of organizational control operationalized to achieve those objectives (standardization, predictability, reliability, certainty, etc.), which are consistently 'corrupted' by particularistic values and interests. To this extent, systems of imperative co-ordination are the primary institutional expression of the inevitable conflict between instrumental and moral modes of social action, and of the dilemmas and ambiguities which are generated as a result of its pervasive influence on the transactions between individuals and groups located at various points in its social structure.

A summary of the analysis provided of each of the three case studies within the terms of reference established by the practice framework is given in diagrammatic form in *Figure 2*.

Figure 2   Studies in organizational practice

areas of analysis	Selznick	Gouldner	Crozier
1 Material and social conditions	'New Deal' era; increased central government intervention; hostile local environment	Tightening of labour and product markets; ebb of rural community; increased corporate dominance and control	Highly structured institutional environment; accelerating pace of socio-economic change
2 Transition in mode of assembly	From 'formal' bureaucracy to 'client-based' bureaucracy	From 'mock' bureaucracy to 'punishment-centred' bureaucracy	From 'strategic' bureaucracy to 'rational' bureaucracy
3 Mechanisms facilitating transition	Co-optation; 'grass roots' doctrine	Strategic replacement; new technology; bureaucratization; indoctrination	Technical and organizational rationalization; managerialist ideology
4 Impact on pattern of intra-organizational power relations	Reinforced dominance of large-scale farming interests; minority interests excluded	Wildcat strike; institutionalization of prevailing pattern of power relations	Increase in 'managerial' power at expense of 'expert' power

areas of analysis	Selznick	Gouldner	Crozier
5 Implications for inter-organizational power relations	Reinforced existing structure of inter-organizational power relations	Closer corporate control by management and trade unions	Dominance of managerial elite; decline in power of traditional bourgeois and bureaucratic technocracy
6 Unresolved tensions and dilemmas	Increased exposure to national criticism; local disaffection from agency 'mission'	Bureaucratization as a solution to and facilitator of industrial conflict	Bureaucratic vicious circles

COMMON THEMES

Three major themes common to each of the case studies discussed in the previous section will be analysed within the frame of reference provided by the practice framework. First, an analytical theme concerned with the necessary theoretical mediation between 'organizational' and 'institutional' levels of analysis in the study of social change. Second, a substantive theme focused on the 'politicization of bureaucracy', the obverse of the 'bureaucratization of politics' outlined by Michels (Burns 1980). Third, an ideological theme highlighting the increasing dominance of a managerialist ideology in the post-1945 era and the underlying instability and fragility of that ideology as a 'solution' to the deep-seated conflicts produced by further phases of technological and organizational rationalization.

Each of the studies illustrates the crucial role of concepts which mediate between 'organizational' and 'institutional' levels of analysis in the study of social change. The conceptual apparatus of structural–functionalist sociology (appropriately modified to fit the circumstances of the cases) provides all the authors with the theoretical tools whereby this mediation can be achieved.[23] Gouldner's argument that we 'know practically nothing about the larger institutional forces underlying the various forms of bureaucracy' (Gouldner 1954a: 243) is developed within a conceptual framework that identifies an operational organizational logic linking together the actions of members and the workings of the institutional environments in which their organizations are situated. This logic is also identified by Selznick and Crozier, as it derives from a conception of bureaucratic organization as a self-sustaining functional mechanism geared to the needs of various social groups located in the wider social structure of which it is a part.

However, this approach presents each author with considerable difficulties when it is stretched to accommodate the complex link between the strategies of social agents and the structure of social relations which they reproduce. In other words, there is a marked tendency for 'strategic analysis' and 'institutional analysis' to become separated from each other so that the deterministic explanatory significance of structural factors is strongly emphasized at the expense of strategic variables (for example, see Selznick 1966: 249–53, Gouldner 1954a: 151–79, and Crozier 1964: 7–9). The theoretical status of the latter becomes increasingly uncertain as the determining role of autonomous structural forces takes on overriding importance in the analysis of organizational change and its institutional sources.

The practice framework avoids this separation of strategic and institutional analysis by developing a conceptual framework and a research orientation that examines structural forms, while simultaneously carrying back reference to the strategies through which they are generated. Within the functionalist framework, organizational change is treated as a process of dynamic equilibrium in which demands or pressures in the organization's institutional environment create sources of tension and disturbance within its

---

23 Clearly, the three authors discussed in this chapter make rather different use of structural–functionalist sociology as a theoretical resource. Selznick's usage is formally closest to that of Parsons, while Gouldner and Crozier diverge substantially from the latter in their interpretation and utilization of the functionalist heritage. However, none of them can be included in the orthodox mainstream of structural–functionalist sociology – one reason why their work continues to invite so much comment and debate.

established pattern of social relations. These internal tensions mediate external pressures and shape the behavioural response that is required of organizational elites to realize a form of structural adaptation which preserves system stability. This leads to the development of new centres of need and power within the organization's institutional environment. The latter provide the catalyst for subsequent periods of reorganization consisting of alternating phases of stability and instability and the development of those mechanisms through which they can be partially controlled and directed. Consequently, structural regularities operating independently of the interventions of social actors provide the explanatory concepts linking the sources, mechanisms, and outcomes of successive phases of organizational change within a long-run cyclical rhythm of dynamic equilibrium.

Within the practice framework, the potential bifurcation between structure and agency endemic to functional analysis is resisted by conceptualizing organizations as social practices in which members are routinely engaged in the course of maintaining or restructuring the systems of social relations in which they are collectively implicated. This suggests that the explanation of organizational change necessarily requires an account of the means and methods whereby actors 'penetrate' the institutional structures in which they are implicated so as to formulate and implement alternative organizational forms to those currently available. In this way, the idea of hidden structural logic which operates 'behind the backs' of practitioners to produce institutional outcomes of which they are completely unaware is replaced by the notion of an explicit social process in which knowledgeable and skilful agents are engaged in social practices aimed at realizing a set of arrangements which more closely reflect their priorities.[24]

This clearly takes us on to the crucial explanatory role that the concept of power plays within the practice framework and its relevance to an understanding of the second major theme which emerges from the reworking of the three case studies conducted in the previous section – the 'politicization of bureaucracy'.

---

24 This recourse to a hidden structural logic is a recurring theoretical theme in the intellectual development of organizational analysis and finds expression in the current enthusiasm, in some quarters, for the explanatory potency of 'deep structures' which can only be unearthed through a painstaking and elaborate decoding of everyday surface realities.

All three case studies point to the dual role of bureaucracy as a solution to and a producer of power struggles within particular organizational units and the wider institutional framework in which they operate. As such, they reinforce one of the central theoretical arguments developed within the field of organizational studies over the last twenty years – that the analysis of organizational change is inseparable from the analysis of those power struggles which generate and direct it (Crozier 1974). As a mode of assembly, imperative co-ordination has been reinterpreted as both a facilitative resource and a regulative mechanism directing power struggles between contending social groups rather than as a rational instrument of administrative regulation which is isolated from conflict over the allocation of normative priorities and the distribution of material rewards within the community.

In part, the politicization of bureaucracy is due to its inevitable failure to achieve the elimination of social conflict through the effective rationalization of all aspects of the organization's operations. This leads to the development of areas of discretion and autonomy that provide sources of power and influence exploited by 'expert groups' which are able to resist the embrace of regulative mechanisms and controls. Crozier describes this as the development of 'parallel power relations':

'Since it is impossible, whatever the effort, to eliminate all sources of uncertainty within an organization by multiplying impersonal roles and developing centralization, a few areas of uncertainty will remain. Around these areas, parallel power relationships will develop, with the concomitant phenomena of dependence and conflict. Individuals or groups who control a source of uncertainty, in a system of action where nearly everything is predictable, have at their disposal a significant amount of power over those whose situations are affected by this uncertainty. Moreover, their strategic position is all the stronger because sources of uncertainty are very few. Paradoxically, in a bureaucratic system of organization, parallel power increases in direct ratio to its rarity.'

(Crozier 1964: 192)

Crozier's summary of this process also points in the direction of a second component of the explanation for the mutation of bureaucratic structures in operational circumstances; that is, the intensified drive for control through more sophisticated and extensive strategies of organizational rationalization attempted by dominant groups striving to remove the sources of power made available to subordinate groups which they originally created. As a result, the increasing social visibility of the coercive and manipulative characteristics of an ostensibly rational administrative instrument serves to demystify the technocratic ideological foundations on which it had been developed. Far from constituting the rational social technologies envisaged by Saint-Simon and those 'administrative scientists' who followed his intellectual lead, bureaucratic organizations are now seen as the primary institutional mechanisms whereby power struggles are carried on in modern industrial societies (McNeil 1978).

Indeed, within the terms of reference provided by the practice framework, the bureaucratic 'vicious circle' can be reinterpreted as the paradigmatic organizational expression of the 'problematic of human agency' which provides the thematic focus for the former. Insofar as all three case studies describe a process whereby 'action succumbs to powers and constraints which are themselves the products of action' (Abrams 1982: xiv), they serve to highlight the conditions under which managerial control structures inevitably threaten the moral commitments generated through voluntary collaboration and involvement. These conditions usually take the form of heightening economic, political, and ideological pressures exerted on managerial practitioners to tighten their control over primary producers in the pursuit of increased organizational efficiency. The measures taken to achieve more effective control necessarily jeopardize moral involvement by intensifying the tensions and conflicts which already exist. The response of managerial practitioners is to redouble their efforts at more effective regulative control through further rationalization and to exacerbate the difficulties which this strategy has created in the first place.[25]

This takes us to the third theme exhibited by the reworking of the case studies – the increasing political dominance of 'managerialist ideology' in the post-Second-World-War era and the underlying instability and fragility of that belief system either as a basis for normative consensus or for operational practice under contemporary socio-economic conditions.

---

25 Other empirical examples of this process are documented in Nichols and Beynon (1977) and Burns (1977).

The rise of a managerialist ideology as providing the legitimatory basis for the exercise of collective power and the maintenance of institutional control through bureaucratic organization is documented in all three case studies. The cluster of ideas associated with this increasingly influential belief system can be divided into two major components: first, a public rhetoric which emphasizes the role of technical expertise as providing the legitimatory sanction for managerial power; and second, a private language that stresses the key political and judicial role of modern management within an 'organizational society' (Crozier 1964: 300). The technocratic rhetoric insists that modern organizations are characterized by the formal rationality of managerial experts who provide the administrative and technical skills necessary to rationalize collective activities in the pursuit of the universal goals of greater operational efficiency and effectiveness (Gouldner 1976). The private language of political bargaining and judicial regulation suggests that the social reality of managerial practice is pervaded by a concern to preserve the status quo through the skilful manipulation of the myriad of conflicting interests found within and without modern organizations to form sustainable human communities (Burns 1961, 1966, Anthony 1984).

Insofar as managerialism necessarily implies the elevation of organizational means (structures, routines, rules, programmes, budgets, etc.) to the status of moral ends, it also runs the risk of undermining the ideological façade which it has helped to construct. This is so to the extent that the rejection of managerial control strategies, wrapped up in moralistic packaging, by subordinates has to be interpreted (by managers) as a moral failure rather than a rational response of avoidance or resistance to a situation which the former perceive in coercive or manipulative terms. If management invests organizational means with an ethical significance which their perceived instrumental purpose belies, then they are forced to take strong measures in support of their control strategy if recalcitrance is encountered. As a result, the process of long-term organizational rationalization (and particularly during crises of managerial succession or environmental adaptation) becomes infused with severe ethical and ideological conflicts which would be much less likely to occur if organizational means were reduced to their instrumental value.

Yet managerialism cannot afford this more relaxed and indulgent attitude to organizational means because they have become the primary symbols and instruments whereby managerial practitioners attempt to legitimize their power and to use that power in the furtherance of their material interests. Thus each of the case studies points to the mutually reinforcing tendencies exhibited in the politicization of bureaucracy and the rationalization of managerial ideology. At the same time, the studies highlight the internal contradictions which these mutually reinforcing processes contain and their inability to provide workable solutions to the endemic material and ideological conflicts characteristic of contemporary work organizations.

Summary

This chapter has applied the practice framework to the reworking of three case studies that illustrate the characteristic dilemmas and contradictions which the process of organizational rationalization creates for managerial practitioners.[26] While facilitating a detailed focus on the specific circumstances of each case, the practice framework has also provided a coherent theoretical analysis of general themes and processes which transcend particular contexts. At the same time, the analysis which has been undertaken in this chapter indicates the broader significance of organizational analysis as an intellectual practice for an informed consideration of those issues which congeal within the 'problematic of human agency'.

In this way, organizational analysis may be better placed to recover and refurbish its links with a tradition of socio-political thinking which has much to offer those attempting to understand and explain contemporary organizational forms and their implications for long-term historical development.

---

26 The focus on managerial practitioners developed here is justified, in theoretical terms, both in relation to their strategic role in assembling and implementing organizational structures, and in respect of their relative neglect within the sociology of work organizations. However, the latter situation is changing as more attention is directed to the role which management play in generating and handling the tensions and contradictions embodied in contemporary organizational forms.

6
New directions in organizational analysis

Introduction

The previous chapters of this book have been focused on two major areas: first, the historical development of organizational analysis as an intellectual practice; and second, contemporary efforts aimed at reshaping the epistemological base and theoretical structure of the former.

This chapter moves on to a consideration of the strategies for future intellectual development which are currently on offer within the field of organizational studies. Four developmental strategies are selected for detailed analysis and certain prescriptive recommendations are made concerning the most appropriate strategy for long-term intellectual advance. Subsequent discussion and assessment of these strategies are carried out in relation to five interrelated areas: first, an exposition of the most significant intellectual challenges thought likely to direct future development; second, a specification of the theoretical responses deemed best equipped to cope with these problems; third, an identification of the major sources of intellectual consensus and conflict generated by these theoretical solutions; fourth, the implications of these solutions for the prescribed relationship between 'analysis' and 'practice'; and fifth, the underlying models of conceptual change which inform each of the strategies.

Four developmental strategies will be analysed in these terms. They have been labelled as 'integrationist', 'isolationist', 'imperialist', and 'pluralist' respectively. Each strategy will be considered in general terms and followed by a discussion of the recent work of individual writers who are treated as representatives of a particular strategy. Subsequently, an overall evaluation of the developmental strategies will be offered from the vantage point provided by the historical, conceptual, and empirical analysis which has been developed in the preceding chapters of this book.

The integrationist strategy

The major intellectual challenge or problem facing contemporary organizational analysis from an integrationist perspective is to provide a more systematic and coherent account of organizational structures as the outcomes of a continuous process in which members attempt to come to terms with the contextual constraints that limit their design options. To the extent that it strives to overcome the traditional theoretical dichotomy between 'voluntaristic' and 'deterministic' theories of organizational structure, integrationism demands that an effort must be made to conceptualize the interrelation between social action and contextual constraint. It also indicates that the strategic research task confronting organizational analysts is to identify those empirical situations in which the scope for choice in the design and implementation of certain structural patterns is much wider as compared to those contextual conditions in which it is more tightly circumscribed.

The theoretical response thought most appropriate to this problem is a greater degree of conceptual reconciliation between theoretical approaches which are often deemed to be incompatible in terms of their underlying philosophical presuppositions and ideological commitments. This is usually interpreted as a requirement to achieve a synthesis of selected conceptual elements from the interactionist and contingency approaches to form a theoretical framework which systematically incorporates actors' stragegies and structural constraints. The latter is to be achieved by focusing on the process whereby institutionalized social relations are produced and reproduced in the everyday interactions of organizational members.

As such, this theoretical response attempts to overcome the conventional break between 'structures' as formal frameworks of institutionalized relations and 'strategies' as informal networks of social interactions. It does this by concentrating on the socio-political processes through which members attempt to come to terms with a range of situational constraints which they are likely to encounter in varied historical contexts. This also implies a critical explanatory role for the concept of power insofar as it identifies the differentially distributed capacity to determine structural outcomes which arises out of the network of dependency relations existing between coalitions located within and without a particular organizational unit. In this way, a concern with the control which actors exercise over scarce resources, and the skill with which this control is deployed to form networks of dependency relations, becomes a central focusing point for understanding and explaining structural change. Such a focus demands a serious interest in the pro-active strategies whereby members construct and reconstruct organizational arrangements, while at the same time retaining a concern with the structural and environmental contingencies which shape the interventions followed by different groups to create a set of arrangements most favourable to their perceived interests.

The most prominent source of potential intellectual consensus and conflict within this programme of selective theoretical synthesis is seen to be the choice of methodological procedures and practices through which a better appreciation of the situational factors shaping the process of organizational design can be achieved. The projected theoretical synthesis of interactionist and contingency approaches also requires a methodological reconciliation of 'interpretative' and 'naturalistic' research strategies which may be difficult to operationalize. This is especially the case when the empirical identification and codification of the contextual constraints which shape actions seem to demand a research design and practice which precludes the painstaking reconstruction of the conceptual frameworks through which actors make sense of their strategic and tactical interventions in particular situations. Consequently, the continued fealty of the integrationist strategy to the need for the application of a modified version of 'scientific method' in the discovery of structural regularities contained in the process of organizational design provides a continuing source of tension and disagreement which will have to be worked through in each research setting.

Integrationism suggests that there is greater scope for much closer collaboration between 'analysts' and 'practitioners' in the realm of organizational design and control than is conventionally assumed in contemporary discussions of this issue. The achievement of a greater degree of theoretical integration serves to consolidate those approaches which are equipped to deal with complex organizational phenomena and to prune the field of perspectives which are unable to provide clear and coherent explanatory theories. Consequently, organizational analysts should be in a much better position to offer practical guidance to managers and administrators on key issues in the area of structural design and control. The integrationist strategy suggests that a more informed managerial choice between competing organizational design philosophies and methods can be realized if the polarized thinking characteristic of recent intellectual development in the field of organizational studies is superseded by an approach which is sensitive to the potential for reconciliation between conflicting perspectives.

Integration is based on the premise that theoretical synthesis will substantially reduce the bewildering array of conflicting vocabularies and perspectives available within the field of organizational studies, and provide the intellectual foundations on which a more intelligent and participatory form of managerial practice can be developed. More reliable and valid information about the consequences of alternative design policies and practices produced by strong theories is thought more likely to facilitate knowledgeable and unconstrained decision-making over critical organizational issues than a plethora of competing approaches which degenerate into a meaningless squabble over philosophical minutiae.

Clearly, the integrationist strategy interprets the extended theoretical and methodological debate released by the break-up of the functionalist orthodoxy during the late 1960s and early 1970s as having reached a point where serious dysfunctional consequences have set in which endanger the survival of organizational analysis as a viable and useful intellectual enterprise. It welcomes the increased scope for theoretical and methodological debate which the break-up facilitated. However, it maintains that the severe fragmentation which this has produced threatens to turn organizational analysis into an inward-looking endeavour obsessed with its own internal intellectual problems and having little, if anything, to say to those engaged in day-to-day organizational practice. It sees that the time is ripe for organizational analysts to turn away from introverted speculation over the philosophical entrails of their intellectual practice and to produce theoretical explanations which can provide the intellectual basis for more effective intervention in the practical affairs of human beings. Albrow's warning about the debilitating consequences of becoming embroiled in the needs of 'men of affairs'

(Albrow 1968) is turned on its head and transformed into an injunction to re-enter the world of practical pursuits and to facilitate the development of a more progressive and enlightened social order.

Integrationism is ground in an evolutionary model of conceptual change and development within the social sciences in general and organizational analysis in particular. This evolutionary model identifies a cumulative process of growth in scientific knowledge whereby successive incremental improvements in the conceptual refinement and methodological rigour of organizational analysis produces formalized theoretical explanations of increasing empirical range and precision. These conceptual and methodological advances are realized in spite of philosophical and ideological controversy which threatens the development of theories with strong predictive value which can be usefully applied in specific organizational settings. This is true to the extent that improvements in the substantive knowledge content of organization theory inevitably accrue as a consequence of the internal logic of the research process which imposes certain procedural imperatives on researchers in regard of both research practice and the criteria by which its products are evaluated. As a result, the rational procedures and principles inherent in the logic of scientific analysis are seen to contain the worst excesses of ideological intrusion and to permit the construction and codification of formal theories which have stood the test of empirical falsification.[27]

The commitment to an evolutionary model of conceptual growth and development tends to favour an 'internalist' account of scientific progress which stresses the importance of logical principles and rational procedures at the expense of 'external' influences which may shape scientific practice such as social context or material interests (see Toulmin 1972). It does not preclude a recognition of the latter and the impact which they may have on the direction and pace of scientific advance, but it does maintain that they will be unable to prevent the steady improvement in scientific knowledge made possible by internal disciplinary controls over the long term. The latter guarantee the progress towards falsifiable, parsimonious, and

---

27 In this sense, integrationists retain a touching faith in the 'objective rationality' of the practice of scientific method which has remained undented by recent developments in the post-empiricist philosophy of science. On the latter see Bernstein (1983).

readily comprehensible theories of organization whatever obstacles or intrusions are put in the way.

The integrationist strategy is well represented in the writings of contemporary organization theorists, even though it has been generally out of favour in recent years. Elements of this position can be discovered in the recent contributions of Ranson, Hinings, and Greenwood (1980), Lammers (1981), Donaldson (1982), and Pfeffer (1982).

Ranson, Hinings, and Greenwood perceive the need for a more unified theoretical and methodological analysis of organization structure which is adequate at the levels of meaning and causality. They draw on theoretical resources located within the action and systems perspectives to construct a comprehensive theory of organizational structuring which conceptually integrates phenomenological analysis of actors' meanings and strategies with a causal analysis of underlying regularities and mechanisms of which actors may be unaware. This integrated conceptual framework is offered as one way out of the confusion and disorder produced by the internecine conflict between competing perspectives and vocabularies in contemporary organization theory. It also seeks to identify the crucial mechanisms which shape the process of structural change as a way of achieving a better understanding of the socio-historical conditions in which the creative interventions of human agents may be most effective.

As such, the analysis which the authors provide is offered as an intellectual solvent to the perpetual strife which characterizes contemporary organization theory and threatens to fragment the 'collective enterprise of adequate understanding' into warring bands of fundamentalists unwilling and unable to articulate the 'latent linkages' that exist between conflicting perspectives.

Lammers also interprets the recent history of organizational sociology (as a more or less distinct speciality within the interdisciplinary field of organizational studies) in terms of improved conceptual definition and empirical delineation across a range of institutional sectors. While sympathizing with many of the recent criticisms made of the contingency approach, he endorses them 'rather more as statements concerning lacunae in the work of the past which have to be filled as soon as possible, rather than as proposals to wipe from the record what has already been achieved' (Lammers 1981: 278). He perceives a definite continuity between work done in the 1960s and early 1970s, even though the latter indicates a more definite switch in the direction of macrosociological concerns which have their intellectual roots in classical social theory. The preservation of organizational sociology, as a distinctive specialism within an inter-disciplinary field, is supported in terms of the indirect contribution which it can make by delivering applicable knowledge that signals problems, dangers, and abuses (Lammers 1981: 366). As a scientific enterprise, it must be justified in terms of its therapeutic uses, as well as the diagnostic advances which it has made possible as a result of empirical research and theoretical analysis.

Consequently, Albrow's view that organizational sociology ought to be detached from practical affairs is firmly rejected. Lammers is aware that the policy advice which social scientists offer may be of the 'soft' variety – that is, of an indeterminate nature. The ideal of clear and definite policy prescriptions founded on a systematic analysis of causal relations subject to practical control has to be replaced by the more limited idea of general intellectual illumination and enlightenment as an aid to practical interventions. Thus the social scientist is seen to provide 'source books' for handy ideas which may prove relevant in getting to grips with practical organizational problems rather than 'recipe books' containing hard and precise policy guidelines (Lammers 1981: 369). Nevertheless, the organizational sociologist (as a social scientist) can contribute to human affairs by 'helping to diagnose the problems of organizational practice' (Lammers 1981: 370) and communicating the knowledge gained through the application of these diagnostic skills and techniques to 'brokers' who act as intermediaries between the producers and users of scientific knowledge.

Donaldson's defence of the contingency approach in organizational analysis also displays many of the features of an integrationist strategy as it has been characterized in previous discussion. It rejects the thesis of 'separate development' advocated by exponents of an action frame of reference such as Schreyogg (1982) and the mis-characterization of the contingency framework which flows from this dichotomous mode of thinking. It recognizes theoretical and methodological deficiencies in the contingency-design view but maintains that these can be rectified by a judicious overhaul of the approach's conceptual apparatus and research strategy. In addition, his defence suggests that this overhaul can be complemented by a theoretical retooling which will equip a revitalized contingency approach with the analytical and methodological insights to be derived from an action perspective. The whole ethos of his analysis is presented in the spirit of reconciliation between modes of thinking which are often treated as if they were totally incompatible. This is underwritten by a belief in the positive implications of valid social scientific information for extending the creative interventions of managers and workers aimed at bringing about better organizational designs which manifests itself in better communication, decision-making, motivation, and intergroup co-operation (Donaldson 1982: 69).

Donaldson's defence concludes with another reconciliation between the epistemological commitments of a humanistic social action-based mode of enquiry and those of a scientistic contingency-based approach. This is achieved by reference to an interpretation of Weberian epistemology which treats general explanatory hypotheses about the typical actions of individuals within particular socio-historical settings as regularities that can be subsumed under more encompassing scientific laws. While the debate about philosophical fundamentals forced by the break-up of the conventional systems-based approach and the increasing prominence of alternative perspectives has led to the clarification of basic issues, Donaldson clearly believes that there is a pressing need to reassert the continuing value of structural and scientific analysis which can accommodate a concern with social action and its grounding in actors' interpretative schemes.

Finally, we come to Pfeffer's recent overview of the field of organizational studies and the advice which he offers on the most fruitful avenues for future growth and development. Pfeffer also believes that contemporary organization theory suffers from a glut of theoretical schemes which are high on conceptual abstraction and methodological novelty and low on empirical demonstration and logical elegance. He frequently uses the metaphor of a garden which is overgrown with weeds and which is in need of severe pruning and the planting of new seeds which are likely to produce a much higher yield of developed plants with strong roots and foliage that can withstand bad weather. In his view, the field of organizational studies 'has tended to move too far from the data and findings. Or, put another way, there is too much ideology and assertion and not enough attention to the results (or lack thereof) of the various empirical investigations that have been undertaken' (Pfeffer 1982: 259).

In particular, Pfeffer suggests that the introspective bent of contemporary work indicates a growing sense of intellectual bewilderment and an almost naive willingness to accept analytical approaches which concentrate on the cognitive and ideological aspects of organizational life to the virtual exclusion of the material and structural properties of organizations considered as 'material entities with physical characteristics, characterized by social relationships and demographic processes' (Pfeffer 1982: 259). This fascination with cognitive processes and ideological frameworks, Pfeffer maintains, has also encouraged a marked disinclination to evaluate competing theoretical perspectives with fundamental criteria common to all scientific study such as parsimony, logical coherence, falsifiability, clarity, and empirical consistency (Pfeffer 1982: 37–40).

The theoretical seed-crop which Pfeffer recommends to produce a more robust and high-quality analytical yield attempts to germinate three strains in one plant – that which treats organizations as physical structures, relational networks, and demographic entities. He argues that each of these 'compelling realities' can provide the conceptual resources from which a more logically coherent and empirically compelling theory of organizations can be developed in the future.

While Pfeffer's analysis tends to concentrate on the internal disciplinary factors which have produced this state of affairs and the remedies it requires, he is not unmindful of the contextual influences which have contributed to the present 'tower of Babel' that confronts organizational analysts. Indeed, the neglect of social structures and the prominence afforded to cognitive and cultural processes is seen to reinforce the 'technical or efficiency-based determinism' (Pfeffer 1982: 258) which resonates with the powerful material interests located in the social context in which organization theory has developed. A focus on these processes at the individual and group level has forged a common bond between producers and users of organizational knowledge which has been much stronger than would have been the case if attention had been directed at larger socio-economic structures and their effect on organizational arrangements. While not wanting to destroy this bond entirely, Pfeffer indicates that the growing and tending of more productive intellectual crops will clearly strengthen the social visibility and role of organizational analysis in modern society.

Yet Pfeffer's treatment of the contextual factors which have shaped intellectual developments is extremely cursory and seems to hold little, if any, relationship to the universal criteria and procedures which are offered as a basis for theory evaluation. They are discussed as distinct and discrete concerns. The interest in the interaction between social context and intellectual change finally boils down to a focus on the careers of individual researchers and the socialization agencies to which they were exposed during their advance from apprentice to journeyman (Pfeffer 1982: 32–3). As in the case of each of the representatives of integrationism reviewed in this section, the overpowering attraction and security of an internalist and evolutionary account of organization theory's historical development and present condition tend to push Pfeffer's interest in external considerations on to the margins of intellectual debate.

The isolationist strategy

Isolationism maintains that the central intellectual problem shaping the agenda on which the future development of organizational analysis will be based is the identification of those 'hidden mechanisms' that produce, sustain, and develop the institutionalized system of social relations on which the integrationist perspective is focused. This demands that the researcher penetrate the immediate surface 'reality' constituted by formalized role structures with the objective of explicating the underlying mechanisms that determine the institutional frameworks in which everyday life is carried on. These mechanisms are seen to be inaccessible to an approach which takes the empirical evidence made available by conventional methodological procedures as providing a scientifically acceptable representation of some bedrock reality beyond which we cannot proceed. The inherent opacity of these fundamental mechanisms can only be removed through the application of a theoretical and methodological strategy which will systematically reveal and clarify the inner nature of the 'real world' that cannot be understood through the categories and procedures of behavioural science. The latter concentrates on the phenomenal world of sense experience and the empirical generalizations which can be formulated by a theoretically informed examination of that experience. The isolationist strategy is predicated on the assumption that the noumenal world of essential mechanisms or structures can only be explicated by rational intellectual constructs which are not constrained by observable entities or processes established by experimental science.

This intellectual task is seen to demand the achievement of 'paradigm closure' so that the theoretical approaches best equipped to provide the required analytical resource and methodological tools are allowed to develop and fructify without any contact with alien perspectives that may introduce conceptual impurities into their theoretical bloodstream. The demand for intellectual isolation and protection rests on two key assumptions. First, that the fundamental incompatibility between the philosophical and ideological presuppositions underlying distinct approaches located within different meta-theoretical frameworks or paradigms necessarily rules out theoretical reconciliation. Second, that previous attempts at interparadigm mixing have resulted in dominant orthodoxies swamping promising heterodoxies and stunting the growth of innovative theoretical development. Thus the isolationist strategy demands paradigm closure on both logical and historical grounds. Separate development is the only viable alternative in a field of study which has been tightly structured and controlled by an intellectual orthodoxy which is always liable to envelop promising rivals within its suffocating theoretical embrace and denude them of any independent identity or growth potential. It is the only way of preserving and developing the comparative intellectual pluralism and freedom which have resulted from the breakup of the 'functionalist hegemony' that reigned until the 1960s.

The focus on philosophical incompatibility as a rationale for paradigm closure and theoretical self-development reflects the emphasis which the isolationist strategy gives to the ontological foundations of competing analytical frameworks and methodologies. Assumptions about the nature of the phenomena to which different approaches attend are seen to provide a basis for some degree of theoretical interaction and combination. Yet this can only take place within, never across, the philosophical boundaries which delimit the sovereign territories and subjects of incommensurable paradigms. Theoretical variation and synthesis are permitted within the range of ontological possibilities which a paradigm lays down. However, the latter also provides a mutually exclusive set of constitutive categories through which the entities in its object domain are clearly defined and delimited. No amount of theoretical 'special pleading' or compromise will allow these ontological boundaries to be transgressed.

In focusing upon the ontological sources of consensus and conflict within organizational analysis, the isolationist strategy also gives overwhelming priority to the meta-theoretical assumptions that direct substantive research and theorizing. Its gaze is fixed on the fundamental presuppositions that shape the world views within which individual researchers and theorists are forced to operate. The latter usually possess little, if any, awareness, much less understanding, of these 'deep' intellectual structures and the pervasive influence which they exert over their work. Yet these alternative views of social reality provide the philosophical frameworks which combine groups of theorists into viable intellectual communities and set them apart from other groups whose work occupies a very different ontological universe.

The most basic ontological disagreement which the isolationist strategy highlights as providing a source of consensus and conflict is that prevailing between a 'constructivist' and 'objectivist' view of social reality.[28] The former maintains that social reality is constituted through the meaningful social interaction engaged in by pro-active human agents. As such, it has to be continually renewed and reaffirmed through human interaction and has no independent ontological status apart from that conveyed through the cognitive process and interpretative practices necessarily engaged in by human agents. Objectivism is founded on the premise that social reality is an objective structural configuration determined by the material conditions in which it develops irrespective and independent of the interventions of human agents. While the latter may engage in cognitive and interpretative processes of various kinds, these only have ontological significance insofar as they directly reflect the objective structures of material processes and relations that determine social interaction.

While there may be some room for manoeuvre within each of these frameworks, the isolationist perspective suggests that the individual theorist is required to follow one or other when providing a basic characterization of the phenomena with which he or she is concerned. This characterization will inevitably determine the epistemological, theoretical, and methodological assumptions which regulate substantive intellectual analysis.[29] Questions concerning

---

28 The tension between these opposed ontologies is resurfacing in current intellectual fashions in organizational analysis such as the recent enthusiasm for 'organizational symbolism and culture'. For a review of various philosophical and sociological positions available within the latter see Allaire and Firsirotu (1984).

29 The isolationist perspective rests on a highly formal and rigid specification of the link between philosophical assumptions, theoretical strategy, and substantive analysis which may be extremely difficult to maintain in practice – as this book has revealed on several occasions.

the nature of the phenomena to be studied are the fundamental issues on which intellectual order is established.

Not only does isolationism call for separate theoretical development as the only viable strategy for intellectual growth in organizational analysis, but it also demands a much more distinctive separation between analysis and practice as a precondition for continued intellectual vitality. This is legitimated on the grounds that the previous intellectual dominance of a paradigm strongly linked to the policy concerns of powerful social groups and classes within industrial capitalist societies had produced a field of study characterized by theoretical somnolence and philosophical inertia. The material interests sponsoring the development of mainstream organizational analysis as an accredited social scientific discipline had ensured that certain ideological restraints prevented the discipline's practitioners from raising questions and searching for answers that challenged the accepted view of complex organizations and their role in contemporary society. Functionalism provided the individual theorist with a conceptual vocabulary which resonated with the conventional ideological assumptions reinforcing the position of dominant interests and a technical apparatus that facilitated limited organizational reforms maintaining their strategic control.

If a return to these conditions is to be avoided, then the traditional Gordian knot between scientific analysis and policy concerns would have to be severed by intellectual practitioners who were committed to the independent value and self-justifying quality of their chosen vocation. This issue cannot be evaded or ignored. It has to be confronted head-on so as to ensure that the intellectual vitality of organizational analysis is not sapped by the wearying ideological encumbrance of class interest masquerading as 'common sense'. Only in this way can the intellectually paralysing effect of ideological convention, mediated by theoretical orthodoxy, be restored.

This does not require a form of organizational analysis which is stripped of all political commitment and ideological force. But it does demand a distinctive separation – intellectually, socially, and morally – between intellectual analysis and technical concerns as a precondition that permits a much more reflective evaluation of the organizational strategies pursued by social groups and classes located at various points within the social structure in which organizational analysis is practised.

Isolationism draws on an exclusionary model of conceptual

change which gives priority to the internal disciplinary conditions and procedures which generate and direct theoretical developments occurring in an independent and self-sustaining fashion. The fundamental presuppositions which structure collective cognitive endeavour into coherent intellectual traditions are also seen to lay down the philosophical tramlines on which theoretical change can proceed within hermetically sealed frameworks which survive and prosper in blissful ignorance of each other.

As a result, the isolationist perspective tends to neglect the contextual determinants of the dynamics of internal theoretical development which have been highlighted in more recent interpretations of organizational analysis's present state and future prospects. It does not totally deny the significance of situational factors in helping to create conditions favourable to intellectual innovation, but relegates them to a subsidiary role when it comes to explaining the origins, courses, and consequences of such novel developments. In this sense, isolationism rests on a rationalist interpretation of cognitive progress and advance which stresses the independent determining force of ideas irrespective of the social settings in which they develop.

The foremost exponents of an isolationist strategy in recent years have been Burrell and Morgan (1979). It is worth quoting them at some length because of the clarity and persistence with which they pursue this line of reasoning:

> 'In essence, what we are advocating in relation to developments within these paradigms amounts to a form of isolationism. We firmly believe that each of the paradigms can only establish itself at the level of organizational analysis if it is true to itself. Contrary to the widely held belief that synthesis and mediation between paradigms is what is required, we argue that the real need is for paradigmatic closure. In order to avoid emasculation and incorporation within the functionalist problematic, the paradigms need to provide a basis for their self-preservation by developing on their own account. Insofar as they take functionalism as their reference point, it is unlikely that they will develop far beyond their present embryonic state – they will not develop coherent alternatives to the functionalist point of view.'
>
> (Burrell and Morgan 1979: 397–98)

This recommendation is based on an analysis of the metatheoretical assumptions informing the range of approaches available

within contemporary research and writing in terms of four paradigmatic frameworks which present mutually exclusive views of the
social world. Their analysis also stresses the ontological commitments informing substantive research and theorizing as providing a
basis for paradigmatic closure and isolation. While the specific
organizational theories developed outside the confines of the functionalist paradigm still remain relatively weak and undernourished
in intellectual terms, they remain embedded within traditions of
social theorizing and analysis which are distinctive, internally coherent, and self-sustaining (Burrell and Morgan 1979: 396).

Burrell and Morgan also provide a somewhat idiosyncratic interpretation of Kuhn's concept of 'paradigm' (Kuhn 1962) which reveals
their relative lack of interest in the process of theoretical change
and development in organizational analysis. Kuhn uses the concept
of paradigm to analyse the socio-historical dynamics of conceptual
and cognitive change in natural science. Burrell and Morgan invoke
the concept to provide intellectual legitimation for a heuristic
framework which has little or nothing to say about the process of
theoretical change in organizational analysis or the contextual factors
which may have influenced its development. The few cryptic remarks which they offer on this issue suggest a commitment to an
internalist view of conceptual change in which intra-paradigm development proceeds in an intellectual climate of 'disinterested hos-
tility' (Burrell and Morgan 1979: 36). This approach diverges quite
sharply from Kuhn's interest in the dynamics of conceptual and
methodological innovation, and the socio-historical factors which
facilitated movement in certain directions rather than others. Indeed,
the use which Burrell and Morgan make of Kuhn's concept to justify
a strategy of 'paradigm closure' in organizational analysis is drastically at odds with both the spirit and the intentions of the former's
analysis.

Burrell (1980) extends this case for an isolationist strategy in
support of a 'radical organization theory' which is in need of careful
intellectual nurturing and protection if it is to avoid the trap of
'theoretical mediation, abasement and emasculation' which has be-
fallen so many other innovatory perspectives. The realization of
paradigm closure is seen as one of the essential preconditions (along
with a realist epistemology and a deeper appreciation of 'radical
theory's' distinctive intellectual roots) for the sustained growth and
development of a radical alternative to conventional perspectives
elaborated within, or in reaction to, functionalist orthodoxy.

There is a similar perception of the fundamental incompatibility and separateness of different paradigmatic frameworks, such that theoretical mediation between paradigms is seen to be futile and prejudicial to the development of a radical alternative. Self-sustained theoretical development in an isolated and protected intellectual environment is the only way in which radical organization theory will be able to develop a creative autonomy of its own that will facilitate independent intellectual progress outside the confines of the orthodox framework or its satellites (Burrell 1980).

In both analyses, previous and prospective intellectual innovation and progress is interpreted in splendid isolation from any systematic consideration of contextual factors and the influence which they may exert over the direction and content of cognitive change. The internalist account of intellectual development associated with the integrationist strategy is reinforced with a vengeance by exponents of isolationism who seem to hold a touching faith in the independent creative power and moral force of ideas.

The imperialist strategy

The theoretical priority at the forefront of an imperialist strategy of intellectual development in organizational analysis is the identification and elaboration of those 'organizing principles' that inhere in the wider social formation in which particular organizational units are located and from which they take their institutional form and direction. Organizational structures and mechanisms are interpreted as the secondary effects of the primary structural patterns which specify the manner in which organizational units will operate and the institutional form within which their reproductive and transformative activities shall be regulated. The analysis of work organizations is justified on the grounds of what it will tell us about the organizing principles of the society in which the former are temporally and socially situated rather than in terms of improving our detailed understanding of their internal characteristics and processes. The engagement in organizational analysis is legitimated only as an integral component of a larger intellectual enterprise aimed at improving our understanding of long-term and large-scale institutional formation and transformation. Organizational analysis loses any claim to separate intellectual identity or purpose and is merged within a wider analytical framework geared to the examination of historical transformations in institutional structures and the principles which underlie these long-term historical movements.

This task is to be realized through a systematic examination of the 'structural logics' or 'modes of rationality' which determine the explicit organizational structures that function at the 'surface level' of everyday social practice and action. These logics or rationalities are treated as objective 'selection rules' which determine how organizational structures develop in relation to the major institutional transformations taking place within the social formations in which they are situated. They can only be articulated and analysed through the formulation and application of analytical models which permit the 'deconstruction' of social action so as to reveal the implicit structures that shape and regulate everyday organizational practice.

In turn, this requires the incorporation of specific theoretical approaches into a more encompassing framework which supersedes the limitations imposed by the former's intellectual history and commitments. While they may have a limited analytical and empirical value, conventional theoretical perspectives must be denuded of their previous intellectual identities and reworked within a synthesizing framework equipped to deal with the structural logic determining organizational change. A focus on long-run transformations in the structure of social organization and the short-run organizational strategies which they generate demands the incorporation of the perspectives provided by mainstream theories into a single unified framework. Only in this way can contemporary theorists and researchers hope to contain the range of macro-level historical, political, cultural, and material factors which shape the specific organizational forms or arenas in which larger societal forces contend and the institutional outcomes they produce.

However, the ideological contexts which shape intellectual practice and development are seen to provide an important source of frustration and opportunity for those wishing to pursue this developmental strategy. The theoretical reworking and relocation of mainstream approaches within a larger framework may prove easier to achieve than a complete restructuring of their ideological foundations. Ideological residues may remain to limit the scope for further theoretical development and restrain intellectual innovation within conventionally accepted parameters. At the same time, a general movement in the direction of an ideological context favouring a systematic focus on macro-societal transformations and their impact on organizational structures and processes may stimulate an irresistible force tearing organizational analysis free from its managerialist roots.

This latter trend is thought likely to be reinforced by a fusion of 'analysis' and 'practice' within a form of socio-political praxis based on a thorough understanding of the underlying structural forces and principles which shape surface-level interventions and arrangements. Within the frame of reference imposed by an imperialist strategy, the conventional technical and managerial interests of mainstream theorizing are redefined in terms of a political struggle to regain control over the organizational mechanisms which mediate societal forces. Individual exponents of the strategy may differ as to how much scope there is for human control in a social world dominated by material and social structures which develop according to their own logical principles. Yet the desire to inform collective political struggle and intervention through an intellectual framework geared to a better understanding of the hidden forces which shape contemporary organizational designs and strategies is a recurring theme in the work of the 'imperialists'.

This objective is also legitimated by the commitment to a revolutionary model of conceptual change within organizational analysis and the potential support which it offers to a form of political praxis aimed at transforming the institutional environment in which organizations conventionally operate. Substantive transformations in the intellectual equipment whereby human beings attempt to gain a better understanding of the institutional structures which shape their lives are seen to be brought about through the continuing struggle between contending communities of theorists as they respond to external developments in their socio-economic context. Consequently, the imperialist strategy offers an 'externalist' account of intellectual development which focuses on the situational conditions which favour the intellectual hegemony of certain 'world views' as opposed to others. These situational constraints are analysed in dynamic rather than static terms; that is, they are treated as inherently unstable features of the socio-economic order in which intellectual production and conflict take place. While they may develop according to an inherent logic or rationality of structural transformation, they are not fixed and determinate entities such that law-like statements can be made concerning their developmental course and outcome. Indeed, they are seen to embody multiple contradictory forces which may occasion dislocations and crises within the intellectual communities attempting to understand and interpret their significance for a wider audience.

In this sense, the imperialist strategy dissolves the traditional boundaries between intellectual analysis and social context which are emphasized by alternative perspectives. It treats organizational analysis as a form of intellectual production which is subjected to the same sort of material and social constraints imposed on other types of productive activity. Substantial alterations to the situational conditions under which intellectual analysis is practised are seen to provide a context favourable to transformations in the cognitive process and conceptual tools through which complex organizations are understood. However, this intimate relationship between social and conceptual change is mediated by the continuing struggle for intellectual dominance taking place between contending groups of theorists who offer contrasting interpretations of the social world which they inhabit. These interpretations often have an influence far beyond the relatively narrow and confined milieu in which they operate.

Thus exponents of an imperialist strategy abjure a simple reductionist account of cognitive and conceptual change within organizational analysis in which intellectual developments are treated as automatic reactions to material transformations. Instead they provide a more complex analytical model in which a process of intellectual struggle and conflict mediates between theoretical and social change to produce contending conceptual approaches which wax and wane in relation to the opportunities offered by a dynamic socio-economic context and the relative skill with which they are utilized by different intellectual communities.

Clearly, present conditions are seen to provide a context disposed towards an intellectual climate and community in which conventional approaches are waning in strength and vitality. Alternative perspectives geared to a better understanding of the organizing principles underlying established organizational forms are increasing in intellectual power and intensity. Nevertheless, the outcome of this conflict between competing perspectives is seen to depend as much, if not more, on the relative skills of contending intellectual communities and the support which they receive from other social groups as on a clinical and rational appraisal of the quality of their respective cases. Intellectual struggle remains a form of ideological conflict in which contending social groups attempt to impose their world view, as the only realistic interpretation, on others.

Elements of the imperialist strategy can be discerned in the works of Benson (1977a), Whitley (1977a), Karpik (1978), and Clegg and Dunkerley (1980).

Benson's call for a dialectical approach to the study of organizations is based on the argument that the major task for organizational analysts in the coming years is to provide a better understanding of the underlying processes through which organizational arrangements are produced and maintained. His approach to this problem is guided by four basic principles – social construction, totality, contradictions, and praxis – which convey a conception of organization as a social whole with 'multiple, interpenetrating levels and sectors' (Benson 1977a: 9) and with intricate linkages to the socio-economic macrostructure in which it functions. The dialectical perspective focuses 'upon the transformations through which one set of arrangements gives way to another. Dialectical analysis involves a search for fundamental principles which account for the emergence and dissolution of specific social orders' (Benson 1977a: 3).

Two levels of organizational reality can be discerned within the dialectical view – organizational morphology and organizational substructure. The former refers to the 'officially enforced and conventionally accepted view of the organization' (Benson 1977a: 10). The latter indicates a concern with the underlying network of social relations and material conditions which provide 'the basis for transformation of the organization's morphology' (Benson 1977a: 12). It includes ties to the larger societal system in which organizations are embedded and bases of economic, political, and ideological dominance which have an intra-organizational source and reference.

Benson indicates that the large body of literature dealing with internal bases of intra-organizational dominance can be incorporated within the wider analytical framework provided by the dialectical approach. The latter incorporates, but transcends, these earlier theories; they 'represent partial perspectives which can be incorporated in a variety of more encompassing arguments. The dialectical view is instead a more nearly complete explanatory framework into which more limited theories may be drawn' (Benson 1977a: 13). The proponents of more conventional perspectives are also committed to an uncritical, unreflexive stance towards organizational realities. In part, Benson maintains, this can be explained in terms of their commitment to a positivist methodology. It is also related to the ideological interests which have influenced their theoretical analyses involving a programme of technocratic rationalization through planning or more sophisticated forms of political manipulation and bargaining:

> 'From a dialectical perspective, then, specific theories are not in any simple sense to be set aside. Rather, they are to be superseded in a more encompassing framework. . . . The dialectician goes beyond such formulations to inquire into the relationships between organization theories and organizational realities – considering the "reality-defining" potential of a theory of administration, the linkage between administrator and theoretician, and the connection of social theories to social movements of various kinds.'
>
> (Benson 1977a: 17)

However, a commitment to a reflexive form of analysis, appreciative of the subtle interconnections between 'theoretical' and 'ideological' work, is not enough. Dialectical analysis must also be concerned with the development of a new form of political praxis through which the reconstruction of existing organizational arrangements can be achieved: 'This reconstruction is aimed toward the realization of human potential by the removal of constraints, limitations upon praxis. This task involves both the critique of existing organizational forms and the search for alternatives' (Benson 1977a: 18). As crucial instruments of material and ideological domination in advanced industrial societies, organizations must be regarded as the strategic social units through which the transformation of the existing social order must be achieved.

Whitley's critique of the various approaches to the analysis of organizational control which have been developed within mainstream literature is predicated on an alternative theoretical strategy that takes institutionalized social relations as problematic and enquiries into the underlying structures through which they are reproduced and changed:

> 'This would mean going beyond the immediate "surface" reality and explicating structural processes which would account for it, such as fundamental relations of productive activity. . . . This theoretical strategy assumes that surface realities should not be taken as given, but as explicable in the light of more fundamental structural processes; instead of treating these processes as a "black box" it considers their elaboration as a major task of scientific inquiry.'
>
> (Whitley 1977a: 170)

Such an alternative theoretical strategy allows Whitley to develop an analytical framework focused on the problem of organizational control which takes valid components of more orthodox approaches and reworks them within a view of organizations as units which mediate changing relations of production and exchange. Thus macrostructural changes to the framework of social relations which define and constrain productive activity are treated as transformations in the modes of organizing and the uses of organizations: 'The point is that organizations do not engage in some sort of mutual competition in a social vacuum; their interrelations are structured and developments in one are connected to those in others in a determinate fashion which can be discerned' (Whitley 1977a: 183).

In the latter part of his paper, Whitley draws particular attention to the legitimatory role which organizations and organization theories fulfil in societies dominated by 'a structural imperative to increase efficiency as indicated by profit and form the locus of class conflicts which impact upon the realization of this imperative' (Whitley 1977a: 181). However, the institutionalization of class conflict which is achieved through formal organization structures and strategies is far from complete and does not preclude the development of alternative ideological interpretations that challenge conventional interpretations of social reality. The latter process is likely to gain in strength and range when changes to certain productive and administrative processes 'dislocate' existing belief systems and undermine the legitimacy which they previously provided for existing power structures.

Whitley concludes with the suggestion that the central task for future research and theorizing in organizational analysis is to construct a set of analytical categories describing organizations and their modes of transformation in terms of different patterns of subordination and the systems of macrosocial power relations in which they are most likely to develop.

Karpik also constructs a conceptual framework which incorporates ideas drawn from a range of approaches developed within mainstream organization theory (decision-making theory, the negotiated-order perspective, political bargaining models) to analyse the 'logics of action' that inform strategies of organizational design and control followed by large corporations in which their operation can most clearly be identified. 'Logics of action', he argues, are principles of regrouping and dispersal which establish similarities and differences between actors and organizations. They represent a wide range of socio-economic principles in terms of which organizational action can take on a distinctive institutional form. They also provide principles of action around which individuals and groups structure their attitudes and behaviour.

As such, Karpik continues, the concept of 'logics of action' allows the organizational analyst to reconstruct the material stakes and general power systems which structure the organizational strategies followed by various interest groups. This process of analytical reconstruction gets behind the 'official view' of social reality presented by powerful groups which attempt to conceal their aims and the organizational means selected to achieve them by projecting their own interpretation of events as the only sensible version available. Thus 'logics of action' are regarded as rationalities which the analyst attributes to actors and coalitions attempting to establish their sectional objectives as universal goals to which all other considerations should be subordinated.

He applies this framework to the analysis of the various strategies followed by multinational corporations within the international economic system. The resulting analysis suggests that corporate strategy is the outcome of a complex interaction between intra-organizational power relations and bargaining process and inter-organizational structures of social domination based on access to and control over economic, technological, and cultural resources. It indicates that 'the logics of action of organizational actors are not arbitrary. That is, organizational coalitions choose preferences that are historically and economically conditioned' (Weiss 1981: 394).

He concludes with the general historical proposition that two major forms or phases of modern capitalist development can be distinguished; 'industrial capitalism' based on market exchange and mass production and 'technological capitalism' based on regulated exchange and the integration of science and technology as the central driving force of institutional transformation. Multinationals are treated as the predominant organizational expression of 'technological capitalism' to the extent that they operate on the basis of a 'logic of action' in which the organization of scientific development and the production of economic goods are systematically combined. This has enabled multinationals to attain a degree of control over their operational environments on an international scale which is unique in the history of economic development. This economic system and the organizational units through which it is reproduced and developed have become the dominant political and cultural realities of the contemporary world which will shape the future of civil society and the state.

Finally, we come to Clegg and Dunkerley's advocacy of a 'political economy' of organizations which bears all the hallmarks of an imperialist strategy for future intellectual development in organizational analysis.

The major problematic directing the future development of organizational analysis, Clegg and Dunkerley maintain, is the construction of a general analytical framework which will identify the 'modes of rationality' that have informed the various forms of organizational control initiated by dominant groups and classes in different historical epochs. In the construction of this framework they attempt to draw on and synthesize a great deal of material which has been produced by theorists operating within more conventional and less ambitious intellectual traditions such as contingency theory and strategic-choice models of organizational design.

The achievement of this Herculean task of theoretical synthesis and abstraction demands a more historically sensitive and less empiricist approach to organizational analysis:

> 'We cannot simply take this entity – the organization – for granted as a real empirical phenomenon which our data simply reports on. We must construct an explicit and theoretical model of our object of analysis which is related to the historical development of our concrete empirical object of organizations. In doing this we may find that if we wish to say anything other than the most general things about empirically visible aspects of its structure (e.g. size, centralization, etc.) our faith in the category of "the organization" may have been premature. Perhaps, after all, there are types of organization which cluster not at the level of empirically given variation, but at the level of specificity within an overall macrostructural context.'
>
> (Clegg and Dunkerley 1980: 502)

This leads them to advocate a reconceptualization of the key concept of 'structure' as the empirical expression or representation of 'modes of rationality' or selection rules which can only be identified through a rational reconstruction of the developmental logic integral to the historical process whereby transformations in capitalist modes of production have been realized (Clegg and Dunkerley 1980: 501–03). The organizational strategies followed by dominant groups and classes have to be 'decoded' to establish the mode of rationality which informed their choices:

> 'This allows subjects considerably more choice, theoretically, at the surface level of social practice and action. Nonetheless, this freedom, like all freedom, is conditioned, and one can hypothesize rules which condition the selection of strategies of action.'
>
> (Clegg and Dunkerley 1980: 503)

Considered in these terms, organizations are redefined as 'historically and temporally complex sedimented structures' (Clegg and Dunkerley 1980: 509) which maintain control over the labour process in the interest of the owners of capital and their agents. This approach then provides the basis for Clegg and Dunkerley's analysis of various forms of 'hegemonic control' over the labour process imposed by dominant classes since the early decades of the twentieth century. They trace out a general move from 'coercive' to 'manipulative' forms of labour-process control which is in turn related to an increasingly sophisticated strategy of organizational co-optation on the part of the capitalist state as the predominant response to 'systems contradictions' or crises of varying magnitudes and intensities. It is these 'systems crises' that must provide the starting point for any complete explanation of organizational change within the capitalist mode of production as it has passed through various stages of historical transformation.

All of this is based on the proposition that conventional organizational analysis is an intellectual tool which has continued to serve the ideological and material interests of the capitalist class (Clegg and Dunkerley 1980: 58). For Clegg and Dunkerley, organization theory remains an ideological intervention which attempts to obscure the fundamentally and inherently antagonistic nature of class relations within the capitalist mode of production. However, they clearly believe that their brand of theorizing can 'break the mould' of conventional intellectual analysis and offer a general theory of organizational change which is geared to the integral instabilities and contradictions of the capitalist system. In this way, they express a continuing belief in the progressive quality of intellectual change and the opportunity which it provides for more effective intervention in the process whereby structural forms are developed on behalf of subordinate groups and classes. A better understanding of the abstract principles which underlie the selection of certain organizational patterns rather than others may have some contribution to make to extending the scope for action in a social world where the political and economic domination of the capitalist class is experiencing something of an extended crisis of confidence.

The pluralist strategy

The intellectual priority for a pluralist strategy is the need to develop a more subtle appreciation of the complex social processes through which organizational arrangements are constituted. The reproduction of organizational structures is seen to be directly and inextricably tied to the social interaction taking place between participants. Thus a better understanding of the way in which the structuring of organizational arrangements is achieved can only be arrived at through a concerted focus upon how this process is practically accomplished in social situations over a period of time. It cannot be realized through an approach which analytically contrasts 'structural constraint' with 'social action' or one which presumes to identify a set of abstract and universal organizing principles or logics that determine practical interventions by social actors who are completely ignorant of the structural forces which produce their interventions.

The pluralist strategy is grounded in a model of the actor as a knowledgeable and pro-active agent who shapes his or her organizational setting through their interaction with other agents. Consequently, an interest in the 'interpretative schemes' or everyday stocks of knowledge which actors rely upon to produce and modify the social interaction in which they are engaged becomes a central theoretical and empirical concern for exponents of the pluralist strategy. Only through the detailed analysis of the interpretative schemes which facilitate the regularly recurring engagement in social interaction by social actors can the researcher hope to understand and explain the structures of social relations which are reproduced as a result of this engagement. The process of structuring is logically tied to the constituting of social interaction so that an understanding of the former is necessarily dependent on an in-depth exploration of the latter. This is aimed at revealing the interpretative frameworks which actors draw on and utilize in the production of meaningful social interaction. Concepts such as 'organizational structure' or 'control mechanism' only assume any descriptive or explanatory significance when they emerge from concrete social practices engaged in by social actors in specific socio-historical situations.

This does not lead exponents of the pluralist perspective to deny the fact of structural constraint and conditioning or its practical and theoretical importance. What it does commit them to is the fundamental ontological proposition that this conditioning is produced by knowledgeable human agents involved in meaningful interaction rather than by abstract structural forces or principles which are independent of that process and assume a determinant explanatory status. In this sense, the pluralist focus on the social processes through which organizational structures are reproduced and transformed rests on an ontological premise that necessarily requires a rejection of the conception of human beings as 'determined objects' informing the imperialist strategy. Indeed, the major aim for exponents of the pluralist strategy is to restore the concept of social interaction to a central theoretical role and practical significance in organizational analysis in sharp contrast to 'objectivist approaches that have effaced the knowledgeability of the human subject' (Giddens 1981: 65).

The theoretical response thought most appropriate to the realization of this objective is the continued diffusion of a wide range of theoretical approaches and research methodologies concentrating on different, but interrelated, aspects of the structuring process. This does not preclude the possibility of some degree of integration between distinctive approaches; neither does it suggest that legitimate attempts at partial synthesis should turn a blind eye to the basic philosophical and ideological differences which underpin the former. Rather, the support for a strategy of continued theoretical diffusion is based on the desire to prevent a premature theoretical closure which is likely to result if the comparative diversity of conceptual frameworks and research methodologies of recent years is superseded by a 'paradigmatic mentality' (Hammersley and Atkinson 1983) which demands intellectual imperialism or isolationism.

The pluralist case maintains that the inherent complexity and diversity of the structuring process demand the development and application of a sufficient range of theoretical approaches which will allow its subtleties and paradoxes to emerge. It rejects the search for comprehensive explanation which motivates the attempt at total theoretical synthesis and is extremely wary of the desire for theoretical exclusivity as a precondition for intellectual development. The former is seen to legitimate an extreme form of conceptual abstractionism and explanatory determinism. The latter is thought likely to produce a field of study populated by theoretical perspectives which are unable to face the rigours of critical scrutiny and debate because of this protected status.

Pluralism takes partial understanding and explanation as a defining characteristic of social scientific analysis. It prefers one-sided accounts which reveal part of the complexity and ambiguity of specific social phenomena such as organizations over the totalizing predilections of explanatory frameworks which willingly sacrifice empirical richness and conceptual subtlety on the altar of theoretical synthesis and explanatory comprehensibility. The choice between a range of theoretical perspectives which have been elaborated and worked through in a critical dialogue with alternative approaches provides one necessary guarantee for the continued development of an intellectual practice which is sensitive to the recurring dilemmas of organizational life.

In place of the revelatory imagery of imperialism and the relativistic leanings of isolationism, the pluralist strategy offers a range of contrasting insights into the characteristic contradictions and tensions embodied in contemporary work organizations. It recognizes the risks which have to be run in maintaining this position: an over-abundance of contending theoretical approaches; the severe difficulties encountered in attempting to achieve some degree of integration as a basis for cumulative growth in knowledge; the obstacles which stand in the way of a more meaningful dialogue between the intellectual community and the public as a result of the confusion created by the theoretical anarchy that seems to characterize the present state of organizational studies. Yet these risks are treated as an acceptable price to pay for the preservation of that degree of intellectual freedom and choice which the 'theoretical smorgasbord' of contemporary organizational studies offers.

One area in which exponents of the pluralist strategy identify a tendency towards intellectual convergence is around the development of a non-positivistic epistemological foundation for current and future work in the field of organizational studies. The attempt to construct a general theory of organizations based on a combination of empiricism and naturalism during the course of the 1950s and 1960s is seen to have petered out in the 1970s. This has been replaced by a number of epistemological interventions on the part of organization theorists who have an interest in the philosophical foundations of organizational analysis which stress the interpretative schemes and procedures which inform all scientific investigation whether in the natural or social worlds (for a recent review see Bernstein 1983).

However, this collective rejection of positivism has not produced a single epistemological doctrine around which organizational theorists can unite. Indeed, this development would be rather surprising from a pluralistic perspective, given its belief in the necessarily disputatious quality of intellectual argument whether at the philosophical, theoretical, methodological, or ideological levels of discourse. Thus the continuing debate over the relative merits of 'conventionalist' and 'realist' philosophies of science (Keat and Urry 1975) proceeds between organizational theorists who are ostensibly committed to a pluralistic strategy of long-term intellectual development (Astley and Van de Ven 1984).

On the whole, advocates of the pluralist strategy have been suspicious of too close a relationship between intellectual analysis and technical interests in the field of organizational studies. Too intimate a relationship is seen to compromise the intellectual integrity of a field of study which has undergone a process of historical development dominated by technical and managerial concerns up until the last twenty years or so. On the other hand, pluralism does not demand the strict institutional and intellectual separation between theoretical and practical concerns advocated by the exponents of isolationism.

Indeed, it sees a continuing interconnection between analysis and practice as an inevitable and positive feature of future development in the field. What the pluralist strategy requires is that this relationship be managed through a more explicit recognition of the necessary tensions which exist between theoretical and technical concerns, and a most sophisticated appreciation of the practical methods through which the resulting conflict may be regulated. In responding to a far wider range of practical interests than has traditionally been the case with a 'technocratically oriented' organizational analysis, future generations of researchers and writers will have to get used to the unavoidable tensions between the painstaking search for knowledge and the pressure for something that works. They will have to develop social arrangements and communicative structures in which a number of mutually suspicious groups may be able to engage in a joint search for improved understanding and enlightenment. Researchers will need to treat organizational members less as respondents and more as informants who need to be regularly exposed to, and encouraged to comment on and use, the findings which social investigation generates. Members will need to be less distrustful of and more sympathetic to the 'peculiar' interests and needs of the researchers who will be amongst them on a regular basis.

Pluralists realize that the obstacles standing in the way of a more meaningful dialogue between the research community and the organizational community are formidable, but their arguments indicate a preference for practical action over academic rhetoric extolling the virtues of 'humanistically oriented' research programmes *ad nauseam*.

The pluralist strategy rests on a developmental model of conceptual change in organizational analysis which is focused on the dynamic interaction between intellectual community and social context. This model indicates that the elaboration and assessment of new ideas and methods cannot be understood, much less explained, without an appreciation of the contextual factors which shape the direction and outcome of conceptual innovations. However, it attempts to avoid the reductionist leanings of the imperialist strategy by striking a balance between the internal disciplinary constraints and opportunities generated through intellectual practice and the external conditions that influence the historical sequences by which new ideas are proposed, developed, modified, and decay.

In a similar vein, Toulmin (1972) has argued that a serious interest in the patterns of events through which conceptual frameworks are created, develop historically, and fall into disuse is best pursued through an analytical model which forges connections between disciplinary procedures and socio-historical processes. His model takes theoretical perspectives, rather than isolated concepts, as its basic unit of analysis and attempts to trace the complex interaction between rational procedures and contextual processes through which these perspectives come to displace one another in the course of an intellectual discipline's historical development. Rather than present a revolutionary explanation of intellectual change which sets out to show how entire paradigmatic frameworks succeed one another, the pluralist strategy attempts to provide a narrative account of how theoretical perspectives become progressively transformed. While the former stresses the discontinuous nature of conceptual change, the latter emphasizes the continuities which can be discerned when innovative perspectives displace the currently accepted wisdom within a particular field of study.

This development model suggests that the analysis of intellectual change needs to focus on the factors which encourage the carriers of an intellectual tradition to propose new ways of moving ahead. It also directs attention to those factors which lead them to select certain innovations in preference to others as a basis for modifying the tradition with which they are identified. In both cases, the developmental model presumes an interaction between disciplinary and contextual factors rather than treating either as having a decisive independent effect on the eventual outcome.

In certain respects, it is possible to argue that the pluralist strategy exercises a pervasive, if partial, influence within contemporary organizational analysis to the extent that many of those advocating alternative strategies still retain vestiges of the former in their arguments. In particular, those who argue for isolationism at the meta-theoretical level are prepared to court pluralism at the theoretical level; paradigm intermediation may be firmly rejected, but the proliferation of metaphorical alternatives is just as strongly supported (Morgan 1980). Others accept the basically antithetical nature of paradigm commitments in organizational analysis, while advocating some degree of theoretical integration around central issues concerned with the nature and structuring of organizations (Astley and Van de Ven 1983). Indeed, there is something to the claim that 'we are all pluralists now' in some degree or another.

However, the commitment to a pluralist strategy of future intellectual development in organizational analysis is unlikely to be fully supported by those who approach the issue with a 'paradigm mentality' that emphasizes the intellectual and ideological incommensurability of different world views. This mentality rules out the partial reconciliation between contending perspectives and approaches supported by exponents of the pluralist strategy. In stressing the overriding ideological function of intellectual analysis, it also excludes the rational assessment of conflicting approaches through a process of critical scrutiny and debate. In other words, it is ill equipped to steer a middle course between structural determinism and cognitive relativism which is the primary mission for the pluralist strategy.

A number of theorists who have already been discussed at some length in this book can be regarded as prime exponents of the pluralist strategy, such as Burns, Crozier, Gouldner, and Child. However, it should be evident by now that the pluralist strategy resonates most strongly with the historical and theoretical analysis which has been elaborated in previous chapters of this book. The following section attempts to provide an overall evaluation of the four developmental strategies which have been outlined in this chapter from the perspective provided by the preceding analysis. A diagrammatic summary of the four strategies is provided in *Figure 3.*

Evaluation

The major danger which threatens the comparative intellectual pluralism and innovation released by the decline of the functionalist orthodoxy and the flowering of alternative perspectives is the 'paradigm mentality' which infects a great deal of contemporary discussion and debate. This mentality grossly overstates the philosophical and ideological incompatibilities between different conceptual frameworks. It directly encourages a form of intellectual isolationism and protectionism which severely circumscribes the potential for creative theoretical development through the imaginative confrontation between contending approaches. In addition, this mentality also generates a relatively static and myopic vision of organization theory's historical development in which the subtle and complex interaction between intellectual change and social context tends to be ignored in favour of a single-minded concentration on internal factors. Finally, in denying the possibility of rational comparison and assessment across paradigm boundaries this mode of thinking facilitates an extreme form of cognitive relativism in which intellectual production and evaluation are seen to be subordinate to ideologically mediated interests that contend in a wider social arena.

This critique does not provide an indirect justification for a mindless integrationism in which the intellectual and practical significance of the domain assumptions underlying substantive organizational theories is either blithely ignored or strenuously denied in favour of an arid 'methodological puritanism' which quickly degenerates into technical manipulation bereft of theoretical insight or meaning (on this latter point, see Whitley's critique of the Aston studies in Whitley 1977a). Indeed, the analysis conducted within these covers has continually emphasized the crucial importance of an appreciation of underlying philosophical and ideological commitments for an understanding of intellectual development in organization studies.

Figure 3 Alternative developmental strategies

strategy	central intellectual issue	theoretical response	sources of consensus and conflict	'analysis'/ 'practice' relationship	model of conceptual change
Integrationist	organizational structures	reconciliation	methodology	collaboration	evolutionary
Isolationist	organizational mechanisms	closure	ontology	separation	exclusionary
Imperialist	organizational principles	incorporation	ideology	fusion	revolutionary
Pluralist	organizational processes	diffusion	epistemology	tension	developmental

However, the analysis presented here suggests that the 'paradigm mentality' which is so strongly entrenched in current considerations of future intellectual development in organizational analysis is the most intractable obstacle standing in the way of progress towards an intellectual community in which a meaningful dialogue between conflicting approaches can take place. In the concluding pages of his critical review of post-empiricist philosophy, Bernstein argues that:

'Such a vision [of rational dialogue] is not antithetical to an appreciation of the depth and pervasiveness of conflict – of the agón – which characterizes our theoretical and practical lives. On the contrary, this vision is a response to the irreducibility of conflict grounded in human plurality. But plurality does not mean that we are limited to being separate individuals with irreducible subjective interests. Rather it means that we seek to discover some common ground to reconcile differences through debate, conversation and dialogue.'

(Bernstein 1983: 223)

He also suggests that the beginnings of this 'common ground' through which the deterministic predilections of objectivism and the reductionist tendencies of relativism are to be most forcefully resisted can be discovered in the concept of 'practical discourse' and its implications for the practice of social analysis. Practical discourse, Bernstein suggests, is evident when 'there is choice, deliberation, interpretation, judicious weighing and application of "universal criteria", and even rational disagreement about which criteria are most relevant and important' (Bernstein 1983: 172). It is a form of practical decision-taking which is reflected in the social practices in which communities are collectively engaged and reinforced by the shared understandings and experiences which bind the members together. Far from being inimical to conflict or attempting to impose a unitary perspective on all participants, practical discourse enables a rational dialogue to take place between contending viewpoints without reducing them to emotional spasms or the ideological weapons of sectional interests. The open contest between contending perspectives strengthens and revitalizes the community through the continuous revision of interests and opinions by rational means:

'What is to count as evidence and reasons to support a proposed theory can be rationally contested – even what is to count as proper criticism. Hunches, intuitions, guesses all have a role to play in scientific inquiry, but the scientist never escapes the obligation to support his or her judgements with the best possible reasons and arguments. Communal decisions and choices are not arbitrary or merely subjective. There may be losses and gains in the replacement of one scientific tradition by another, but science does progress.'

(Bernstein 1983: 172)

This may seem a somewhat fragile and slender foundation on which to build a common strategy of intellectual development which is appreciative of the formidable difficulties which lie in the way of comparative assessment and evaluation of conflicting theoretical perspectives. However, it seems to offer a much more attractive prospect than the grudging support for intellectual apartheid advocated by exponents of isolationism or the all-encompassing theoretical synthesis promised by supporters of the imperialist strategy. A Hobson's choice between separate intellectual development or total intellectual unification is not the only possibility available.

If we are inclined to make the attempt to escape from the 'paradigm mentality' which is so influential within contemporary organizational analysis, then we must be prepared to countenance the risks that this involves. A judicious balance between incremental conceptual integration and contained theoretical pluralism would seem to offer the best prospect for developing the field of organizational analysis as an intellectual community in which practical discourse can flourish. This may seem rather unexciting, not to say downright boring, when compared to the dazzling prospectus on offer from those who have fixed their gaze on the paradigmatic discontinuities which are to be unearthed through archaeological excavations of organization theory's intellectual past. However, Bernstein's plea that we should 'learn to think and act more like the fox than the hedgehog[30] – to seize upon the experiences and struggles in which there are still the glimmerings of solidarity and the promise of dialogical communities in which there can be genuine mutual participation and where reciprocal wooing and persuasion can prevail' (Bernstein 1983: 228)-would seem to provide a sensible guideline for

---

30 On the distinction between the fox and the hedgehog see Berlin (1969). On the whole, hedgehogs seem to have been rather more influential in the development of organizational analysis than foxes.

us to follow in a field of study in which the unavoidable ambiguities and dilemmas of organizational life form the substantive core for our intellectual endeavours.

Organizational analysis has travelled some intellectual distance since the relative theoretical sterility of the heyday of the functionalist orthodoxy between the late 1930s and the early 1960s. Postinterregnum organizational studies are a much more pluralistic and innovative affair. The conventional model of formal organization as a rational instrument of technical control has been subverted from within and a range of interesting alternatives have been developed. Nevertheless, the intellectual diversity and uncertainty characteristic of the present situation invite new attempts at theoretical synthesis or unification, or they encourage a grim determination to 'cut adrift' from the mainstream of intellectual development in the search for theoretical self-fulfilment. The analysis provided in this book suggests that both of these understandable but avoidable tendencies should be resisted in favour of a developmental strategy which looks for limited theoretical reconciliation where it is feasible and regards intellectual pluralism as a precondition for practical discourse rather than a licence for theoretical anarchy.

Summary

This chapter has provided a review and assessment of the major strategies of intellectual development which are on offer within contemporary organizational analysis. It has argued that the drift towards intellectual and ideological polarization encouraged by the 'paradigm mentality' which currently infects organizational analysis should be resisted in favour of a pluralistic strategy which attempts to strike a sensible balance between incremental conceptual integration and contained theoretical proliferation.

It is within the wider intellectual frame of reference provided by this developmental strategy that the conceptual framework constructed and applied in the previous two chapters should be located. The former also provides a perspective on intellectual change and development within organizational analysis which has informed the historical reconstruction attempted in the first three chapters. As one contribution to the furtherance of a pluralist strategy in organizational analysis, this book is written in the confident expectation that there will be many others to follow.

Conclusions

In the course of developing the analysis presented in this book a fundamental intellectual dichotomy has emerged which is of far greater significance for the interpretation and assessment of organizational analysis as an intellectual practice than the paradigmatic divergences emphasized by other commentators. This underlying intellectual cleavage relates to the manner in which the historical location and intellectual role of organizational analysis are characterized and the implications of this characterization for the practice of organizational analysis.

On one side are those who have treated organizational analysis as a constituent element of that general body of socio-political theory which has been developed in Western society since the time of Plato. On the other side stand those who have interpreted organizational analysis as a distinctive disciplinary or technical specialism which began to take shape as a social-scientific hybrid in America during the late 1930s and early 1940s.

Those who regard organizational analysis as a branch of Western socio-political theory emphasize the deep intellectual and historical roots of such an intellectual practice in the struggle to understand and explain the dynamics of institutional change beginning with the Greeks. For them, organizational theory is part and parcel of an evolving grammar and vocabulary aimed at improving our understanding of socio-political practices and the characteristic human dilemmas which they embody.

This position is clearly reflected in the writing of Wolin (1961), Stretton (1969), and, more recetly, Ramos (1981). It firmly rejects an instrumentalist view of organizational studies as a technical specialism geared to the needs and problems of a managerial elite struggling to cope with the seemingly insurmountable complexity of organizational life. The rejection of this interpretation rests on the contention that instrumentalism merely reinforces an uncritical acceptance of the organizational status quo. In Ramos's phrase, it turns organizational analysts into a breed of 'academic clerks' who document and record a pre-reflective view of organizational reality (Ramos 1981: 100). The latter is worked up into an 'official theory' of organization consumed by students in schools of business and public administration without as much as a second thought as to its empirical veracity and intellectual validity.[31]

Supporters of a technicist reading of organization theory's historical location and intellectual role regard their protagonists' obsessive interest in archaic academic disputes with a mixture of morbid intellectual curiosity and outright ideological disdain. They tend to treat such archaic intellectual ramblings as an unpleasant historical residue of an applied discipline which has long cut itself free from the debilitating limitations imposed by academic rectitude and established its credentials as a useful decision-making tool in the hands of men of affairs.[32]

The analysis developed in this book has shown that the historical development of organizational theory is impregnated with themes, issues, problems, categories, and concepts which are integral components of the Western tradition of socio-political thought which stretches over a period of more than two millennia. While a number of attempts have been made to obscure, if not to deny, the historical roots of organizational analysis in this intellectual tradition, none

---

31 The distinction between 'official theory' and 'real theory' in organizational analysis is also outlined in Anthony (1984). The former refers to the model of the business organization as a rational instrument of economic calculation and control, while the latter emphasizes the essential nature of business organization as a human community generated and sustained through shared normative and symbolic systems. Anthony further suggests that the ideological and pedagogical utility of the former is coming under increasingly critical scrutiny as the theoretical and practical significance of the latter grows. This argument is also advanced, in a rather different theoretical idiom, in Reed (1984).

32 For a recent elaboration of this position see Hood and Dunsire (1981).

have been able to sustain a technicist interpretation that excludes any consideration of the themes and problems which crystallize within the former. The more immediate historical origins of organizational analysis in the institutional dislocations engendered by the political and industrial revolutions of the eighteenth and nineteenth centuries can now be seen as part of a much larger process of intellectual maturation in which successive generations of social and political theorists attempt to come to terms with institutional crisis and its social consequences.

Insofar as they reinforce a general move to re-establish contact with this broader tradition of socio-political theorizing, the arguments advanced in this book are in keeping with the prevailing intellectual mood and tenor of contemporary analysis. However, the case developed in the previous chapters of this book has also included a warning against over-indulgence in the kind of intellectual 'tub-thumping' which threatens the return of a quasi-scientific instrumentalism as dangerous (if not more so) as the positivism it has overturned. This warning is offered in support of a conception of the human sciences which is both intellectually defensible and practically efficacious. Such a conception has found one of its clearest expressions in Dunn's brief, but pungent, review of Western political thought:

'To recognize the intrinsic fluidity of the epistemic field of the sciences of man and to recognize the central role of counterfactual analysis,[33] not merely in validating the candidates for explanatory laws within these sciences, but also, and at least equally importantly, in characterizing adequately what is humanly the case at a particular time, enforces on us a very different understanding of the character of these sciences from that which at present prevails. It demands that we conceive them as irretrievably moral sciences, cognitive enterprises committed to the necessarily *humble* assessment of social and individual potentiality under extraordinarily refractory conditions, sciences which are not entitled to and which should not expect the protection of professional authority and

---

33 By 'counterfactual analysis' Dunn is referring to the method of positing and evaluating opposed factual conditions and outcomes to those entailed and predicted by explanatory theories. For a further statement of the nature and significance of counterfactual analysis in the social sciences see Runciman (1983).

routinization, but which place awesome demands for sensitivity
and moral self-discipline on those who aspire to practise them.'

(Dunn 1979: 103)

A conception of organizational analysis as a moral science or
intellectual practice focused on the ways in which social practices are
assembled to form coherent and sustainable institutional structures
and human communities need not fall prey to the intellectual para-
lysis or overbearing ideological disputation which seems to characterize so much of contemporary writing in the field. Rather, it can
attempt to get on with the job of formulating explanatory accounts
of organizational life which 'achieve an understanding of social
behaviour and social institutions which is different from that current
among the people through whose conduct the institutions exist; an
understanding which is not merely different but new and better'
(Burns 1970: 72).

Burns's characterization of sociological explanation is framed
within a conception of sociology as an intellectual practice attempting to provide a critical analysis of conventional patterns of thinking
and acting: 'It is the business of sociologists to conduct a critical
debate with the public about its equipment of social institutions'
(Burns 1970: 72). He thought that engagement in this debate was of
crucial importance at a time (the second half of the 1960s) when the
pace of scientific and technological change demanded a better understanding of human behaviour in all its contexts as one contribution to
overcoming 'the disparity between man's understanding and control
of nature and his insight into and command over his own conduct
and his own affairs' (Burns 1970: 73).

This task is as pressing at the present time (if not more so) as it was
when Burns originally developed these ideas. Organizational analysis has a substantial contribution to make in improving our understanding of organizational forms and their impact on organizational
action. It is in a very different intellectual condition now than it was
little more than ten years ago; a condition of upheaval over fundamentals and their implications for the practice of analysis. The
intellectual and social space which has been created as a result of this
continuing debate over the terms and conditions under which
organizational analysis can be practised needs to be turned to good
account in furthering the dialogue over institutional equipment. It
would indeed be a travesty, not to say a farce, if we were simply to
exchange one intellectual straitjacket for another when the opportunity for widening and deepening the dialogue is still there.

References

Abrams, P. (1982) *Historical Sociology*. Somerset: Open Books.
Albrow, M. (1968) The Study of Organizations – Objectivity or Bias? In J. Gould (ed.) *Penguin Social Sciences Survey*. Harmondsworth: Penguin. Reprinted in G. Salaman and K. Thompson (eds) (1973) *People and Organizations*. London: Longman.
Albrow, M. (1974) Is a Science of Organizations Possible? In *Perspectives on Organizations*. DT 352 Unit 16. Open University: Longman.
Allaire, Y. and Firsirotu, M. (1984) Theories of Organizational Culture. *Organizational Studies* 5(3): 192–226.
Allen, V. L. (1975) *Social Analysis: A Marxist Critique and Alternative*. London: Longman.
Anthony, P. D. (1984) Managerial Culture. Mimeograph. University College, Cardiff.
Astley, W. G. and Van de Ven, H. (1983) Central Perspectives and Debates in Organization Theory. *Administrative Science Quarterly* 28(2): 245–73.
Attwell, P. (1974) Ethnomethodology since Garfinkel. *Theory and Society* (1): 179–210.
Barnard, C. (1938) *The Functions of the Executive*. Cambridge, Mass.: Harvard University Press.
Bauman, Z. (1973) On the Philosophical Status of Ethnomethodology. *Sociological Review* 21(1): 5–23.
Bell, D. (1960) *The End of Ideology*. New York: Collier Macmillan.
Bell, D. (1973) *The Coming of Post-Industrial Society*. New York: Basic Books.
Benson, J. K. (1975) The Inter-Organizational Network as a Political Economy. *Administrative Science Quarterly* 20(2): 229–49.
Benson, J. K. (1977a) Organizations: A Dialectical View. *Administrative Science Quarterly* 22(1): 1–21.

Benson, J. K. (1977b) Innovation and Crisis in Organizational Analysis. *Sociological Quarterly* 18 (Winter): 229–49.
Berlin, I. (1966) Does Political Theory Still Exist? In G. Laslett and W. Runciman (eds) *Philosophy, Politics and Society*. Oxford: Oxford University Press.
Berlin, I. (1969) Historical Inevitability. In I. Berlin, *Four Essays on Liberty*. Oxford: Oxford University Press.
Bernier, R. (1983) *Political Judgement*. London: Methuen.
Bernstein, R. J. (1983) *Beyond Objectivism and Relativism*. Oxford: Basil Blackwell.
Bhaskar, R. (1978) *A Realist Theory of Science*. Brighton: Harvester.
Binns, D. (1977) *Beyond the Sociology of Conflict*. London: Macmillan.
Bittner, E. (1965) The Concept of Organization. *Social Research* 32(3): 239–55. Reprinted in G. Salaman and K. Thompson (eds) (1973) *People and Organizations*. London: Longman.
Bittner, E. (1967) The Police on Skid Row: A Study of Peace Keeping. *American Sociological Review* 32(5): 699–715.
Blackburn, R. (1972) The New Capitalism. In R. Blackburn (ed.) *Ideology in Social Science*. London: Fontana.
Blau, P. (1955) *The Dynamics of Bureaucracy*. Chicago: University of Chicago Press (revised edition 1963).
Blau, P. (1968) The Study of Formal Organizations. In T. Parsons (ed.) *American Sociology*. New York: Basic Books.
Blau, P. (1974) *On the Nature of Organizations*. New York: Wiley.
Blau, P. and Schoenherr, R. A. (1971) *The Structure of Organizations*. New York: Basic Books.
Bordieu, R. (1977) *Outline of a Theory of Practice*. Cambridge: Cambridge University Press.
Bradley, D. and Reed, M. (1980) The Study of Organizational Change and the Concept of Practice. Mimeograph. University of Strathclyde.
Bradley, D. and Wilkie, R. (1980) Radical Organization Theory. *British Journal of Sociology* 31(4): 514–79.
Braverman, H. (1974) *Labour and Monopoly Capitalism: The Degradation of Work in the Twentieth Century*. New York: Monthly Review Press.
Bucher, R. and Stelling, J. (1969) Characteristics of Professional Organizations. *Journal of Health and Social Behaviour* 10(1): 3–15.
Burawoy, M. (1979) *Manufacturing Consent*. Chicago: University of Chicago Press.
Burns, T. (1961) Micropolitics: Mechanisms of Institutional Change. *Administrative Science Quarterly* 6(3): 257–81.
Burns, T. (1963) Industry in a New Age. *New Society* 18: 17–20.
Burns, T. (1966) Introduction to second edition of *Management of Innovation*. London: Tavistock Publications.
Burns, T. (1969) On the Plurality of Social Systems. In T. Burns (ed.) *Industrial Man*. Harmondsworth: Penguin.
Burns, T. (1970) Sociological Explanation. In D. Emmet and A. MacIntyre (eds) *Sociological Theory and Philosophical Analysis*. London: Macmillan.

Burns, T. (1974) On the Rationale of the Corporate System. In R. Marris (ed.) *The Corporate Society*. London: Macmillan.

Burns, T. (1977) *The B.B.C.* London: Macmillan.

Burns, T. (1980) Sovereignty, Interests and Bureaucracy in the Modern State. *British Journal of Sociology* 31(4): 491–506.

Burns, T. (1981) A Comparative Study of Administrative Structure and Organizational Processes in Selected Areas of the National Health Service. Social Science Research Council Report. HRP.6725.

Burns, T. and Stalker, G. M. (1961) *The Management of Innovation*. London: Tavistock Publications.

Burrell, G. (1980) Radical Organization Theory. In D. Dunkerley and G. Salaman (eds) *The International Yearbook of Organizational Studies*. London: Routledge & Kegan Paul.

Burrell, G. and Morgan, G. (1979) *Sociological Paradigms and Organizational Analysis*. London: Heinemann.

Carey, A. (1967) The Hawthorne Studies: A Radical Criticism. *American Sociological Review* 32(3): 403–16.

Child, J. (1969) *British Management Thought*. London: Allen & Unwin.

Child, J. (1973a) Organizational Structure, Environment and Performance: The Role of Strategic Choice. In G. Salaman and K. Thompson (eds) *People and Organizations*. London: Longman.

Child, J. (1973b) Organization: A Choice for Man. In J. Child (ed.) *Man and Organization*. London: Allen & Unwin.

Cicourel, A. V. (1964) *Method and Measurement in Sociology*. New York: Free Press.

Cicourel, A. V. (1968) *The Social Organization of Social Justice*. New York: Free Press.

Clegg, S. (1975) *Power, Rule and Domination*. London: Routledge & Kegan Paul.

Clegg, S. (1977) Power, Organization Theory, Marx and Critique. In S. Clegg and D. Dunkerley (eds) *Critical Issues in Organizations*. London: Routledge & Kegan Paul.

Clegg, S. and Dunkerley, D. (1977) *Critical Issues in Organizations*. London: Routledge & Kegan Paul.

Clegg, S. and Dunkerley, D. (1980) *Organization, Class and Control*. London: Routledge & Kegan Paul.

Cohen, G. A. (1978) *Karl Marx's Theory of History: A Defence*. Oxford: Oxford University Press.

Collins, R. (1980) Weber's Last Theory of Capitalism: A Systematization. *American Sociological Review* 45(6): 925–42.

Crouch, C. and Pizzorne, A. (eds) (1978) *The Resurgence of Class Conflict in Western Europe since 1968*: vol. 1, *National Reports*; vol. 2, *Comparative Studies*. London: Macmillan.

Crozier, M. (1964) *The Bureaucratic Phenomenon*. Chicago: University of Chicago Press.

Crozier, M. (1969) *The Stalled Society*. New York: Viking Press.

Crozier, M. (1974) Recent Trends and Future Trends for Sociology of

Organizations. In M. Archer (ed.) *Current Research in Sociology*. Paris: Mounton Hague.

Crozier, M. and Frieberg, M. (1980) *The Actor and the System*. Chicago: University of Chicago Press.

Dahrendorf, R. (1959) *Class and Class Conflict in Industrial Society*. London: Routledge & Kegan Paul.

Dahrendorf, R. (1975) *The New Liberty*. London: Routledge & Kegan Paul.

Dalton, M. (1959) *Men Who Manage*. New York: Wiley.

Dawe, A. (1970) The Two Sociologies. *British Journal of Sociology* 21(2): 207–18.

Dawe, A. (1979) Theories of Social Action. In T. Bottomore and R. Nisbet (eds) *A History of Sociological Analysis*. London: Heinemann.

Day, R. A. and Day, J. V. (1977) A Review of the Current State of Negotiated Order Theory: An Appreciation and a Critique. *Sociological Quarterly* 18 (Winter): 126–42.

Dickson, D. (1974) *Alternative Technology and the Politics of Technical Change*. Glasgow: Fontana.

Donaldson, L. (1976) Woodward, Technology, Organizational Structure and the Universal Generalization. *Journal of Management Studies* 13 (October): 255–73.

Donaldson, L. (1982) Comments on 'Contingency and Choice in Organization Theory'. *Organization Studies* 3(1): 65–72.

Donzelot, J. (1980) *The Policing of Families*. London: Hutchinson.

Dore, R. (1973) *British Factory – Japanese Factory*. London: Allen and Unwin.

Douglas, J. (1971) *Understanding Everyday Life*. London: Routledge & Kegan Paul.

Dreitzel, H. P. (ed.) (1970) *Patterns of Communicative Behaviour*. London: Macmillan.

Dunn, J. (1979) *Western Political Theory in the Face of the Future*. Cambridge: Cambridge University Press.

Durkheim, E. (1938) *The Rules of Sociological Method*. New York: Collier Macmillan.

Edwards, R. (1979) *Contested Terrain*. London: Heinemann.

Eisen, A. (1978) The Meanings and Confusions of Weberian 'Rationality'. *British Journal of Sociology* 29(1): 57–70.

Eldridge, J. E. T. (1971) *Sociology and Industrial Life*. London: Nelson.

Eldridge, J. E. T. (1980) *Recent British Sociology*. London: Macmillan.

Eldridge, J. E. T. and Crombie, A. (1977) *A Sociology of Organizations*. London: Allen & Unwin.

Elger, A. (1975) Industrial Organizations: A Processual Perspective. In J. B. McKinley (ed.) *Processing People: Cases in Organizational Behaviour*. New York: Holt, Rinehart, & Winston.

Emerson, R. T. (1962) Power Dependence Relations. *American Sociological Review* 27(1): 31–41.

Emmet, D. and MacIntyre, A. (1970) *Sociological Theory and Philosophical Analysis*. London: Macmillan.

Etzioni, A. (1961) *A Comparative Analysis of Complex Organizations*. New York: Free Press (second edition 1975).

Feldman, A. and Moore, W. (1969) Industrialization and Industrialism: Convergence and Differentiation. In W. Faunce and W. Form (eds) *Comparative Perspectives on Industrial Society.* Boston: Little, Brown.

Filmer, P., Phillipson, M., Silverman, D. and Walsh, D. (1972) *New Directions in Sociological Theory.* London: Collier Macmillan.

Friedman, A. L. (1977) *Industry and Labour: Class Struggle at Work and Monopoly Capitalism.* London: Macmillan.

Friedrichs, R. W. (1970) *A Sociology of Sociology.* New York: Free Press.

Galbraith, J. K. (1967) *The New Industrial State.* Harmondsworth: Penguin.

Garfinkel, H. (1967) *Studies in Ethnomethodology.* Englewood Cliffs: Prentice-Hall.

Geertz, C. (1979) From the Native's Point of View: On the Nature of Anthropological Understanding. In P. Rainbow and W. M. Sullivan (eds) *Interpretive Social Science: A Reader.* Berkeley: University of California Press.

Gerth, H. H. and Mills, C. W. (1952) A Marx for the Managers. In R. K. Merton *et al.* (eds) *Reader in Bureaucracy.* New York: Collier Macmillan.

Geuss, R. (1981) *The Idea of a Critical Theory: Habermas and the Frankfurt School.* Cambridge: Cambridge University Press.

Giddens, A. (1971) *Capitalism and Modern Social Theory.* Cambridge: Cambridge University Press.

Giddens, A. (1973) *The Class Structure of the Advanced Societies.* London: Hutchinson.

Giddens, A. (1976) Classical Social Theory and the Origins of Modern Sociology. *American Journal of Sociology* 81(6): 703–29.

Giddens, A. (1977) *Studies in Social and Political Theory.* London: Hutchinson.

Giddens, A. (1979) *Central Problems in Social Theory.* London: Macmillan.

Giddens, A. (1981) *A Contemporary Critique of Historical Materialism.* London: Macmillan.

Gidlow, B. (1972) Ethnomethodology: A New Name for Old Practices. *British Journal of Sociology* 23(4): 395–405.

Goffman, E. (1959) *Asylums.* Harmondsworth: Penguin.

Goldman, P. and Van Houten, D. (1980) Bureaucracy and Domination: Managerial Strategy in Turn-of-the-Century American Industry. In G. Salaman and D. Dunkerley (eds) *International Yearbook of Organizational Studies.* London: Routledge & Kegan Paul.

Goldthorpe, J. H. (1964) Social Stratification in Industrial Society. In P. Halmos (ed.) *The Development of Industrial Societies.* Keele: University of Keele.

Goldthorpe, J. H. (1971) Theories of Industrial Societies: Reflections on the Recrudescence of Historicism and the Future of Futurology. *European Journal of Sociology* 12(2): 236–88.

Goldthorpe, J. H. (1973) A Revolution in Sociology? *Sociology* 7(4): 449–62.

Gospel, H. (1983) Managerial Structure and Strategies: An Introduction. In H. Gospel and C. Littler (eds) *Managerial Strategies and Industrial Relations.* London: Heinemann.

Gouldner, A. (1954a) *Patterns of Industrial Bureaucracy*. New York: Collier Macmillan.

Gouldner, A. (1954b) *Wildcat Strikes*. New York: Antioch Press.

Gouldner, A. (1959) Organizational Analysis. In R. K. Merton (ed.) *Sociology Today*. New York: Basic Books.

Gouldner, A. (1971) *The Coming Crisis of Western Sociology*. London: Heinemann.

Gouldner, A. (1973) *For Sociology: Renewal and Critique in Sociology Today*. Harmondsworth: Allen Lane.

Gouldner, A. (1976) *The Dialectic of Ideology and Technology*. London: Macmillan.

Gouldner, A. (1980) *The Two Marxisms*. London: Macmillan.

Habermas, J. (1972) *Knowledge and Human Interests*. London: Heinemann.

Habermas, J. (1974) *Theory and Practice*. London: Heinemann.

Habermas, J. (1976) *Legitimation Crisis*. London: Heinemann.

Haddon, R. (1973) Foreword to *Industrialism and Industrial Man* by C. Kerr, J. T. Dunlop, F. Harbison and C. A. Myers. Harmondsworth: Penguin.

Hall, S. (1980) Cultural Studies: Two Paradigms. *Media, Culture and Society* (2): 57–72.

Hammersley, M. and Atkinson, P. (1983) *Ethnography: Principles in Practice*. London: Tavistock Publications.

Harré, R. (1979) *Social Being: A Theory for Social Psychology*. Oxford: Basil Blackwell.

Harris, C. C. (1969) Reform in a Normative Organization. *Sociological Review* 17(2): 167–85.

Harris, C. C. (1980) *Fundamental Concepts and the Sociological Enterprise*. London: Allen & Unwin.

Heydebrand, W. (1977) Organizational Contradictions in Public Bureaucracies: Toward a Marxian Theory of Organizations. *Sociological Quarterly* 18 (Winter): 83–107.

Hollis, M. (1977) *Models of Man*. Cambridge: Cambridge University Press.

Hood, C. and Dunsire, A. (1981) *Bureaumetrics*. Farnborough: Gower.

Hyman, R. (1972) *Strikes*. London: Fontana (third edition 1984).

Jehenson, R. (1973) A Phenomenological Approach to the Study of Organizations. In G. Psthas (ed.) *Phenomenological Sociology*. New York: Wiley.

Jessop, B. (1982) *The Capitalist State*. Oxford: Martin Robertson.

Karpik, L. (1977) Technological Capitalism. In S. Clegg and D. Dunkerley (eds) *Critical Issues in Organizations*. London: Routledge & Kegan Paul.

Karpik, L. (1978) Organizations, Institutions and History. In K. Karpik (ed.) *Organizational Environment: Theory, Issues and Reality*. London: Sage.

Keat, R. (1981) *The Politics of Social Theory*. Oxford: Basil Blackwell.

Keat, R. and Urry, J. (1975) *Social Theory as Science*. London: Routledge & Kegan Paul.

Kerr, C. and Fisher, L. (1957) Plant Sociology: The Elite and The Aborigines. In M. Komarovsky (ed.) *Common Frontiers of the Social Sciences*. Chicago: Free Press.

Kerr, C., Dunlop, J. T., Harbison, F., and Myers, C. A. (1960) *Industrialism and Industrial Man*. Cambridge, Mass.: Harvard University Press.

Krupp, S. (1961) *Patterns in Organizational Analysis*. Philadelphia: Chilton.

Kuhn, T. (1962) *The Structure of Scientific Revolutions*. Chicago: University of Chicago Press (revised edition 1970).

Kumar, K. (1978) *Prophecy and Progress: The Sociology of Industrial and Post-Industrial Society*. Harmondsworth: Penguin.

Lammers, C. J. (1974) The State of Organizational Sociology in the United States: Travel Impressions by a Dutch Cousin. *Administrative Science Quarterly* 19(4): 422–30.

Lammers, C. J. (1981) Contributions of Organizational Sociology, Parts I and II. *Organization Studies* 2(3): 267–86 and 361–76.

Landsberger, H. A. (1958) *Hawthorne Revisited*. New York: Cornell University Press.

Lane, D. (1977) Marxist Class Conflict Analyses of State Socialist Society. In R. Scase (ed.) *Industrial Society: Class, Clevage and Control*. London: Allen & Unwin.

Lassman, P. (1974) Phenomenological Perspectives in Sociology. In J. Rex (ed.) *Approaches to Sociology*. London: Routledge & Kegan Paul.

Lawrence, P. R. and Lorsch, J. W. (1967) *Organization and Environment*. Cambridge, Mass.: Harvard University Press.

Lipset, S. M. (1960) *Political Man*. London: Heinemann.

Littler, C. (1982) *The Development of the Labour Process in Capitalist Societies*. London: Heinemann.

Littler, C. and Salaman, G. (1982) Bravermania and Beyond: Recent Theories of the Labour Process. *Sociology* 16(2): 251–69.

Lukes, S. (1977a) Alienation and Anomie. In S. Lukes, *Essays in Social Theory*. London: Macmillan.

Lukes, S. (1977b) Power and Structure. In S. Lukes, *Essays in Social Theory*. London: Macmillan.

McDonald, G. and Pettit, P. (1981) *Semantics and Social Science*. London: Routledge & Kegan Paul.

MacIntyre, A. (1981) *After Virtue: A Study in Moral Theory*. London: Duckworth.

McNeil, K. (1978) Understanding Organizational Power: Building on the Weberian Legacy. *Administrative Science Quarterly* 23(1): 65–90.

Mandel, E. (1975) *Late Capitalism*. London: New Left Books.

March, J. and Simon, H. (1958) *Organizations*. New York: Wiley.

Marcuse, H. (1971) Industrialization and Capitalism. In O. Stammer (ed.) *Max Weber and Sociology Today*. Oxford: Blackwell.

Marglin, S. (1980) The Origins and Functions of Hierarchy in Capitalist Production. In T. Nichols (ed.) *Capital and Labour*. London: Fontana.

Massie, J. (1965) Management Theory. In J. March (ed.) *The Handbook of Organizations*. New York: Rand McNally.

Mayntz, R. (1964) The Study of Organizations. *Current Sociology* 13(3): 95–156.

Mead, G. H. (1936) The Problem of Society – How We Become Selves. In

M. N. Moore (ed.) *Movements of Thought in the Nineteenth Century*. Chicago: University of Chicago Press.

Mennell, S. (1975) *Sociological Theory: Uses and Unities*. London: Nelson.

Merton, R. K. (1940) Bureaucratic Structure and Personality. *Social Forces* 17(4): 560–68.

Merton, R. K. (1949) *Social Theory and Social Structure*. New York: Free Press.

Merton, R. K. *et al.* (1952) *Reader in Bureaucracy*. New York: Free Press.

Miliband, R. (1977) *Marxism and Politics*. London: Oxford University Press.

Mintzberg, H. (1977) Review of H. A. Simon's The New Science of Management Decision (revised edition). *Administrative Science Quarterly* 22(2): 342–51.

Morgan, G. (1980) Paradigms, Metaphors and Problem-Solving. *Administrative Science Quarterly* 25(4): 605–22.

Mouzelis, N. (1967) *Organization and Bureaucracy*. London: Routledge & Kegan Paul.

Nichols, T. (1969) *Ownership, Control and Ideology*. London: Allen & Unwin.

Nichols, T. (1980) *Capital and Labour*. Glasgow: Fontana.

Nichols, T. and Beynon, H. (1977) *Living with Capitalism*. London: Routledge & Kegan Paul.

O'Connor, J. (1973) *The Fiscal Crisis of the State*. New York: St Martin's Press.

Offe, C. (1976) *Industry and Inequality*. London: Edward Arnold.

Parkin, F. (1981) *Marxism and Class Theory: A Bourgeois Critique*. London: Tavistock Publications.

Parsons, T. (1951) *The Social System*. New York: Collier Macmillan.

Parsons, T. (1956) Suggestions for a Sociological Approach to the Theory of Organization I and II. *Administrative Science Quarterly* 1(1/2): 63–85 and 225–39.

Parsons, T. (1960) Social Strains in America. In T. Parsons, *Structure and Process in Modern Societies*. Chicago: Free Press.

Parsons, T. (1967) On the Concept of Political Power. In R. Bendix and S. M. Lipset (eds) *Class, Status and Power*. London: Routledge & Kegan Paul (second edition).

Perrow, C. (1967) A Framework for the Comparative Analysis of Organizations. *American Sociological Review* 33(3): 194–208.

Perrow, C. (1972) *Complex Organizations: A Critical Essay*. Illinois: Scott Foresman (first edition).

Perry, N. (1977) Recovery and Retrieval in Organizational Analysis. Mimeograph. University of Strathclyde.

Pettigrew, A. (1973) *The Politics of Organizational Decision-Making*. London: Tavistock Publications.

Pettit, P. (1979) *Judging Justice*. London: Routledge & Kegan Paul.

Pfeffer, J. (1982) *Organizations and Organization Theory*. Boston: Pitman.

Phillipson, M. (1972) Phenomenological Philosophy and Sociology. In P. Filmer *et al.* (eds) *New Directions in Sociological Theory*. London: Macmillan.

Pugh, D. (1966) Modern Organization Theory. *Psychological Bulletin* 66(4): 235–51.

Pugh, D. and Hickson, D. (1976) *Organization Structure in its Context: The Aston Programme I.* Farnborough: Saxon House.

Pugh, D. S., Hickson, D. J., and Hinnings, C. R. (1969) The Context of Organization Structure. *Administrative Science Quarterly* 14(1): 91–114.

Radice, H. (ed.) (1973) *International Firms and Modern Imperialism.* Harmondsworth: Penguin.

Ramos, A. G. (1981) *The New Science of Organizations.* Toronto: University of Toronto Press.

Ranson, S., Hinings, B., and Greenwood, R. (1980) The Structuring of Organizational Structures. *Administrative Science Quarterly* 25(1): 1–17.

Reed, M. (1984) Management as a Social Practice. *Journal of Management Studies.* Special issue. *Critical Perspectives on Management Studies and Management Science* 21(3): 273–85.

Roethlisberger, F. J. and Dickson, W. J. (1939) *Management and the Worker.* Cambridge, Mass.: Harvard University Press.

Rose, M. (1975) *Industrial Behaviour: Theoretical Development Since Taylor.* Harmondsworth: Penguin.

Ross, A. M. and Hartman, P. T. (1960) *Changing Patterns of Industrial Conflict.* New York: Wiley.

Runciman, W. G. (1983) *A Treatise on Social Theory:* vol. 1, *The Methodology of Social Theory.* Cambridge: Cambridge University Press.

Said, A. and Simmons, L. R. (eds) (1975) *The New Sovereigns: Multinational Corporations and World Power.* Englewood Cliffs: Prentice-Hall.

Salaman, G. (1978) Towards a Sociology of Organizational Structure. *The Sociological Review* 26(3): 519–54.

Salaman, G. (1979) *Work Organizations: Resistance and Control.* London: Longman.

Salaman, G. (1981) *Class and the Corporation.* London: Fontana.

Saunders, P. (1981) *Social Theory and the Urban Question.* London: Hutchinson.

Schreyogg, G. (1980) Contingency and Choice in Organization Theory. *Organization Studies* 1(4): 305–26.

Schreyogg, G. (1982) Some Comments about Comments: A Reply to Donaldson. *Organization Studies* 3(1): 73–8.

Schutz, A. (1964) *Collected Papers:* vol. 2. The Hague: Martinus Nijhoff.

Schutz, A. (1967) *The Phenomenology of the Social World.* Evanston: North Western University Press.

Scott, W. G. (1961) Organization Theory: An Overview and an Approach. *Journal of the Academy of Management.* April: 7–26.

Selznick, P. (1949) *TVA and the Grass Roots.* Berkeley: University of California Press.

Selznick, P. (1966) *TVA and the Grass Roots* (second edition). New York: Harper.

Silverman, D. (1968) Formal Organizations or Industrial Sociology: Towards a Social Action Analysis of Organizations. *Sociology* 2(3): 221–38.

Silverman, D. (1970) *The Theory of Organizations*. London: Heinemann.
Silverman, D. (1972) Some Neglected Questions about Social Reality. In P. Filmer (ed.) *New Directions in Sociological Theory*. London: Macmillan.
Silverman, D. (1975) Accounts of Organizations: Organizational Structure and the Accounting Process. In J. B. McKinley (ed.) *Processing People: Cases in Organizational Behaviour*. New York: Holt, Rinehart, & Winston.
Silverman, D. and Jones, J. (1973) Getting In: The Managed Accomplishments of Correct Selection Outcomes. In J. Child (ed.) *Man and Organization*. London: Allen & Unwin.
Silverman, D. and Jones, J. (1976) *Organizational Work: The Language of Grading and the Grading of Language*. London: Macmillan.
Simon, H. (1945) *Administrative Behaviour*. New York: Collier Macmillan.
Simon, H. (1964) On the Concept of Organizational Goal. *Administrative Science Quarterly* 9(1): 1–22.
Simon, H. (1965) *The New Science of Management Decision-Making*. Englewood Cliffs: Prentice-Hall.
Smith, J. H. (1975) 'The Significance of Elton Mayo.' Foreword to E. Mayo (1975), *The Social Problems of an Industrial Civilization* (second edition). London: Routledge & Kegan Paul.
Storey, J. (1983) *Managerial Prerogative and the Question of Control*. London: Routledge & Kegan Paul.
Storing, H. (1962) The Science of Administration. In H. Storing (ed.) *Essays on the Scientific Study of Politics*. New York: Holt, Rinehart, & Winston.
Strauss, A. (1978) *Negotiations*. New York: Wiley.
Strauss, A. *et al.* (1963) The Hospital and its Negotiated Order. In E. Friedson (ed.) *The Hospital in Modern Society*. New York: Macmillan.
Stretton, H. (1969) *The Political Sciences*. London: Routledge & Kegan Paul.
Sudnow, D. (1965) Normal Crimes: Sociological Features of the Penal Code in a Public Defenders Office. *Social Problems* 12(3): 255–76.
Thompson, J. D. (1956) On Building an Administrative Science. *Administrative Science Quarterly* 1(1): 102–11.
Thompson, J. D. (1967) *Organizations in Action*. New York: McGraw-Hill.
Thompson, P. (1983) *The Nature of Work*. London: Macmillan.
Tillet, A. (1970) Industry and Management: A Historical Perspective. In A. Tillet, T. Kempner, and G. Wills (eds) *Management Thinkers*. Harmondsworth: Penguin.
Tomlinson, J. (1982) *Unequal Struggle: British Socialism and the Capitalist Enterprise*. London: Methuen.
Toulmin, S. (1971) Rediscovering History: New Directions in the Philosophy of Science. *Encounter* 36(1): 53–64.
Toulmin, S. (1972) *Human Understanding*: vol. 1. Princeton: Princeton University Press.
Touraine, A. (1974) *The Post-Industrial Society*. London: Wildwood House.
Trist, E. L., Higgin, G. W., Murray, H., and Pollock, A. B. (1963) *Organizational Choice*. London: Tavistock Publications.
Tugenhadt, C. (1973) *The Multinationals*. Harmondsworth: Penguin.
Vernon, R. (1973) *Sovereignty at Bay*. Harmondsworth: Penguin.

Waldo, D. (1948) *The Administrative State*. New York: Knopf.

Wallerstein, I. (1974) *The Modern World System: Capitalist Agriculture and the Origins of the European World Economy in the Sixteenth Century*. London: Academic Press.

Weinberg, I. (1969) The Problem of the Convergence of Industrial Societies: A Critical Look at the State of a Theory. *Comparative Studies in Society and History* 11(1): 1–15.

Weiss, J. W. (1981) The Historical and Political Perspective on Organizations of Lucien Karpik. In M. Zey-Ferrell and M. Aiken (eds) *Complex Organizations: Critical Perspectives*. Illinois: Scott Foresman.

Whitley, R. (1977a) Organizational Control and the Problem of Order. *Social Science Information* 16(2): 169–89.

Whitley, R. (1977b) Concepts of Organizational Power in the Study of Organizations. *Personnel Review* 6(1): 54–9.

Willmott, H. (1981) The Structuring of Organization Structure: A Note. *Administrative Science Quarterly* 26(3): 470–74.

Winch, P. (1958) *The Idea of the Social Science*. London: Routledge & Kegan Paul.

Wolin, S. (1961) *Politics and Vision*. London: Garnett & Evans.

Wood, S. (ed.) (1982) *The Degradation of Work*. London: Hutchinson.

Woodward, J. (1958) *Management and Technology*. London: HMSO.

Woodward, J. (1965) *Industrial Organization: Theory and Practice*. London: Oxford University Press.

Worsley, P. (1974) The State of Theory and the Status of Theory. *Sociology* 8(1): 1–17.

Zeitlin, M. (1974) Corporate Ownership and Control: The Large Corporations and the Capitalist Class. *American Journal of Sociology* 79(5): 1073–119.

Zimblast, A. (ed.) (1979) *Case Studies on the Labour Process*. New York: Monthly Review Press.

Zimmerman, D. (1971) The Practicalities of Rule Use. In J. Douglas (ed.) *Understanding Everyday Life*. London: Routledge & Kegan Paul.

Zwerman, W. L. (1970) *New Perspectives on Organization Theory*. Connecticut: Greenwood.

Name index

Abrams, P., 102–03, 114, 143–44, 171
Albrow, M., 3, 46, 61, 107–09, 178, 180
Allaire, Y., 185
Allen, V. L., 78
Anthony, P. D., 172, 211
Astley, W. G., 202, 204
Atkinson, P., 200
Attwell, P., 56

Barnard, C., conceptualization of
    organizations, 16, 20–2, 25–7,
    29–30, 46n, 113; 'dual vision', 22,
    61; 'founding father' of
    organizational theory, 6, 13, 18;
    neo-rationalism, 40
Bell, D., 79, 102
Benson, J. K., 45, 55, 64, 71, 74, 105,
    131; on business corporations, 76;
    concept of contradiction, 78–80;
    dialectical approach, 91, 193–94; on
    functionalism, 65–7
Berlin, I., 135, 208
Bernier, R., 117
Bernstein, R. J., 117, 178, 202, 207–08
Beynon, H., 171
Bhaskar, R., 75
Bittner, E., 44, 56–8
Blackburn, R., 69
Blau, P., 3–4, 17, 19, 30–2, 68, 97
Bordieu, R., 117
Bradley, D., 90, 108

Braverman, H., 82, 85–6, 157
Bucher, R., 53
Burawoy, M., 85, 89
Burns, T., 46, 60, 97, 100, 167, 171;
    conception of organizations,
    127–28, 129, 138, 213; conception
    of social practice, 117; on
    managerial practice, 172; on
    pluralism, 134, 139, 204; on
    sociology or process, 114–15
Burrell, G., concept of contradiction,
    78–9; critical theory, 64–5, 67, 69,
    73, 78, 90; isolationism, 187–89;
    radical structuralism, 83–4, 91, 130

Carey, A., 24
Child, J., 13n, 46, 100, 106–07, 148,
    204
Cicourel, A. V., 55
Clegg, S., 16, 63, 65–6, 106, 193; on
    class relations, 68–9, 198; political
    economy of organizations, 197–98;
    on power relations in capitalism,
    70–2, 77, 82–3, 113
Cohen, G. A., 76
Collins, R., 15, 133
Crombie, A., 109
Crouch, C., 102
Crozier, M., 11, 17, 33, 46; pluralism,
    204; study of public bureaucracies,
    147, 159–62, 164, 165–68, 170,

Subject index